This book pursues the complex qu[estion of]
the nature of the controversy surro[unding]
monetarist theory and evidence, and the
reasons for the persistence of this
controversy.

The theory of monetarism is examined in its
old guise as the Quantity Theory of Money,
and subsequent chapters look at the evolution
of the theory to its present form in the period
since the 1950's. On this topic in particular
the author weaves together issues of theory
with those of econometric evidence. Such a
survey of econometric and economic
theoretic issues reveals much disagreement
concerning the criteria by which one decides
whether a theory has been validated by data
or not. As much of the controversy since
1963 has been about econometric results, it is
important that the criteria for choosing
between rival formulations are stated explicitly
and that these criteria are applied in a
consistent fashion. Such has not been the
practice in many cases in the past, which is
one reason for the persistence of the
controversy.

Chapter 4 brings together the various results
on testing monetarism. This is arranged by
looking in turn at major predictions of
monetarism. In each case the author critically
examines the claims made in the literature in
the light of his discussion of the methodology
of testing theories and notices that the
empirical support for monetarism is much
weaker than it seems. Indeed he finds the
claims of monetarism invalid.

The concluding chapter surveys recent
developments in the UK economy where a
monetarist policy has been pursued by
governments in one form or another for the
last five years. The reason for tackling this
political subject is the recognition that
relevance and urgency in economic
discussions must be allowed prominence
sooner or later over the aesthetic and
scientific satisfaction of conducting a debate
objectively and at leisure.

Meghnad Desai is Reader in Economics at the London School of Economics. He is the author of *Marxian Economic Theory, Applied Econometrics,* and *Marxian Economics*. He has written extensively on economic theory, economic history and political economy in numerous journals. His books have been translated into several foreign languages, and he has acted as a consultant to UN agencies and private and public corporations.

Testing Monetarism

Testing Monetarism

Meghnad Desai

St. Martin's Press, New York

All rights reserved. For information write:
St. Martin's Press, Inc., 175 Fifth Avenue, New York NY 10010
Printed in Great Britain
First published in the United States of America in 1982

ISBN 0-312-79356-1

Library of Congress Cataloging in Publication Data

Desai, Meghnad.
    Testing monetarism.

    1. Money -- Mathematical models.
2. Monetary policy -- Mathematical models.

HG221.3.D48   1982   332.4'6'0724   81-21360
ISBN 0-312-79356-1   AACR2

CONTENTS

PREFACE

One hardly needs to explain at any great length the motivation for writing a book on monetarism. It is no longer a purely academic topic but one of vital concern to all people who are interested in understanding the present economic malaise. I have therefore tried in this book to address the general reader as much as the specialist economist and econometrician. The book tries to explain the nature of monetarism as fully and objectively as is possible. Since much of what is claimed for monetarism is said to be based on solid empirical research, one has to delve into technicalities of econometrics to evaluate these claims. I have tried both to cover these technicalities fully and to convey their flavour in simple language in the hope that the general reader will persist with my presentation even if this means gliding over the algebra.

In writing this book, I have drawn on some of my recent work done under the auspices of the Methodology, Inference and Modelling in Econometrics (MIME) programme at the London School of Economics funded by the SSRC, whose support is gratefully acknowledged. David Blake has been a resourceful Research Officer on this programme, a fruitful collaborator and a great help in a variety of ways which have brought order to my chaotic habits of research. The stimulating and friendly environment of the LSE econometrics group has helped very much. I am grateful as usual to Denis Sargan, David Hendry, Andrew Harvey and members of the Econometric workshop for their interest over the years. Steven Pudney deserves a special word of thanks for allowing the use of his computer programme SNIPE. My efforts to finish this book only moderately after the deadline agreed with my publisher has imposed great pressure on my family as well as friends who have shown great understanding. Jill Duggan typed the manuscript at great speed and with good humour. I should also like to thank Hali Edison, Christine Wills and Dilia Montes for their help. Frances Pinter was a model publisher in making sure that the manuscript was published as speedily as possible, once I had actually managed to deliver it. To this end Jenny Donald and her staff were also extremely helpful. I thank them all.

INTRODUCTION

Monetarism, a word coined but ten years ago, has now become an established part of the economic and political vocabulary. The use of monetarism as an economic theory and its adoption by many governments, most notably that of the UK since May 1979 is a clear illustration of Keynes' dictum about the power of ideas. Here is a notion at once two centuries old and ten years young which is currently synonymous with the persistent refusal of governments of developed capitalist countries to pursue any policy which could counter rising unemployment, falling output and a tidal wave of business failures. While this refusal is justified by the fight against high rates of inflation experienced since 1973, there is some dispute whether the monetarist policies will even curb inflation. The bitterness of the medicine being administered is no proof of its efficacy.

We can expect, however, that such short-run failure to achieve stated objectives will not deter the champions of monetarism. They have reasons and rationalisations which can account for any immediate failure. The recalcitrant economy and the irrational consumer/trade-unionist will no doubt be blamed; we shall be told that such a short run lack of efficacy was anticipated since lags between a cut in money supply and its eventual effect are 'long and variable'.

This latter statement is one way of saying that no one is quite sure what is likely to happen, or when. Though frequently used as a technical or 'scientific' argument, it is a confession of ignorance. The question it raises extends to the entire corpus of monetarist theory and practice. What evidence do we have or did we have that can justify the faith placed by governments around the world in this theory?

Seldom has an intellectual argument been won so quickly and so completely, at the policy level at least, as the monetarist demolition of the Keynesian demand management policies of the fifties and sixties. In 1956, Milton Friedman along with some associates brought out *Studies in the*

Quantity Theory of Money (*Studies* hereafter) a brave attempt to revive a theory which everyone thought had been discredited both on logical and on empirical grounds. Whatever its ultimate impact, little notice was taken of *Studies* at the time. A belief in the quantity theory of money was thought in the late fifties and early sixties to be a peculiar Chicago madness, indulgently mocked by others but thought to be harmless. Simultaneous publication of two works co-authored by Milton Friedman took place in 1963. One was an econometric study with David Meiselman (Friedman and Meiselman (1963)) which claimed that a quantity theoretic explanation of movement in nominal income was more stable and had greater predictive power than the hitherto dominant Keynesian explanation. The money multiplier based on a stable demand function for money, it was argued, was more stable than the Kahn-Keynes investment multiplier based on the Keynesian income-expenditure model. This study used US data on income, investment and money supply for the 63 years between 1897 and 1959. The argument for a monetary explanation was based in this instance not upon its *theoretical* merits but upon a superior *econometric* performance. The use of econometric techniques (of arguable quality as we shall see later) to settle a long-standing debate in economics demonstrated the extent to which the econometric revolution had progressed in economics. It was also an innovation in being the first such attempt to use econometrics to answer such an important substantive question.

The Friedman-Meiselman (FM) paper aroused immediate and widespread controversy. The debate which we shall survey below can be described at best as a draw or at worst as a claim not convincingly established. The other work published that year was however a slow fuse. This was *A Monetary History of the United States* written in collaboration with Anna Schwartz (Friedman and Schwartz (1963)). This achieved the status not, as with the FM paper, of a gauntlet thrown down, but of a monumental scholarly work. It established, with a combination of narrative history, econometric and pre-econometric (National Bureau) techniques, the proposition that movements in the stock of money were the major determinant of movement in nominal income. A major chapter in the book tried to provide an alternative explanation to the Keynesian one for the Great Depression of 1929–33. Friedman and Schwartz sought to show that it was due to a reduction in the money stock by the Federal Reserve authorities that the subsequent decline in prices, employment and output occurred. The traditional Keynesian argument had been that monetary policies had been ineffective in pulling the economy *out* of the Depression — a primarily theoretical argument but with some empirical support. This then meant that only fiscal policy — an increase in the government's autonomous expenditure — could get an economy out of a high unemployment equilibrium. Friedman and Schwartz argued that far from being ineffective, monetary policy got the economy *into* the Depression, and not until fiscal policy had had an expansionary effect on money supply could one claim that economic recovery had taken place.

Friedman's innovation with respect to the old-fashioned quantity theory of money at this stage (1963) was to alter its emphasis from an explanation of *prices* to an explanation of *nominal income*. Indeed this was the main argument in his 'The Quantity Theory of Money: A Restatement' of 1956. By shifting the emphasis away from Irving Fisher's equation of exchange (MV = PT) to the Cambridge (Marshallian) theory of the proportion of income held in liquid form by economic agents, Friedman was able to recast the quantity theory as a theory of the demand for money. Adding an exogenous determination of the money supply to this, he obtained a theory of the determination of nominal income.

At the same time however there was another debate centering around the relationship between money wage changes (and by implication, inflation) and unemployment. This was the celebrated Phillips Curve based on the work of A.W.H. Phillips with British data for nearly a hundred years between 1861 and 1957 (Phillips (1958)). Attempts had been made earlier, most notably by A.J. Brown in his *The Great Inflation* (1954) to trace the connection between the *level* of the unit labour cost and the level of unemployment and then between prices and wages, but though illustrated with empirical information, no econometric evidence was advanced by Brown. Once again it was the pioneering *econometric* relationship established by Phillips and his demonstration about the stability of the relationship over the long period which explains the appeal of the Phillips Curve. Phillips also explained the *rate of growth* of money wage rates and the percentage rate of unemployment. This made the subsequent link with the *rate of growth* of prices (inflation) easier.

It was the debate about the economic theoretic foundation of this established empirical regularity — the Phillips Curve — which led to the crucial next step in Friedman's argument about the monetary causes of inflation, which thus took his theory back to the original emphasis of the quantity theory of money. The resurgence of the monetary explanation of *inflation* (rather than nominal income) is thus a later event in the (contemporary) history of ideas. Phillips' original work hinted at the usefulness of his discovery to an explanation of inflation but he did not make the connection explicitly. It was, as often happens in the history of ideas, the subsequent simplification and extension of Phillips' argument (most notably by Samuelson and Solow (1960) in their *Analytics of an Anti-Inflation Policy*) that launched the Phillips Curve as an important tool of public policy. The argument was made that by controlling aggregate demand and therefore the level of unemployment, a government (on behalf of society) could choose the rate of inflation it felt was desirable. Inflation and unemployment were both evil, but were seen as alternatives between which there could be some trade-off. By choosing an optimal combination of inflation and unemployment, and by using the stable, objective, empirical relationship between the two variables derived from Phillips' work, governments, it was said, could deal with both inflation and unemployment.

The high point of the Phillips Curve's reputation in academic economic circles as a possible panacea was in the first half of the sixties. It is doubtful if any government planned its policy instruments precisely or deliberately using the Phillips Curve as its basis. But the use of deflationary techniques to achieve a *disinflationary* outcome was bandied about in public debate. (It was perhaps most forcefully advanced as a policy prescription in the UK by Frank Paish, and an expression, 'margin of unused capacity' as a euphemism for unemployment gained in currency in the mid-sixties. The US economy throughout the period 1961–70 had high levels of employment and reached near full employment levels after 1966; the inflation rate was also quite mild then by later standards, at least until 1968).

Friedman's challenge to the Phillips Curve was on *a priori theoretical* rather than empirical grounds. At this juncture (1966), the *empirical* stability of the Phillips Curve was not as yet questioned (as it was to be five years later). The Phillips Curve had provided the missing explanation for price changes in the textbook Keynesian model,[1] which had until then operated on fixed price assumptions. This challenge on theoretical grounds was more successful in making a serious inroad into the Keynesian complacency than Friedman's earlier econometric efforts. By relying on a neoclassical and decidedly non-Keynesian theory of labour market equilibrium,[2] Friedman questioned the validity of the observed empirical trade-off between *nominal* wage changes and unemployment. He first put forward the standard neoclassical view that it was relative prices — and hence real wages — rather than absolute prices which were determined in the labour market. So unemployment cannot *causally* influence nominal wage changes without taking into account information on expectations about inflation. This assertion relies on the classical dichotomous separation between real and monetary sectors which is also at the heart of the quantity theory of money. While the neoclassical micro-economic theory was accepted by economists — Keynesian or otherwise — the inexorable link between this micro theory and the quantity theory of money was never fully admitted by most economists. By establishing this link, Friedman provided an explanation of the Phillips Curve in line with textbook micro theory, emphasised the importance of inflationary *expectations* on actual behaviour, argued that the equilibrium (natural) rate of unemployment was immune to nominal price changes as well as to government stimulus and introduced the notion that inflation was caused by governments' attempts to use the Phillips Curve to buy a temporary reduction in unemployment at the cost of future rises in inflation. The theoretical ascendancy of neoclassical theory, unquestioned in micro theory, was established thereby in macro theory. An explanation of inflation in terms of government interference with private economic equilibrium was provided, thus reintroducing laissez faire arguments at the macro-economic level whence they had been driven away by Keynesian theory. But most important, Friedman linked together a monetary explanation of inflation — the old quantity theory concern — with that of nominal income and unemployment — the theme of his earlier 'Restatement'.

The key concept was that of the natural rate of unemployment. This concept goes back to Adam Smith's Invisible Hand, resuscitated in modern economics by Walras's concept of general equilibrium. The free optimising choices of individuals as consumers and producers, as buyers and sellers of labour and other commodities, clear all markets at positive (at least non-negative) prices. This is essentially the realm of barter where money plays no role. This market clearing private equilibrium established by the Invisible Hand yields a natural rate of unemployment. This is the rate of *voluntary* unemployment, the Keynesian notion of *involuntary* unemployment being inconsistent with *Walrasian* general equilibrium theory. No wage bargaining behaviour on the part of workers, unions or employees nor any government attempt to stimulate the economy by purely macro-economic budgetary actions could alter this natural rate. The natural rate is not constant, but changes only as a result of long-run structural changes in tastes, market processes etc. It provided Friedman with the missing link between the influence of monetary changes on *nominal income* movements and on *price* movements. It simply said that *changes in real output of a long-run equilibrium kind were independent of the changes in the money stock.* In the short run, some changes in real output could be caused by monetary changes but ultimately such changes would be cancelled out by changes in the opposite direction. No *permanent* change in real output (or the natural rate of unemployment) could result from changes in the money stock. Thus the enduring consequence of money supply changes was inflation.[3]

Thus, by the time of Friedman's Presidential address to the American Economic Association in December 1967, the monetarist argument was complete in its essentials. It re-established the pre-Keynesian economic theory of the capacity of the economy to arrive at an equilibrium level of employment independently of government interference. It offered to those who desired such neatness, a consistent micro-economic and macro-economic theoretical framework. It interpreted the evidence of the ill effects of governmental interference in market processes taught in micro-economic textbooks with the inflationary consequences of governments' desire to achieve a full employment level inconsistent with the natural rate at the macro-economic level. It offered a complete and coherent alternative model to the Keynesian one, not by innovating new ideas, but by going back to older theories and restating them more cogently. The Keynesian model in theory, in econometric specification and in the policy makers' version had by this time become a patchwork of neoclassical micro-theory, of arguments about institutional price rigidities and of the allegedly inelastic nature of certain crucial behavioural relationships which became harder to sustain empirically, and became a prop and justification for the growth of executive power.

Although the theoretical work had been completed, the time for the popular triumph of monetarism had not come by 1968. There were other strands to the debate which were incidental to the main one but which were tagged on. One was the argument deriving from the FM paper that monetary policy was quicker in making its impact and more reliable than fiscal policy. This was the debate which centred around the St. Louis model of Andersen and Jordan (1968). A related but somewhat confused pair of econometric methodological issues were those of the relative merits of small econometric models as against large econometric models and of structural form estimation as against reduced form estimation (of which more later). The argument about the efficacy of monetary policy relative to fiscal policy goes back to the debates surrounding the *General Theory*. Keynes was supposed to have demoted monetary policy relative to fiscal policy. But as early as 1952, Howard Ellis was already discerning in the contemporary economic scene 'The Rediscovery of Money'. Earlier, authors such as Haberler had also tried to hold the ground for monetary policy. This preference for monetary over fiscal policy has long been a hallmark of politicians and economists with a conservative bent. Thus upon the Conservative Party's return to power in 1951, Lionel Robbins reaffirmed the primary role of the Bank Rate as a policy instrument (See Dow (1964)

Chapter 2).

The Phillips Curve had its heyday as a policy tool in the second half of the sixties and the early seventies. Faced with a stark choice between full employment and moderate inflation, many governments tried to break the link between the two by 'going off' or tilting the Phillips Curve.[4] Thus wages and incomes policies, either statutory or voluntary, were seen as a way out of the dilemma. Both in the UK and the USA, it was perhaps paradoxically governments of a conservative bent that tried these policies, either by a statutory freeze on wages and prices or by some other device. It was also at this time that complaints began to be heard that the Phillips Curve, so stable for so long, had shifted and was drifting. Instead of a negative correlation between inflation and unemployment, a positive association began to be discerned between the two. The era of stagflation had arrived.

The breakdown of the Bretton Woods arrangements as signalled by President Nixon's New Economic Policy announcement of 15 August 1971, led to the adoption of the monetarist prescription of floating exchange rates between the USA and its trading partners. The UK in the meantime witnessed a deliberate use of the monetary instrument in the Heath–Barber government's dash for high employment and rapid growth during 1971–3. In October 1973 came the OPEC price rise. Now had come the days of *rapid* inflation and the hour of the monetarists had arrived.

There had been an attempt in December 1972 on the part of a small group of economists and one MP to argue the monetarist case that the projected PSBR (net borrowing requirement as they called it then) for 1972–3 was too high at £3 billion compared to its historical average of £200 million for 1945–70 and even the £500 million in 1971–2. This *Memorial to the Prime Minister*[5] was signed by, among others, Harry Johnson, Alan Walters, David Laidler and Brian Griffiths. They put the case for the control of money supply growth (6 to 8%) and argued that only by controlling PSBR could money supply be controlled. They said the incomes policy then in operation was unlikely to be more than a short-term palliative ('a lump of ice that dams up the flow of a river'). They queried the basis of the unemployment statistics.

Thus, what were to become the standard monetarist arguments were rehearsed in this short letter. It is hard to know whether any notice was taken of it at that time. The Bank's policy of money supply-fuelled expansion was successful (belying the old Keynesian adage that you cannot push on a string). Unemployment fell to a low, reminiscent of the 1950s (2% in 1973 IV). The growth rate of real GDP was 7.2% in 1973 over 1972, almost treble the historical average for the postwar period. The growth of money supply (M3) was 6.2% in 1970, 11.9 in 1971, 22.5 in 1972 and 25.9 in 1973. Inflation was by later standards still mild. In annual average terms it was 6.4% in 1970, 9.4 in 1971, 7.1 in 1972 and only 9.2 in 1973. (Some credit for this should be given to the government's much maligned incomes policy for its success in the short run at holding down inflation in the face of a fiscal policy which was exerting a lot of upward pressure on wages).

A prophet has to be right only once for his reputation to be secure forever. Although real growth rather than inflation occurred in 1973, the property speculation mania and the subsequent collapse of the secondary banks, the Miners' action, the Three Day Week in December 1973–January 1974 and the double digit inflation that followed in 1974 gave the monetarists the opportunity to vindicate themselves. In the aftermath of the political and economic debacles (for different reasons) of the Nixon and Heath governments, monetarism as a serious argument came to make its impact on policy-making circles. Evidence for the precise timing of the arrival of monetarism as an orthodoxy is hard to gather, but a few pointers are evident between 1974 and 1976. The first, after the 1972 *Memorial*, is the House of Commons Select Committee on Public Expenditure hearings on monetary policy in 1974. Alan Walters acted as a specialist adviser to the committee for this set of hearings. At that time, monetarism was sufficiently a curiosity for the Chairman to describe David Laidler in the singular as 'our monetarist witness'. Laidler's evidence is a lucid presentation of the monetarist view at this time (House of Commons Expenditure Committee Ninth Report, 1974).

The Institute of Economic Affairs had been arguing the general case for a market oriented policy and it sponsored a number of pamphlets. Now Milton Friedman, whose Wincott Memorial lecture *The Counter-Revolution in Monetary Theory* had been published as an IEA occasional paper in 1970, returned to the theme of inflation and unemployment in another IEA occasional paper published in June 1975 with an appendix on British experience by David Laidler. Friedman's influence was reinforced by the award of the Nobel Prize to him in 1976 and his Nobel lecture was published by the IEA as another occasional paper. The Nobel prize awards to Hayek and Friedman meant that the anti-Keynesian, free market position for long out in the cold, was again dominant and not just tolerated by the economics profession. By 1976, the battle for the hearts and minds of policy-making groups in the UK — Treasury, Bank of England, Treasury Ministers — was won.

A sign of this victory was in the changed stance of *The Times*. Its editor, William Rees-Mogg, in an article on 13 July 1976 popularised the notion that inflation follows the money supply growth with a lag of two years. He did this by comparing 'excess' money growth for 1965–73 (9.4% by his definition) with inflation rates for 1967–75 (also 9.4%). Perfect correlation, which anyone trained in statistics would find suspicious, has a fascination for the amateur. (Similar was the reaction in education circles to the perfect fit produced by Sir Cyril Burt for educational ability and class. This was exposed only after three decades by careful investigative journalism on the part of Oliver Gillie). Rees-Mogg went on to argue his more pronounced views of the deleterious effects of inflation on democracy in an IEA paper. Peter Jay, the Economics Editor of *The Times* was also a convert to monetarism as his IEA pamphlet, *Employment, Inflation and Politics*, of January 1976 showed. By this time, the UK was borrowing such large sums from the IMF to meet its payments deficit that the latter was able to insist that a monetarist approach be adopted by the UK Treasury. This was done perhaps with more seeming than real protest by the Callaghan government. The Prime Minister himself pronounced the standard monetarist doctrine of high wages causing unemployment to the Labour Party Conference in 1976. The Labour movement, divided and demoralised over the EEC referendum, caved in to this onslaught. The Conservative Party had by now already disowned the Heath–Barber policy and the dominant group, led by Mrs Thatcher and Keith Joseph, were hard-line monetarists. The changing allegiances of the economics profession was by now discernible in academic journals and in textbooks. Anyone comparing the pamphlets *CRISIS 1975* and *CRISIS 1976* put out by the IEA would see the swing. While some older Keynesians (Kahn, Kaldor, Joan Robinson) stuck to their guns, the majority of the younger economists were now willing to admit the relevance if not superiority of the monetarist framework in explaining the hyperinflation of 1974 and 1975. The high prestige of demand management policies was laid low. The battle for monetarism, fought since 1974, was won within two years.

Since 1976 then, monetarism has been a well established economic theory. Its proponents, especially Milton Friedman, have claimed extensive if not universal empirical support for its central position.[6] This proposition is that every observed experience of inflation has a monetary explanation. Put this way, the monetarist theory reverts fully back to the old quantity theory of money. This main proposition of the quantity theory was thought to have been logically refuted by Keynes, and economists had convinced themselves that the quantity theory was only a tautology. What then has caused this complete reversal of opinion? Keynesian theory was also said to have provided a better explanation of the workings of the modern economy, and it was said that never again would we witness high levels of unemployment being accepted as inevitable (not to say desirable) by governments. These results now appear to have been completely overturned. How could this have come about?

This rehabilitation of an old theory (under a new label) in academic opinion as well as in policy making raises a number of important issues. At one level there is the most vital question to ask of a policy which accepts high unemployment as a necessary price for lower inflation: what if the theory on which such a policy is based were to prove, *yet again*, to be logically faulty or empirically unsound? The real economic and social costs of such mistakes are obviously high and one would like some assurance that there were a reasonable chance of success for such a policy.

This question while extremely important for citizens is at the same time very hard to answer. After all, it can be argued that policy makers have to make policy choices in the present based on imperfect information and cannot wait till economists have settled (if they ever can) such matters. The question we shall seek to ask and answer as thoroughly as possible here concerns the process by which a theory once thought to be logically faulty and lacking any empirical support can be transformed into its very opposite. Can this rise of monetarism and the corresponding decline of Keynesianism be understood in terms of objective scientific criteria for choosing between rival explanations of the same observable phenomena? If we can answer the question in the affirmative then it raises further questions, even harder to answer.

If monetarism is superior on logical and empirical grounds, why did it lose out to its rival theory less than forty years ago? Was it merely a matter of a different generation having less exact standards of judgement or more skilful proponents on its side? That would make the ascendancy of different theories at different times purely a sociological matter. On the other hand it could be argued that Keynesian theory 'fitted' the facts of the thirties but failed to match those of the sixties, whereas the quantity theory/monetarism explanation fits the present facts better. The superiority of one theory over another is then a cyclical matter of historical conjuncture and not one of logical or empirical merits.

Another way to present this complex question is as follows. The controversy between a monetarist and a Keynesian explanation of events is not recent; only the labels are different. A controversy has persisted about certain basic propositions which are central to the two theories. Monetarism accords with the Laissez-Faire/Invisible Hand/Quantity Theory arguments championed by Adam Smith, David Hume, David Ricardo through to modern economists such as Cassel, Irving Fisher and in his early years even by Keynes. This tradition denies the possibility of a free enterprise economy being for any noticeable length in a state of excess supply (demand) in any of its markets and hence denies the possibility of involuntary unemployment as an *equilibrium* phenomenon. It believes in the classical dichotomy of real and monetary variables and explains relative prices in a barter context and absolute prices by a quantity theoretic framework. This tradition has been opposed by another theoretically less-prominent and more heterogeneous group. Part of it has been the underground tradition in economic theory that Keynes talked about. One strand of the critique of the quantity theory of Locke, Hume and Ricardo has been that this is too simple a view of the world, that the classical dichotomy, by imposing a one-good model at the macro level, substitutes a mechanistic view of a price level–money supply link. This tradition can claim Cantillon, Thornton, Wicksell, Mises, Hayek (in his 1930's works), Myrdal and Keynes of the *Treatise on Money*. Another strand has questioned the mechanism whereby sustained periods of excess supply/excess demand are ruled out in the classical theory. Malthus, John Stuart Mill in some of his writings, Marx, Hobson and Keynes of the *General Theory* belong to this strand. An argument was even made by some that a monetary economy *by its very nature* would be prone to cycles and hence never achieve the Ricardo–Say equilibrium. This argument was made by some monetary 'cranks' who sought the root cause of their problems in the powers of bankers and governments who, by controlling money, caused unemployment and misery. Among them were people such as Cobbett, well known for his dislike of the deflation of the 1820s caused by Ricardian policies, or the Attwood brothers Mathias and Robert, or the monetary reformers Douglas and Gesell. It was cogently argued in a Marxist framework by Rosa Luxemburg. (See Corry (1962), Luxemburg (1951), Cobbett (1830).)

Why does such controversy persist? Can we not seek to formalise the rival theories and use our well developed quantitative techniques to settle the arguments one way or another? Econometric evidence has been extensively used, as we noted above, during the last two decades of the Keynesian–monetarist controversy but with no immediate sign of any settlement. It is possible for prominent economists to totally and publicly disagree about whether the money supply–inflation connection has been established beyond doubt or is a spurious correlation. (See for example, the controversy in *The Times* (London) started by Hahn and Nield which evoked replies by Friedman and Minford with rejoinders from Hahn and Nield. *The Times* (1980)).

We shall pursue this question, complex as it is, of the nature of the controversy surrounding monetarist theory and evidence and the reasons for the persistence of this controversy in the following chapters. Our aim is to survey a body of research for the US and UK economies both for the long run over the last hundred years and the short run of the past twenty years. We shall look at some explicit models of monetarism, some of which are available in the literature and some of which are developed by extending available models in more general ways. We shall use the best available econometric techniques as is possible to evaluate the evidence about the validity of the monetarist model, especially concerning the transmission mechanism posited by that model.

The first chapter surveys the theory of monetarism in its old guise as the quantity theory of money since the writings of Hume. Then Chapter 2 looks at recent developments in the theory and its evolution to its present form in the period since the fifties. In this chapter especially we shall have to weave together issues of theory with those of econometric evidence. Such a survey of econometric and economic theoretic issues will reveal that there is much disagreement concerning the criteria by which one decides whether a theory has been validated by data or not. We therefore, in Chapter 3, take up the questions of econometric methodology involved in testing theories. We outline the problem of testing restrictions in a maximum likelihood context. This chapter is by its nature technical but absolutely necessary in our opinion if our results are to be reproducible as they must be to undergo objective criticism. (On the other hand, readers who want to concentrate on the empirical results may wish to skip it if they are willing to grant that the methods used in obtaining these results are appropriate.) Since much of the controversy since 1963 has been about econometric results, it is best in our view to state explicitly the criteria for choosing between rival formulations and to stick to these criteria in a consistent fashion. As we shall see, such has not been the practice in many cases, which is one reason for the persistence of the controversy.

Chapter 4 brings together the various results on testing monetarism. This is arranged by looking in turn at major predictions of monetarism: the constancy of the velocity of circulation, the stability of the demand for money, the exogeneity of the supply of money, the possibility of crowding out, the Natural Rate Hypothesis, the hypothesis about influence of unanticipated changes in the money stock and the law of one price. In each case we critically examine the claims made in the literature in the light of our discussion of the methodology of testing theories and notice that the empirical support for monetarism is much weaker than it seems.

In the concluding chapter we survey the recent developments in the UK economy where a monetarist policy has been pursued by governments of different persuasions for the last five years. This is obviously a topic on which there is bound to be much disagreement and as is inevitable in evaluating something still in progress, premature judgement is hard to avoid. So this chapter has a more tentative air than the previous ones. It also, by the same token, tackles a more political subject than previous chapters. Our reason for including it is that we recognise that relevance and urgency in economic discussions must be allowed prominence sooner or later over the aesthetic and scientific satisfaction of conducting a debate objectively and at leisure.

Notes

1. As in many instances throughout this long debate, it would be appropriate to distinguish between what came to be taught in universities as the Keynesian model and Keynes' own exposition in the *General Theory*. In Book V of the *General Theory*, Keynes discusses the effects of wage changes and the causes of price changes in great detail. The Hicks-Hansen-Modigliani version of the Keynesian model as apotheosised in textbooks and journals ignored this as well as other aspects of Keynes' model. Already in the late fifties and early sixties, isolated authors, especially Sidney Weintraub (1960), had been pointing this out, to no avail.
2. Edmund Phelps was at the same time questioning the Phillips Curve. His work is often bracketed with Friedman's, but for our purposes it was the connection Friedman made between a critique of the Phillips Curve and a monetary theory of inflation which is important.
3. It should be added that the more abstract and mathematically demanding work of Arrow and Debreu has illustrated that it is difficult, if not impossible, to satisfy the assumptions required to prove the Invisible Hand result. Frank Hahn has most eloquently argued the many objections on these grounds to a naive appeal to Walras to justify the natural rate hypothesis (Hahn (1980a), (1980b))
4. Thus in an influential paper Lipsey and Parkin (1970) saw incomes policy as tilting the Phillips Curve in a flatter direction. Influential though it was, the paper's evidence of such tilting was traced to an econometric misspecification (Wallis (1971), Desai (1976)).
5. *Memorial to the Prime Minister* by Harry Johnson et al. published by the Economic Radicals (London, 1972).
6. Friedman has claimed universal empirical support for this central proposition in various places. See for example, *Free to Choose* and his evidence before the UK House of Commons Select Committee on the Treasury and the Civil Service: *Memoranda on a Monetary Policy*, Session 1979–80 (720) (July 1980).

1. THE QUANTITY THEORY OF MONEY

Monetarism as a word was coined around 1968 or 1969,[1] but as an idea it is clearly much older. Its origins can be traced back to the quantity theory of money. As Friedrich Hayek said in a letter to *The Times* on 5 March 1980, 'The new fangled word monetarism means of course no more than the good old name "quantity theory of money", as it was formulated in modern times by the late Professor Irving Fisher and reformulated by Professor Milton Friedman.'

The rudiments of the idea contained in the quantity theory of money can be traced very far back, but perhaps the first modern treatment of it was by John Locke when he wrote on this as on many other matters. This makes the doctrine one of at least three hundred years' standing. This long lineage has been claimed as one of the arguments in favour of the quantity theory. As we shall see below, opposition to the quantity theory is an equally long standing tradition. There is also some evidence, not least that provided by Keynes in his 'Notes on Mercantilism' that there may be equally old roots to the argument that the rate of economic activity — the growth of prices and quantities determine changes in the stock of money rather than the opposite. This perhaps only shows that merits of one theory as against another cannot be decided by how old a theory is.[2]

David Hume then formulated in his celebrated article 'Of Money' what would nowadays be called the homogeneity postulate: If the quantity of money in every citizen's pockets should double overnight, although trade may be stimulated in the short run, prices would eventually double.

> It seems a maxim almost self-evident, that the prices of everything depend on the proportion between commodities and money, and that any considerable alteration on either has the same effect, either of heightening or lowering the price. Increase the commodities, they become cheaper; increase the money, they rise in their value.

Hume thus not only sets forth the basic monetarist proposition but also shows two characteristics of the subsequent debate. First, he talks of all commodities as if they were a single entity — what we should today call a one-good model. Second, he leaves sufficient ambiguity both about the size of the change necessary to bring about the stated consequences ('any *considerable* alteration') and leaves the primary moving-agency — money or commodities — unidentified.

But Hume not only stated the basic tenet of the quantity theory; he also outlined *a transmission mechanism* whereby an increase in money brings about a rise in commodity prices via its effect on wages, labour input and productivity.[3] According to Hume an influx of money to begin with increases employment at the prevailing wage. The workmen so employed would 'never dream of demanding higher wages, but are glad of employment from such good paymasters'. But if workers become scarce, the manufacturer gives higher wages but also demands greater effort which is happily provided by the worker 'who can now eat and drink better'. The effect of higher purchases by workmen at the old prices encourages 'the farmer and gardener'. They produce more and are able at the same time to buy 'better and more cloths from their tradesmen'. 'It is easy to trace the money in its progress through the whole commonwealth; where we shall find, that it must first quicken the diligence of every individual, before it increase the price of labour'. [Hume: Of Money, p. 48 in Rotwein (1970)]

So the immediate effects of an increase in the quantity of money are favourable to employment, effort and output. The long run effects are however unfavourable. 'At first, no alteration is perceived; by degrees the price rises, first of one commodity, then of another; till the whole at last reaches a just proportion with the new quantity of specie which is in the Kingdom'.

Again as in modern discussions, the length of the lag is unspecified but taken to be long. Hume was also clear that it was the money in active circulation (not 'coin locked up in chests') and commodities on offer in the market (not 'hoarded in magazines and granaries') which interact. Thus Hume would exclude hoards though he had no theory of the hoarding of either money or commodities. But then what determines the quanitity of money in active circulation? Could it be that the 'needs of trade' — the volume of commodities and the prices at which they are being offered — determine the quantity in active circulation?

This basic question (is the quantity of money in active circulation supply determined and exogenous to the supply of commodities or is it demand determined and hence endogenous?) is one which has throughout the history of monetary theory divided economists. Hume was opposed by James Steuart who doubted the proportionality between quantity of money and prices. Indeed he made much of the determinants of the quantity of money in active circulation. If there were excess money, he said, it will be hoarded up. If the gold and silver stock fall short of 'the *proportion* of the produce of industry *offered to sale*', resort will be had to 'symbolical money' (credit?) to fill the gap.

> Whatever be the quantity of money in any nation, in correspondence with the rest of the world, there never can remain *in circulation*, but a quantity nearly proportional to the consumption of the rich, and to the labour and industry of (its) poor inhabitants
> (Steuart, *Principles* (Skinner Edition) p. 350 italics in the original).

The Hume-Steuart debate illustrates that while the quantity theory of money is a doctrine with a long history, a claim made in its favour, so is the opposition to the quantity theory. Such opposition consists not as is often alleged in denying money a role in the economy (i.e. that money does not matter) but in tracing a different transmission mechanism between money, output and prices. Locke was opposed by Cantillon as Hume was by Steuart. Steuart's view would be dubbed today (in the UK at least) the Radcliffe Report view. It was argued in the nineteenth century by Tooke, and to some extent by Marx.

Hume's writings were not occasioned by any immediate monetary crisis. There had been the long price revolution of the sixteenth and seventeenth centuries but there was nothing of urgency in mid-eighteenth century which could have caused him to put the quantity theory forward. (Steuart on the other hand had been engaged by the East India Company to study the causes of the economic depression in Bengal in the 1760s which he linked to gold drain, among other things). Ricardo, however, was initially attracted to active economic writing by the events following the suspension of convertibility of Bank of England notes in 1797 at the start of the Napoleonic wars. This depreciation of the paper currency was accompanied by a rise in the price of corn. The inflation caused a sufficient controversy for a Parliamentary Committee to be appointed which in 1809 issued its famous Bullionist Report. Depreciation of the currency had meant a high price for gold, a price above the official mint price prevailing at the time the Bank of England suspended specie payment (a price fixed by Isaac Newton at £3.17.10½d and unchanged since the seventeenth century). In 'On the High Price of Bullion' Ricardo outlined the quantity theory of money in its most rigorous form to date.

Ricardo refused to identify the excess supply of money with all the paper currency issued since suspension in 1797. This was to refute any mechanical connection between the excess supply of money and the high price of bullion. But he did say that the observed fall of Sterling on the Amsterdam Exchange or, equivalently, the high price of bullion was caused by the excess quantity of money above what it would have been had the suspension not taken place. Thus some part of the actual changes in quantity were clearly needed to accommodate the changing economic activity, though Ricardo did not say how this was determined. But there must have been excess paper issue, according to Ricardo for otherwise the pound would not have fallen.

Ricardo's theoretical power clearly dominated the Bullionist group, which also contained Francis Horner. The Bullionists were, by and large, an antigovernment group. The AntiBullionists had no theorist of even moderate competence to oppose Ricardo. They did point out that the English economy had been at war for about fifteen years by the time Ricardo was writing. During this time, they had spent a lot of gold abroad paying for the assistance given by minor European powers, and in general financing of the war. There had also been some bad harvests. To put it in modern terms, the AntiBullionists were trying to show that there had been a decline in commodities available for consumption (due to war, bad harvest, etc) and that internationally England was demanding gold to pay for the war. The commodities side of the question was dismissed by Ricardo by invoking the now famous Ricardian long run. Whatever such short run factors, eventually all price rises must be due to excess quantity of money; price rises had been observed, hence there must have been excess issue of paper money by the Bank of England: *post hoc, ergo propter hoc.*

(This tendency to neglect the commodities side of the equation of exchange persists when discussing many war-induced inflations or inflation in countries recovering from the effects of war. Thus, it is seldom pointed out that the celebrated German hyperinflation was accelerated if not initiated by the French occupation of the Ruhr and other German territories, which produced up to *one third* of German output. The price of the dollar in marks had risen from 4.2 marks in July 1914 to 14.0 marks by July 1919 and 493.2 by July 1922. In January 1923 this rose to 17,972 and in the next ten months it rose to 4,200 billion marks. An *exogenous* reduction of one third in output cannot easily be said to have no effect on prices, whatever the course of the money supply. See Stolper, (1940, Part IV). The hyperinflation in Kuomintang China in the 1940s was also preceded by a long period of Japanese occupation of Manchuria since 1933, the Second World War and the Civil War. Large parts of Chinese territory were occupied by Mao Tse Tung's forces and the loss of output could not have been negligible.)

Ricardo not only restated Hume's quantity theory much more precisely but also provided in his other works a theory of output determination. Thus the short run increase in output, effort and employment as a result of an increase in money pointed out by Hume is lost in Ricardian and post-Ricardian statements of the quantity theory. The classical and neo-classical notion of an automatic tendency for all markets to clear provided prices are flexible — the impossiblity of a sustained excess supply in any market, the absence of any problem of effective demand — was forcefully stated by Ricardo in his debates with Malthus.

Ricardo decisively formed the opinions of his generation and those of subsequent generations on the questions concerning the impact of money on economic activity. He not only restated Hume's theory but fundamentally changed it. In Hume's model, increases in the money supply have favourable effects in the short run on effort, employment and output. Only eventually do prices rise and they do not rise proportionately to increases in money supply. Hume thus provides a transmission mechanism for changes in money to affect prices and output. Ricardo changed all that. In his theory the determination of output in the short run becomes an uninteresting if not an irrelevant question. His theory of output is designed to answer questions of the long run level of output. This 'long run' is not necessarily 'long' in the sense of calendar time though it may be so. It is the long run in the sense of achieving the (full employment) equilibrium level of output.

This long run output is determined by real factors — labour supply, capital stock and natural resources. Movements in the money stock, either autonomous or induced by government policy, can have no influence on the real output level. What is more, for Ricardo short run fluctuations in output were temporary transient disturbances around the long run level. Thus he is dismissive of factors such as bad harvests which may cause output to deviate from its normal level (or equivalently its growth path). Economic theory thus becomes a theory of the long run, and questions of nominal changes in the value of output become divorced from questions of real changes. The classical dichotomy between real and monetary aspects of the economy is achieved by Ricardo. Real factors determine real output and money becomes a veil.

This dichotomy plus the emphasis on the long run equilibrium means that Ricardo has no theory of the transmission of monetary shocks to nominal values. Hume's complex sequence of effort, employment and output variations is replaced by an equi-proportionate increase in prices following an increase in money stock. Thus short run output movements cannot be caused by monetary movement, they are transient and unsystematic. The transmission mechanism is unimportant since the eventual influence of money on prices — its long run equilibrium effect — is all that matters for Ricardo.

Ricardo's influence on macro-economic policy, especially on policy concerning money supply, was decisive for 125 years from 1815 to 1940 and indeed continues to exert its influence today. The British economy was subjected to the first of its many long bouts of deflation following Ricardo's recommendation in the period immediately after 1815. After that, self-denial on the part of governments, whenever contemporary economic conditions cried out for some palliative measure, became the official orthodoxy.

In the *General Theory*, Keynes describes Ricardo's impact very eloquently,

> The completeness of the Ricardian victory is something of a curiosity and a mystery. It must have been due to a complex of suitabilities in the doctrine to the environment into which it was projected. That it reached conclusions quite different from what the ordinary uninstructed person would expect, added, I suppose, to its intellectual prestige. That its teaching, translated into practice, was austere and often unpalatable, lent it virtue. That it was adapted to carry a vast and consistent logical superstructure, gave it beauty. That it could explain much social injustice and apparent cruelty as an inevitable incident in the scheme of progress, and the attempt to change such things as likely on the whole to do more harm than good, commended it to authority. That it afforded a measure of justification to the free activities of the individual capitalist, attracted to it the support of the dominant social force behind authority.
>
> But although the doctrine itself has remained unquestioned by orthodox exonomists up to a late date, its signal failure for purposes of scientific prediction has greatly impaired, in the course of time, the prestige of its practitioners. For professional economists, after Malthus, were apparently unmoved by the lack of correspondence between the results of their theory and the facts of observation; — a discrepancy which the ordinary man has not failed to observe, with the result of his growing unwillingness to accord to economists that measure of respect which he gives to other groups of scientists whose theoretical results are confirmed by observation when they are applied to the facts.
>
> The celebrated *optimism* of traditional economic theory, which has led to economists being looked upon as Candides, who, having left this world for the cultivation of their gardens, teach that all is for the best in the best of all possible worlds provided we will let well alone, is also to be traced, I think, to their having neglected to take account of the drag on prosperity which can be exercised by an insufficiency of effective demand. For there would obviously be a natural tendency towards the optimum employment of resources in a society which was functioning after the manner of the classical postulates. It may well be that the classical theory represents the way in which we should like our economy to behave. But to assume that it actually does so is to assume our difficulties away

[*General Theory*, pp. 32–4]

Much of what Keynes says about Ricardo's analysis rings true today. Its deliberate contrariness to ordinary experience, its austerity and unpalatibility to the ordinary public making it all the more attractive to those in authority, the beauty of its logical superstructure and its usefulness to laissez faire philosophy are all evident today under the altered name of monetarism. This is why governments can stand by while unemployment steadily mounts, why they can put priority on cutting expenditure in the face of excess capacity and widespread bankruptcy of business and and why the tenets of monetarism appeal to conservative governments.

As we shall see below the Hume/Ricardo divide persists today in the various schools of monetarism. There are those who deny any short term benefits from money stock changes and those who deny that such benefits can be permanent. This disagreement expresses itself in the different importance given by various schools to the specification of the transmission mechanism. It also leads to different views about the possible good (harm) that a sensible (irresponsible) monetary policy can do.

Ricardo's triumph was complete for over a hundred years. An opposite view failed to take hold, even to the extent of denying Hume's doctrine of short term benefits in output from a monetary change. Technical progress, rapid accumulation, the opening out of world markets through imperial expansion and trade meant that for Britain during much of this period prices were stable if not falling. The terms of trade were to Britain's advantage as cheap sources of primary products were opened up by migrating British capital. The problem if any in these years was not inflation but business fluctuations heralded by financial crises.

In one respect however Keynes' strictures against the Ricardian orthodoxy may seem misplaced to a modern reader. This is in his statement that Ricardo's doctrine has been a 'signal failure for purposes of scientific prediction', and that it led to a 'lack of correspondence between the results of . . . theory and the facts of observation'. (General Theory). This is because one claim of modern monetarism is to have ample empirical support stretching over long periods of time and many countries. A major step in this direction was Irving Fisher's translation of the Ricardian proposition into a mathematical formula suitable for statistical testing. As an economic theorist of money and interest rates and a pioneer in the statistical theory of index numbers, Fisher was well equipped to formulate the basic quantity theoretic proposition mathematically. In his monumental book *The Purchasing Power of Money* written in 1911 he formulated the celebrated Equation of Exchange:

$$MV = PT \tag{1}$$

where M is the stock of money, V its (transactions) velocity of circulation,

P the general price level, and T an index of the volume of trade.[4]

Fisher derived the equation from the obvious notion that all sales or purchases must have an equivalent monetary counterpart. Most of these transactions will be in newly-produced goods and services (flow of current income) but some would be sales and purchases of old durable goods or paper claims to existing goods especially land and machinery.

Thus Fisher included in his definition of transactions purchase or sale of wealth (real estate, commodities), property (bonds, mortgages private notes, bills of exchange) and services (of rented real estate, of rented commodities, of hired workers). These various terms aggregated to $\sum_i P_i Q_i$ where P_i are prices and Q_i are 'quantities'. On the money side, Fisher included currency (M) with its velocity (V) as well as bank deposits (M') with their velocity (V'). So we have

$$MV + M'V' = \sum_i P_i Q_i \qquad (1a)$$

To reduce $\sum_i P_i Q_i$ to a manageable term, Fisher used the concept of a general price level and defined a base year price weighted sum of quantities as a single variable called transactions. Thus

$$(\sum P_i Q_i)_t = P_t T_t \qquad (2)$$

where

$$P_t = \sum (P_i Q_i)_t \Big/ \sum (P_{io} Q_{it}) \text{ and } T = \sum_i P_{io} Q_{it}$$

Thus T is a quantity index of current quantities weighted by base year prices and P_i is a price index using current quantities as weights.

Fisher realised however that both (1) and (1a) were identities — definitional equations which are true as tautologies. According to him, the identity became an equation — a causal relationship — only when we further add that a change in M produces a proportional change in M'. But the variables V and V' are independent of changes in M and M'. What is most crucial and is a direct echo of Ricardian theory: variations in M and M' produce no changes in Q. Fisher thus argued not the constancy of V and V' but their independence of M and M', and by implication of P or T. Similarly T is independent of M, M', V, V' and P.

It is best at this stage to let Fisher speak for himself

(T)he volume of trade, like the velocity of circulation of money, is independent of the quantity of money. An inflation of the currency cannot increase the product of farms and factories, nor the speed of freight trains or ships. The stream of business depends on natural resources and technical conditions, not on the quantity of money

(Purchasing Power, p. 155)

The full statement of the theory then follows:

> Since then, a doubling in the quantity of money: (1) will normally double deposits subject to check in the same ratio and (2) will not appreciably affect either the velocity of circulation of money or of deposits or the volume of trade, it follows necessarily and mathematically that the level of prices must double. While therefore, the equation of exchange, of itself, asserts no causal relation between the quantity of money and price level, any more than it asserts a causal relation between any other two factors, yet, when we take into account conditions known quite apart from that equation, viz. that a change in M produces a proportional change in M', and no changes in V, V' or the Q's, there is no possible escape from the conclusion that a change in the quantity of money (M) must normally cause a proportional change in the price level (the P's)
>
> (Purchasing Power p. 156–7)

> We may now restate then in what causal sense the quantity theory is true. It is true in the sense that *one of the normal effects of an increase in the quantity of money is an exactly proportional increase in the general level of prices*
>
> (Purchasing Power p. 157)

Fisher as a pioneering theorist and econometrician placed the quantity theory on an algebraic and statistical footing. In his book, he derived estimates of M, M', V, V', T and P and then compared the actual movements in P with those predicted by $(MV + M'V')/T$. He found close correspondence in these series over long periods of time for Britain and the USA. What he did not test however was his subset of hypotheses concerning the independence of T and M or of V and V' of M and of the rate of inflation. He assumed this independence.

While Fisher maintained the classical dichotomy and strictly separated real output determination from any influence of money, he did not entirely ignore the short run effects of changes in prices. In a chapter of his book entitled 'Disturbance of Equation and of Purchasing Power During Transition Periods', he tackles this question. His chain of links is as follows,

> 1. Prices rise. 2. The rate of interest rises but not sufficiently. 3. Enterprises encouraged by large profits expand their loans. 4. Deposit currency (M') expands relative to money (M). 5. Prices continue to rise, that is, phenomenon 1 is repeated. Then No. 2 is repeated and so on.
>
> In other words, a slight initial rise of prices sets in motion a train of events which tends to repeat itself. Rise of prices generates rise of prices, and continues to do so, *as long as the interest rate lags behind its normal figure*.
>
> (Purchasing Power p. 60)

Fisher's contribution to the quantity theory of money is to have formalised the basic notions of the classical theory. Thus it is not the constancy of V (or V') but its independence of M, P and T which is crucial to the causal interpretation of the equation of exchange. Similarly he makes it explicit that the volume of trade is unrelated to the money supply. He thus reiterates the fundamental importance of the classical dichotomy — money has no influence in real output determination but only in the determination of the absolute price level.

The tension between the short run and long run aspects of the theory persists in Fisher. Thus his discussion of the transition does not make clear as to whether real output is affected by the movements in interest rates lagging behind prices. He does maintain the expansion in business loans which will have output consequences if used for productive rather than purely speculative investment. If one assumes that output is continuously at the full employment level in the short run as well as in the long run, deviations of interest rates from price changes can have no systematic effects; they must be random. If one admits short run output effects of money supply changes via interest rate movements, then, in the equation of exchange, T cannot be taken to be independent of M.

Much more significant however is the threat to the proportionality proposition of the QT. If prices are to rise exactly in the same proportion as money supply in the long run, then any positive output effects in the short run due to money supply changes must be *offset exactly* by negative output effects before the long run equilibrium is attained. Otherwise the effect of money supply increase will be split in the long run between price increases *and* output increases. Once this is admitted, the theory loses much of its force as then it becomes a conjectural matter as to how much price changes and how much output changes will combine to equal a given change in money supply.

The independence of Q from M in the short run and/or in the long run is a basic point at issue in the two hundred year old debate surrounding the quantity theory. Many economists wedded to the Ricardo/Say doctrine of a long run theory of output determination still sought a monetary explanation of the trade cycle and financial crises. Thus trade cycle theories were the first attempts to graft a theory of short run output variation onto a long run Ricardian steady state. A certain inconsistency between the short run and long run, or rather loose thinking, was bound to creep in here since otherwise the short run observable output movements would be in flat contradiction to the economic theory underlying the long run.

Attempts were made at the turn of the century, most notably by

Marshall and Wicksell to bridge this gap. We concentrate here on Marshall, leaving Wicksell till later, because Marshall's formulation of the short run is crucial to modern monetarism. Marshall explicitly endorsed the equation of exchange as a long run theory. For the short run he proposed the cash balance approach. With this he provided a micro-economic argument (though not quite a theory) as to why people held money and how much. With his renowned lack of precision, Marshall related cash balances held by the public to its income, wealth and property. He said that a stable fraction of the nominal value of one or all three of these magnitudes was held as cash balances. Thus he mentions at one stage that people held a tenth of annual income and one-fiftieth of property in cash. (For Marshall, cash, of course, means coins and currency and not bank deposits.)

Marshall related the motives for holding money to convenience and the desire to take advantage of expected changes in prices. Thus in terms of Keynes' General Theory he talked of the transaction and precautionary motives. He also clearly formulated the problem of money holding in terms of returns foregone on other assets. But Marshall also had a full employment theory of output. He thought that the cash balance equation was better able to relate price fluctuations to money supply movements *in the short run*. In the long run, business practices, factor supplies etc. changed, which accounted for the long run price changes. Thus as Eshag points out in his study of Marshall's theory

> The primary reason for these long period price fluctuations are 'changes in the methods of business and the amount of commodities' which constitute the 'commercial environment'. In other words, it is the variations in 'the volume of business' and 'the habits of business', rather than the supply of the precious metals, which are, according to [Marshall], largely responsible for the long period price fluctuations
>
> (Eshag (1963) pp. 5–6)

By contrast, the short period fluctuations in prices from one year to the next are explained by Marshall in terms of the cash balance equation. These fluctuations are accompanied by 'inflations and contractions of credit' caused by 'wars and rumours of war, good and bad harvests, changes in business expectations and confidence' etc. Marshall complained that the quantity theory 'does not explain the causes which govern the rapidity of circulation', i.e. no theory of why money is held and for how long. His cash balance equation was designed to do just that. (All citations from Marshall taken from Eshag (1963) pp. 6–7).

Marshall never formulated the cash balance equation mathematically but his writings did succeed in focusing attention on aggregate measures of income and wealth rather than the sum of transactions as in Fisher. Thus, although he was not offering a theory of aggregate output determination, he cleared the way towards thinking in terms of aggregate income flows related to money stocks. His ideas were formulated variously by his Cambridge pupils. Thus the following formulae are listed by Eshag as all describing the cash balance equation.

Pigou formulated the equation and extended it to include bank deposits:

$$M = k P A \ [\ c + b \ (1-c)] \tag{3}$$

where A is real resources expressed in terms of a single good ('wheat'), P is the price of the good or the reciprocal of the value of money in terms of 'wheat', k is the proportion of resources held in money form, c is the proportion of money balances held in cash, b is the banking system's cash reserve ratio and $(l-c)$ is the amount held in bank deposits.[5]

Keynes wrote a simpler version of (3) in his articles for the *Manchester Guardian* which became *A Tract on Monetary Reform*. Thus he had

$$M = k P A \tag{4}$$

On the other hand Robertson in his book *Money* (1928) tried to preserve the Marshallian distinction by having two separate equations. He replaced R with y, real national income,

$$M = k P_y \ y \tag{5}$$

as well as

$$M = k' \ P_T T \tag{6}$$

Where P_Y and P_T are income and transactions price levels, T is the annual volume of transactions and $k, \ k'$ two proportions. It is in Robertson's formulation given in equation (5) that the Cambridge equation has come down to us to this day.

It is tempting to treat (5) as a simple rewriting of (1) with k being the reciprocal of V and y just another name for T. But we have described in detail Fisher's definition of T which makes clear that for Fisher T includes more than the flow of real income. Also these two formulations relate to the short run and long run in separate ways. Thus the same level of real income may generate different levels of transactions depending on frequency of wage payments, of settlement of contracts, on the degree of vertical integration in the economy etc. Very little work has been done connecting y to T in any systematic way. (The only treatment of this is in Hayek's discussion of 'the coefficient of money transactions' in his *Prices and Production* (1931), see also Desai (1981b), For whatever reason, the Cambridge formulation in terms of equation (5) is the currently accepted formulation of the quantity theory.

The seeds of dissatisfaction planted by Marshall in the quantity theory as a behavioural explanation of the impact of money on prices persisted and matured in Keynes' work in the *Treatise on Money*.

Robertson's distinction between a price level implied in the Cambridge cash balance equation (P_y) and the price level implied in Fisher's equation of exchange was clarified and developed further by Keynes in his *Treatise*. But not only was there a multiplicity of price levels to consider. Once Marshall had emphasised the behavioural roots of money holding, it was inevitable that there would be dissatisfaction with the myth of a single consumer whose behaviour was captured in k. Hawtrey pointed out that consumers and traders had different motives for holding money balances which would imply different k's. Keynes in the Treatise carried this dis-aggregation of money balances by type of holder further.

The *Treatise* contains a very exhaustive discussion of index number problems involved in measuring the purchasing power of money. Keynes starts with the obvious point that since money is not held for its own sake but for purchasing goods, one measure of the value of money is obviously an index of consumer goods prices appropriately weighted. Keynes reserves the name *purchasing power of money* for this measure which he also labels the *consumption standard* (P_C). An alternative measure is what Keynes calls the *labour power of money* or the *earning standard* (P_L). As he puts it

> This standard aims at measuring the purchasing power of money over units of human effort as contrasted with units of commodity, so that the purchasing power of money divided by its labour power furnishes an index of real earning power and hence of the standard of life
>
> (*Treatise* p. 56).

Thus if the hourly money wage is £2, then £1 buys half an hour of effort. If £1 buys, say, one tenth of a basket of consumer goods, it would take five hours to buy such a basket. Keynes adds that in measuring consumer prices for the working class as a group, we arrive closer to the real wage since such an index is a better deflator for money wages. Of course any such index captures the purchasing power of money not over all consumer goods but a subset which is socially and culturally thought to be 'necessities'.

The most important point however is that neither the price level in Marshall's equation nor the price level in Fisher's equation measures either the consumption standard or the labour standard. Keynes calls these the *cash balance standard* and the *cash transaction standard*. Thus Fisher's standard since it weights prices by transactions would give greater weight to consumer goods which pass through various stages of manufacture than to consumer services sold directly by the individual service provider to the consumer. In a consumption standard these two may have equal importance. Thus the P of equation (2) or P_T of (6) does not measure the purchasing power of money. Also stock market transactions or sale and purchase of commercial property will generate large transactions per unit sold but they are not relevant to consumers.

Similarly there is a divergence between the cash balance standard (P_y) and the consumption standard (P_C). In modern discussions where some version of equation (5) is taken as the demand for money, it is usual to take the consumer price index P_C as a measure of P_y but this does not match the behavioural mechanism underlying (5). This is because money is held in this equation to take advantage of bargains or likely falls in goods prices. Thus predictable expenditure — the monthly rent, insurance payments — should generate no demand for such balances as they are foreseen.[6] Thus in a cash balance standard, the unpredictable or infrequent items may have a greater weight than the predictable items though both types of goods may be equally important in the consumer's budget.

These different price indices may move parallel in the long run though even this is not certain if we mean by long run calendar time rather than the stationary state (for which it is trivially true). Thus technical progress in the financial and banking industry is making it possible to economise on cash balances and substitute interest-bearing, near-money assets, e.g. building society deposits in UK, NOW deposits in US. Also with the passage of time, concentration of industry may make for much fewer inter-firm transactions and the Fisher index would move differently due to that. But whatever the long run parallelism, in the short run these price indices move divergently. Thus investment fluctuations or even movements in wages will lead to differential changes in transactions than in consumer expenditure. When the prices of services are increasing faster than the prices of goods as has happened in recent years, the P_y, P_T and P_C prices will move differently.

This differentiation between different price measures means that even at a high level of aggregation the connection between money and inflation is not simple. Money wages rising faster than productivity implies a decline in the labour power of money (rise in P_L) or what Keynes calls *income inflation*. The rise of consumer goods prices is for Keynes *commodity inflation* or what is normally called simply inflation. The rise of capital goods prices which is not of much immediate concern to consumers but important in income distribution is called by Keynes *capital inflation*. Commodity inflation and capital inflation represent the relative rise in profits compared to other incomes so Keynes labels these two *profit inflation*. In making these distinctions, one is immediately made aware that inflation does not hit all goods and all individuals equally as is the impression given by equations such as (1) or (5). Inflation has distributional implications and even if money were the sole cause of inflation, we need to know who receives the additional money to know which prices will rise first and who will be affected.

Besides differentiating between price levels, Keynes also talks of three types of bank deposits. Thus *income deposits* are demand deposits held by consumers and *business deposits* are held for transactions purposes by producers and traders. The determinants of the demand for these two types are bound to be different and recent attempts to base the demand for money on consumer theory has led to a relative neglect, if not total obliteration, of business deposits in economic analysis. These business deposits are likely to be the proportionally larger and more volatile of the two. The third category is of course *savings deposits* or time deposits. These would today comprise of a variety of interest bearing liabilities issued by banks and other financial intermediaries which are withdrawable at a stated short notice.

Now if the Cambridge equation is taken seriously as a behavioural relationship, one should only speak of income deposits and their velocity. This is of course frequently ignored and starting with some theory of consumers' demand for real balances, economists seek to explain all of M_1 or even M_3. Keynes however makes a careful distinction between these deposits and the different price levels to provide a better account of the transmission mechanism. This is what Keynes undertook in his fundamental equations in the *Treatise*.

In Chapter 10 of the *Treatise* , 'The Fundamental Equations for the Value of Money', Keynes begins by stating what in his view is the inadequacy of the Fisher/Marshall approach:

> The fundamental problem of monetary theory is not merely to establish identities or statistical equations relating [e.g.] the turnover of monetary instruments to the turnover of things traded for money. The real task of such a theory is to treat the problem dynamically, analysing the different elements involved, in

such a manner as to exhibit the causal process by which the price level is determined and the method of transition from one position of equilibrium to another. The forms of quantity theory, however, on which we have all been brought up are but ill adapted for this purpose. They are particular examples of the numerous identities which can be formulated connecting different monetary factors. But they do not, any of them, have the advantage of separating out those factors through which, in a modern economic system, the causal process actually operates during a period of change.

(Keynes (1971) p. 120)

In order to account for different types of inflation, Keynes adopts here as he did later in the General Theory, a two sector classification of all goods into consumption goods and investment goods. Let us call their prices respectively P_C, P_I. Their quantities are measured in such a way that they are commensurable, i.e. in terms of equal unit costs of production. (Our notation differs from that used by Keynes in order to make it compatible with later chapters.) Thus let the total cost of production of consumer goods be C' and that of investment goods be I'. Keynes' method of measuring volumes of output then requires us to measure investment goods in terms of units of consumer goods. If C is output of consumption goods, then let $C' = aC$, a being the unit cost. We then measure investment goods I so that $I' = aI$. Then $C + I = Q$ is real output. Let total money income (factor earnings) be E' and nominal savings S'. According to Keynes' definition in the *Treatise*, profits are not a part of income.

Keynes then puts forward two equations for the price of consumer goods P_C and the general price level P. W is the rate of earnings per unit of effort and a is the rate of earnings per unit of output. Then we have first an identity of expenditure on consumer goods and the revenue of consumer goods producers.

$$P_C C = E' - S' = \frac{E'}{Q}(C + I) - S' \tag{7}$$

From this we have the first of the fundamental equations

$$P_C = \frac{E'}{Q} + (I' - S')\big/ C \tag{8}$$

Since E' is total money earnings, $E'/Q = a$ and hence the price of consumer goods is related to unit factor cost of all output plus a disequilibrium term relating to the gap between the cost of production of investment goods (i.e. its 'output') and the savings which will be spent on buying them. This leads to the second fundamental equation.

$$P = (P_C C + P_I I)\big/ Q = E'\big/ Q + (P_I I - S')\big/ Q \tag{9}$$

where $P_I I$ is the money receipts of investment goods producers. Thus if investment goods producers are making profits $P_I I > I'$ then the price level will exceed the unit labour cost of output.

Implied in these equations is Keynes' definition of profit. Thus profits (R) of consumer and investment goods industries can be defined as

$$R_C = I' - S' \tag{10a}$$

$$R_I = P_I I - I' \tag{10b}$$

$$R = R_C + R_I = P_I I - S' \tag{11}$$

combining (11) with (9) we get

$$P = a + R \big/ Q \tag{12}$$

Equations (10a), (10b) make clear that profits are the disequilibrium windfall elements in this system, and they are caused by the divergence between investment expenditure and savings. Equation (12) gives an expression for the price level in terms of incomes of labour and entrepreneurs per unit of output.

These equations would be identities except for the disequilibrium interpretation of profits. Prices would be equal to the unit labour cost of output and the standard of living (real wage) would be equal to the productivity of labour in *equilibrium*. In much of the recent discussion this is a condition of equilibrium defined in terms of rates of change of prices and productivity rather than levels. Thus equilibrium in this system requires that I be equal to S. But these decisions are made independently and mediated by the financial system. So it becomes a requirement of monetary policy 'that the banking system should so regulate its rate of lending that the value of investment is equal to savings'. This is required because the determinants of the investment expenditure involve the rate of lending and the extent to which the banking system is willing to take a 'countercyclical' stance or 'lean against the wind'. Much of chapters 11, 13 and 15 of the *Treatise* spell out this mechanism but it will take us too far out of our way to follow this line.

What we can now establish is the connection Keynes makes between P_C, P_y, P_T and his classification of bank deposits. Let M_{1Y} be income deposits and M_{1B} business deposits. Let M_2 be savings deposits. Keynes then shows that in *equilibrium* at least, it is possible to establish a connection between these various measures. Thus in equilibrium $I = I' = S$ we have

$$P = P_C = E'/Q = (M_{1Y}V_Y/Q) \tag{13}$$

In equation (13) we are using equation (5) and $V_Y = k^{-1}$. Now equation (13) can be related to P_T as follows. Let w be the proportion of cash deposits ($M_{1Y} + M_{1B}$) to total deposits ($M_1 + M_2 = M$). Then

$$M_{1Y}V_Y + M_{1B}V_B = w\,MV$$

This lets us write (13) as

$$P_C = M\,w/Q \tag{14}$$

Now equation (1) can be written as

$$P_T T = MVw$$

So

$$P_C = P_T\,(T/Q)\,(V_{1Y}/V) \tag{15}$$

Though this is rather a messy expression, what it illustrates at least in equation (13) is that in equilibrium there may be a direct relationship between money and the price of consumer goods if money is defined narrowly. The definition of equilibrium as stated by Keynes is interesting.

> This means, indeed, that in equilibrium — i.e. when the factors of production are fully employed, when the public is neither bullish nor bearish of securities and is maintaining in the form of savings deposits neither more nor less than the 'normal' proportion of its total wealth, and when the volume of saving is equal both to the cost and the value of new investments — there is a unique relationship between the quantity of money and the price level of consumption goods and of output as a whole, of such a character that if the quantity of money were to double the price levels would be double also.
>
> (Keynes (1971) p. 132).

Then equation (15) points out that there is only a rather indirect relationship between the price level in the old fashioned quantity theory and the purchasing power of money.

When Keynes wrote the *Treatise*, he was not unsympathetic to the main tradition of monetary theory. Indeed he was engaged in clarifying and enriching the Cambridge tradition. He arrives however at the revolutionary notion that the cash balance equation (or the equation of exchange) is useless for analysing the impact of money on prices out of equilibrium. Thus the homogeneity postulate that he asserts in the quotation given above does not say anything about how the economy gets from one equilibrium to another. Indeed only trivial changes in the quantity of money (defining one hundred old francs as one new franc etc.) are understandable in that context. This is because price change involves disequilibrium and happens via the act of the banking system which changes the supply of credit to entrepreneurs relative to the hoarding propensity of savers. Thus equation (13) tells us about a single equilibrium price level, but not about price *change*, particularly about price change away from the dynamic equilibrium path.

Thus even before the publication of the *General Theory*, Keynes working with the Cambridge tradition had arrived at conclusions which restricted the scope of the quantity theory to periods of full employment equilibrium. He found that the quantity theory framework was not enough to understand the relationship of money to economic activity. But he was not alone in this respect. Indeed parallel with the publication of the *Treatise* was the appearance of two other books concerned with monetary theory: by Myrdal (*Monetary Equilibrium*) and Hayek (*Prices and Production*). Both these books also sought to explore the interrelationship of money and economic activity outside the quantity theoretic framework. Of these two, Myrdal went further in construction of a theory of a monetary economy along non-neoclassical lines but unfortunately his book had little impact on subsequent work.

For our purposes the more interesting work is that of Hayek. Hayek's work is worth discussing in some detail because of the recent revival of interest in his theories and his reappearance as an adviser to politicians. It is also of interest because, by his own reckoning, Hayek was not a simple quantity theorist when he gave the lectures at LSE in 1931, which later became his *Prices and Production* (1931).

Indeed given his current status as one of the senior proponents of monetarism (a misleading view of his theory in my opinion), it is interesting to see that Hayek is quite trenchant in his critique of the quantity theory. Hayek views Fisher's attempts to quantify the quantity theory with evident disapproval at the outset of his book. While he grants that the 'elementary propositions of the quantity theory' should never be forgotten, he adds

what I complain of is not only that this theory in its various forms has unduly usurped the central place in monetary theory, but that the point of view from which it springs is a positive hindrance to further progress.

(*Prices and Production* pp. 3–4).

Hayek considers that to trace the effect of money on economic activity mainly through the movement of the general price level is a futile attempt. He denies that categories such as the *total* quantity of money, the general level of all prices and the total amount of production have any influence on the decisions of individuals. In a sense he is saying in modern terms that the quantity theory is a macro-economic view without any micro-economic foundations. Indeed, he questioned the validity of the concept of a general price level and hence, by implication, of a one-good model as a suitable framework for study of monetary theory.

A quantity theory is, according to Hayek, only a crude early stage in monetary theory. Developments occur when theorists try to trace the mechanism whereby money influences different categories of economic activity. Hayek traces this more complex tradition to Cantillon's critique of Locke. He also outlines how Thornton in his *Paper Credit* first brought in the connection between profitability of investment and the cost of credit. Then through a series of classical authors such as Thomas Joplin, Bentham, Malthus, J.S, Mill, Hayek arrives at Wicksell's view. Wicksell, it may be recalled, traced the influence of credit through the gap between market and natural rates of interest. The former equilibrates the demand for and supply of loanable funds and the latter equilibrates saving and investment. A gap between these starts off a cumulative disequilibrium of upward or downward movement of prices. The impetus for the movement of prices comes through the fact that the gap between market and natural rates provides incentive for entrepreneurs to accumulate or de-cumulate.

Hayek then developed the next stage of the argument, due originally to von Mises, that it is not the supply of credit as such but its distribution between producers of capital goods and those of consumer goods which causes what Marx would call a disproportionality between the two sectors. Hayek's attempt in *Prices and Production* is to trace this insight through a rigorous development of the Austrian theory of capital. Thus for Hayek, it is the effect of money on the *production structure* especially the lengthening of the period of production that is crucial. This can explain the inflation in consumer goods prices, the lag between money wages and prices once the credit cycle starts and the eventual collapse of the boom caused by the credit expansion.

Thus Hayek constructs a complex model of the influence of money on the relative prices of goods via the disproportionality in the growth of consumer goods as against capital goods caused by the lowering of the price of credit. He is looking not for stability of the general price level but for a monetary arrangement that will make money neutral, i.e. preserve that allocation of output and that structure of relative prices which would have prevailed in the absence of the disturbing influence of money, for instance, in a barter economy. Thus his policy desideratum is not a stable price level but neutral money — a condition far more difficult to achieve on his own admission. This is because neutral money is not so much a desired stock of money as its appropriate distribution between different activities. Until such a desired distribution is obtained, distortions in factor and product markets prevail because individuals receive false signals from the price system. This means that unemployment is for him a sign of monetary pathology: it is a sign of the maldistribution of money. Such problems can be cured by stopping the growth of money stock altogether immediately rather than gradually and letting the market take its time to adjust until these distortions disappear and economic agents begin to get proper signals from the price system. Hayek was frankly sceptical in his lectures that this was a feasible policy but this is a view he has consistently propounded over the fifty years since the original lectures which became *Prices and Production*.

Thus by the early 1930s there was a great deal of activity in the field of monetary theory. The works of Robertson, Keynes, Hayek, Myrdal and others had begun to integrate monetary theory with the theory of prices and the theory of production. Indeed such integration of money, production and prices in a dynamic theoretical framework was the explicitly stated intention of Keynes, Hayek and Myrdal. The quantity theory framework whether in its Ricardo/Fisher version or in its Marshallian version was superseded if not rejected because it proved to be inadequate on theoretical grounds; 'a positive hindrance to further progress' as Hayek called it. It is often said that it was the Keynesian Revolution i.e. the publication of *The General Theory of Employment, Interest and Money* and its success in persuading the economics profession of a new way of thinking about income and employment that caused the downgrading of monetary theory and policy. If this is taken to be synonymous with the decline of the quantity theory, then this is surely a misrepresentation of the history of economic ideas. The quantity theory was in decline *before* the Keynesian Revolution. It was found to be theoretically inadequate and too mechanical or simplistic as a framework for understanding the role of money in the economy. But the rich harvest of new formulations of monetary theory by Hayek, Keynes and Myrdal sustained no further work after Keynes' *General Theory* changed the agenda of questions economists were to think about in the next thirty years.

Notes

1. Parentage is attributed to Karl Brunner (1968) by Purvis (1980) and to David Fand (1970) by Mayer (1975). Despite this, the label was slow to gain in use. Thus, it does not appear in the index of Gordon (1974), which is devoted to Friedman's monetary theory. Indeed Friedman has never been happy with the word, as he has said on many occasions.
2. For ideas of a quantity theoretic nature and mercantilist ideas, see Blaug (1964), Chapter 1, pp. 8–24. Blaug deals with Locke's ideas. For references to Locke's work on money and prices, see Laslett's 'Introduction to Locke's Two Essays' in Laslett (1962). As for the longevity of a doctrine being no guide to its merit, one may only point to the belief in witchcraft, which was strong for about seven centuries and had its supporting system of theory (in St. Thomas Aquinas), a body of quantitative evidence diligently gathered and its policy applications. See Kors and Peters (1972), especially the section 'St. Thomas Aquinas and the Nature of Evil', pp. 51–74. This collection also cites the evidence that contemporaries had gathered 'proving' the existence of witches. See also Trevor-Roper (1969) and Cohn (1976).
3. Recently Mayer has examined Hume's work in light of Mayer's earlier listing of some twelve basic monetarist beliefs. Mayer (1980).
4. Keynes in his *Treatise on Money* vol. 1, attributes the original algebraic formula to a mathematician, Simon Newcomb to whom Fisher dedicated his book. Keynes (1971) p. 209, footnote.
5. While for Pigou, the choice of wheat as the standard commodity to measure the purchasing power of money had no significance, Keynes points out that this is one method of devising a suitable index, Keynes (1971) p. 97, footnote 2.
6. Recall that Marshall's focus is on cash balance or what we would call today M_1. Predictable expenditure (say the monthly rent payment) can be met by regular withdrawal from time deposits or savings accounts and does not require M_1 balances to be maintained for any appreciable length of time.

2. FROM THE QUANTITY THEORY TO MONETARISM

As we saw in the last chapter, the status of the quantity theory of money on the eve of the publication of Keynes' *General Theory* was no longer secure. The hundred years between 1815 and 1914 saw its untramelled rule. By the time Irving Fisher formulated it algebraically and tested it, in 1911, one could be forgiven for thinking that the quantity theory of money was the capstone needed to furnish the magnificent edifice of classical and neoclassical economics. Whatever the differences regarding value theory between say, Ricardo and Walras, both schools believed in the ability and the desirability of the market mechanism, left to itself, to achieve market clearing outcomes in the labour, commodity and money markets. Price flexibility and perfect mobility of resources unhindered by state interference were supposed to achieve the desired market equilibrium automatically. Both classical and neoclassical schools also shared the assumption of the dichotomy of real and monetary relations. Thus all real decisions are functions of relative prices in a moneyless (barter) context and the money equation only sets the absolute price level. The quantity theory embodies this dichotomy.

This was a century of remarkable economic growth, of a whole series of innovations spanning two industrial revolutions, of the growing dominance of western capitalist countries over the countries of Asia, Africa, Latin America and Australasia. In British experience this meant increasing prosperity though this was beginning to be threatened by a relative loss of competitive power from the 1880s onwards. Keynes described this century of economic experience eloquently:

> During the nineteenth century, the growth of population and of invention, the opening of new lands, the state of confidence and the frequency of war over the average of (say) each decade seem to have been sufficient, taken in conjunction with the propensity to consume, to establish a schedule of the marginal efficiency of capital which allowed a reasonably satisfactory average level of employment to be compatible with a rate of interest high enough to be psychologically accept-

able to wealth-owners. There is evidence that for a period of almost one hundred and fifty years the long run typical rate of interest in the leading financial centres was about 5 per cent, and the gilt-edged rate between 3 and 3½ per cent; and these rates were modest enough to encourage a rate of investment consistent with an average of employment which was not intolerably low. Sometimes the wage unit, but more often the monetary standard or the monetary system (in particular through the development of bank-money), would be adjusted so as to ensure the quantity of money in terms of wage-units was sufficient to satisfy normal liquidity preference at rates of interest which were seldom below the standard rates indicated above. The tendency of the wage-unit was, as usual, steadily upwards on the whole, but the efficiency of labour was also increasing. Thus the balance of forces was such as to allow a fair measure of stability of prices; – the highest quinquennial average of Sauerbeck's index number between 1820 and 1914 was only 50 per cent above the lowest. This was not accidental. It is rightly described as due to a balance of forces in an age when individual groups of employers were strong enough to prevent the wage-unit from rising much faster than the efficiency of production, and where monetary systems were at the same time sufficiently conservative to provide an average supply of money in terms of wage-units which allowed to prevail the lowest average rate of interest readily acceptable by wealth-owners under the influence of their liquidity-preferences. The average level of employment was, of course, substantially below full employment, but not so intolerably below it as to provoke revolutionary changes.

(*General Theory*, pp. 307-8).

In this long statement Keynes interprets nineteenth century experience in terms of the *General Theory* model but we also see a number of special circumstances which helped the smooth working of the classical mechanism. Perhaps most important among these was the relative weakness of workers vis-a-vis employers. Through this period, most countries had severe limitations on adult franchise, not to say on trade union rights. Britain granted universal adult suffrage only *after* the First World War. Thus the state was immune to democratic pressure from groups which suffered from the cyclical variations in employment. Britain was also in the pivotal position in the International Gold Standard both through the ability of the Bank of England to attract gold via small variations in the Bank Rate and the important position of the Indian Empire in the Gold Standard Mechanism.[1]

The First World War changed all this. The tranquility of the previous hundred years was shattered. Most countries abandoned the Gold Standard, industries were started in the peripheral countries of the Empires and in the 'newly industrialising countries' of Latin America, Japan and China. The pre-eminent position of Britain in the world economy was irretrievably lost; Russia was taken out of the international capitalist nexus, the German economy was ruined. The First World War and the dislocations following it brought flexible exchange rates and in many countries experience of hyper-inflation. The First World War had brought unprecedented low levels of unemployment in capitalist countries (in Britain as low as ½%

in 1915-16) and this had led to the strengthening of labour's position.[2] Across Europe, the growing power of labour and of socialist parties seemed to threaten the stability of the state. Everywhere wages rose dramatically in the years 1914-20, as did prices. Although these political changes had their economic impact, contemporary economists fell back on the pre-1914 economic system to understand what was happening, which was interpreted in the light of the quantity theory. Domestically, the absence of the discipline of the Gold Standard was blamed for inflation and, internationally, the doctrine of purchasing power parity (PPP) was proposed as an extension of the quantity theory for interpreting the course of the exchanges. The political dimension was completely ignored.

As Keynes himself described the inflationary experience in 1924 in *The Tract on Monetary Reform*, there seemed to be a close connection between prices and money supply. It was in the decade following 1924 that many economists began to be dissatisfied with the explanations of classical theory and of the quantity theory in particular. In Britain in 1921 severe deflation, along classical monetary lines, brought a severe rise in unemployment which showed no sign of diminishing through the next fifteen years. Britain had special problems after returning to the Gold Standard with an over-valued pound, in the especially large hangover of Public Debt contracted during World War I by a government shy of raising resources by taxation and in the large number of declining industries in the capital goods sector. But also elsewhere in Europe, unlike in the USA, the twenties were not prosperous. The French economy managed marginally better by keeping the Franc undervalued, but the German economy did not become prosperous even after the end of hyperinflation.

To a weak European economy battered by war and never fully recovered, the Great Crash and its financial and economic aftermath in the Great Depression brought severe suffering. Unemployment high through the twenties (relative to pre-1914 experience) increased even more in the thirties. The Gold Standard was abandoned, protectionist measures were adopted by most countries and the banking system was brought into disrepute everywhere due to the many crashes and closures.

It was in this period of severe economic deflation — 1924-1938 for European countries and 1929-1938 for the USA — that the search for alternative explanations became intense. Hayek in *Prices and Production*, Keynes in *The Treatise on Money* as well as Myrdal in *Monetary Equilibrium* and, before them all, Robertson in *Banking Policy and Price Level* sought better theoretical frameworks for understanding the persistently low level of economic activity Europe was experiencing. They did this by following on the various links between money, saving and investment. But they all rejected the quantity theory, either in its Fisherian or in its Marshallian version, as inadequate. Hayek, Myrdal and Keynes all dealt with money and its role in production and accumulation, tracing cyclical fluctuations to changes in business confidence and in monetary conditions. Paradoxes of underconsumption and oversaving ruled out by the Ricardo-Walras system reappeared in economic discussions.

The Ricardo-Walras system could not accommodate persistent unemployment. In a world of flexible wages and prices, markets were supposed to clear and re-establish equilibrium if any extraneous cause had disturbed it. Hayek explicitly located the inability of the Walrasian system to account for business cycles in the absence of money in the Walrasian model.[3] Thus the Walrasian model is one of a barter economy where relative prices determine the equilibrium outcome. Money plays no essential role and can play no such role since, uncertainty being entirely absent from the model, all receipts and payments can be foreseen thus obviating the need for anyone to hold money balances. Thus by integrating money into the Walrasian economy, Hayek thought he could explain cycles as short run but disequilibrium dynamic phenomena around a long run Walrasian equilibrium.

Myrdal saw that the Wicksellian version of neoclassical monetary theory was replete with concepts appropriate to a stationary barter economy. He tried to construct a theory appropriate to a monetary economy where *ex ante* magnitudes differed from *ex post* ones and where expectations were a dominant influence on investment. Myrdal did not think much of the Walrasian model and hence did not refer back to that tradition in constructing his model. Keynes also formulated a theory of price dynamics as a disequilibrium phenomenon driven by the incidence of windfall profits and losses. But in Keynes' *Treatise*, there was still in the background an economy capable of returning to equilibrium fairly soon if it were not constantly disturbed by banking policy. In each of these three authors' works, there is an attempt to define the concept of a 'monetary equilibrium' corresponding to a Ricardo-Walras barter equilibrium. The concept though remains elusive and the policy implications unclear. But a beginning was definitely made in this period to fashion monetary theory richer than the nineteenth-century quantity theoretical heritage — a monetary theory which could accommodate production and accumulation in an environment of uncertainty.

This long background is important for appreciating the break that the *General Theory* represents in the history of economic thought. It comes in a period of transition where disaffection with the classical doctrine was widespread and a search for a more complex theory, if not a different theory altogether, had begun. The roots of disaffection lay in Europe's economic experience (I emphasise European experience here for the theorists in this search for alternatives were mainly European). The urgency of the task was due to the changed political atmosphere in which the economic experience was felt. This was the beginning of universal adult franchise in most European countries. Thus, democratic pressures were being felt by Europe's governments which their nineteenth-century predecessors could blithely ignore. The impersonal forces of the market brought hardships to people who, having got their vote, were no longer willing to suffer patiently. The first socialist country (collectivisation, purges and all) had arisen and provided an alternative political threat.

This background of theoretical and political disaffection with the nineteenth-century system is frequently forgotten in current discussions of the Keynesian Revolution. The quantity theory of money had been found inadequate and a search had been made for alternatives. The practical situation of unemployment and financial distress was urgent and disastrous. In Germany and Italy it had already led to an end of political democracy. Economic freedom and political liberty seemed to be an infeasible combination to many.

It is against this background of unemployment and the urgent questions of the capacity of a society politically democratic (i.e. where governments are subject to popular pressure) and economically decentralised (i.e. where wages and prices could not be determined by *diktat*) that we must look at Keynes' revolutionary refashioning of economics. At the heart of the *General Theory* is a central proposition which is the nub of the dispute between Keynesian and monetarist theories. The dispute as we have seen in the Introduction, had briefly flared before between Ricardo and Malthus but had since been settled in favour of the Ricardo-Walras orthodoxy. This proposition states that

> a private enterprise economy cannot be relied on *automatically* (i.e. when the market is left to its own devices) to guarantee that all markets will clear, in particular the market for labour. There will therefore be an equilibrium situation where some workers will be *involuntarily unemployed*. At the same time, producers will find themselves with stocks of unsold goods and excess productive capacity

While many economists admitted that unemployment and excess capacity may be temporary, transient, cyclical, i.e. *disequilibrium* phenomena (as for instance Hayek in his *Prices and Production*), Keynes asserted the possiblity of an *underemployment equilibrium*. This does not mean that the economy is never capable of full employment but that it was likely to get locked into underemployment if outside (government) stimulus was not applied.

The proposition that a private enterprise economy ('economy' for short) can be in underemployment equilibrium is in flat contradiction to the basic theorem of the classical and neoclassical economic theory from Adam Smith and David Ricardo through to Leon Walras and Alfred Marshall. This theorem says that

> as long as there are not external forces which impede the flexibility of prices and of quantities or the ability of economic actors to enter into voluntary contracts for the purchase and sale of goods and services, a competitive economy will establish an equilibrium of demand and supply such that at the equilibrium prices, no buyer will have unfulfilled demand and no seller will have unsold supply.

This theorem was first formulated by Adam Smith in his notion of the Invisible Hand and given rigorous formulation by David Ricardo and Leon Walras. It has been honed to mathematical perfection in the more recent formulations of Kenneth Arrow and Gerard Debreu. If this theorem is a true picture of the way the actual economies operate then there can be no voluntary unemployment except due to price rigidities, imperfections in the competitive mechanism such as cartels, trade unions, minimum price regulations etc.

Since involuntary unemployment is the central issue at dispute, let us see how Keynes established his claim. The classical answer[4] to the existence of unemployed workers is to say that they are either frictionally unemployed — in between jobs and thus in a transitional state — or that they are voluntarily unemployed because they are asking too high a real wage relative to the level which employers find profitable. Thus if the unemployed were to cut the real wage at which they offered themselves, then they will be able to find employment. While there was no quantitative prediction of how much lower the real wage would have to be, there was theoretical certainty that everyone could find employment at some real wage. Thus the excess supply of labour was caused, like all other excess supplies, because the price was above the equilibrium price — the relevant price being the relative price of labour, the real wage. If prices adjusted downwards in response to this excess supply then eventually the excess supply would be eliminated. Fig. 2.1 illustrates the familiar demand-supply equilibrium. At point E, demand and supply are equilibrium in the labour market. Employers who demand labour are able, given their stock of capital equipment, to obtain a level of marginal revenue product from the workers to afford the real wage level $(W/P)^*$ and still maximise profits. Workers on the other hand are in equilibrium in terms of their preferences between consumption (work) and leisure, the marginal disutility of work being matched by the marginal utility of consumption derived

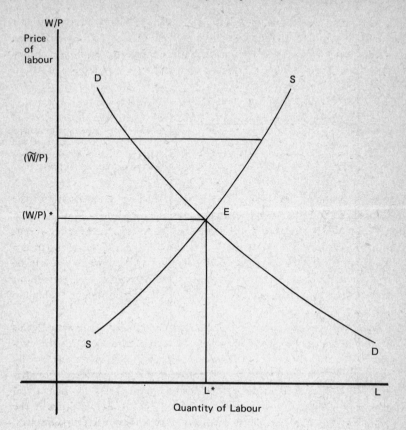

Figure 2.1: The Demand for and Supply of Labour

from the real wage. If for some reason, there is excess supply (unemployment), say at $(\widetilde{W}/P)$, then the price must adjust downwards. This is shown in Figure 2.2. Positive excess supply must generate a negative price change — the real wage must fall till it reaches $(W/P)^*$ and excess supply then vanishes.

Some caveats are in order before we proceed further. In neoclassical economics, one starts with micro-economic optimisation — individual workers and firms who all take the prevailing price as given and make their decisions about supplying or demanding labour. While there may be different types of workers with different skills and tastes, we aggregate them into a single category, labour. Similarly while firms produce different products, some consumer goods and other capital goods, we aggregate their demands for labour into a single demand curve. This transition

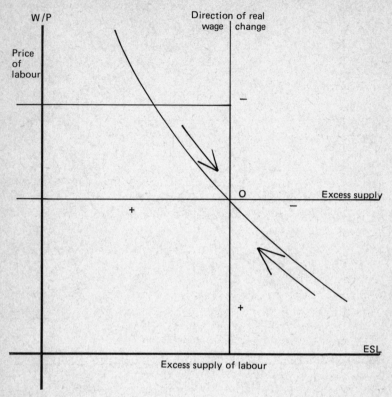

Figure 2.2: The Excess Supply of Labour

from micro-economics to macro-economics involves aggregation but we assume for the time being that no difficulties of aggregation arise. We are in a one commodity, single labour input world. Later we will have occasion to unravel this seamless aggregate economy. In particular we notice that the relative price of labour is the money wage (W) deflated by P — the price level. This price level must be interpreted as what Keynes called the consumption standard in the *Treatise*, especially if we measure the index by weights derived from workers' budgets. With our aggregation, this price is the same price of all output; $P_c = P_y = P$ (where P_c is the consumers' price level and P_y is the producers' price level).

Now Keynes objected to the neoclassical remedy on various grounds. He first pointed out that the neoclassical postulate concerning the individual worker being in equilibrium with marginal disutility of work matching the marginal utility of consumption was true only in a situation of full employment. In situations of involuntary unemployment we had an inequality rather than an equality, i.e.

$$MU \text{ of } (W/P) \geqslant MU \text{ of } (L) \tag{16}$$

MU being marginal utility, where MU of (L) stands for the negative of the marginal disutility of labour. Full equality between the two was the special case of full employment. In situations where the inequality held, workers could not cut their *real* wage in order to increase the demand for their labour.

The first reason for this was that wage bargains were conducted in terms of money wages. This is a characteristic of a money-using economy where goods are exchanged for money rather than as in barter where goods are exchanged for goods. The money wage bargain is also a bargain for income which is going to be spent over some future period for which the goods prices are unknown. Since workers bargain about money wages, they can at best only cut their money wages. But whether real wages fall as a consequence depends on price behaviour. Labour costs were a major part of prime costs and if prices were determined by marginal prime costs, then prices will fall *pari passu*. Thus with money wages and prices both being flexible downwards, the real wage will not go down.

The second reason was that in a decentralised economy, workers did not bargain as a class centrally but in separate groups by industry, occupation etc. This meant that the wages of each group had to be cut separately and this would be seen as a wage cut relative to other groups and workers were sensitive to the loss of wage differentials. Thus while workers were able to cut only their money wage and not their real wage, they would resist piecemeal wage cuts, industry by industry. In this sense there was an assymmetry in workers' attitudes about money wages. While any threat to cut money wages led to strikes and the withdrawal of labour, any rise in consumer goods prices did not lead to such a withdrawal. Since money wages differed across groups but they all consumed roughly the same basket of goods, if one wished to cut real wages across the board, raising the price of goods was an easier, i.e. socially less divisive way of doing so.[5]

This assymmetry in the workers' attitudes about money wage cuts as against price increases meant that labour supply was not a function of the real wage *alone*. Keynes expressed this as follows

[It] may be the case that within a certain range the demand for labour is for a minimum money wage and not for a minimum real wage. The classical school have tacitly assumed that this would involve no significant change in their theory.

But this is not so. For if the supply of labour is not a *function of real wages as its sole variable* their argument breaks down entirely and leaves the question of what the actual employment will be quite indeterminate

(*General Theory*, p. 8, emphasis added).

As we shall see the specification of the labour supply or the wage bargaining relationship is one of the most controversial items in the debate between Keynesians and monetarists.

Keynes' most fundamental objection to the neoclassical remedy of wage cutting was that the aggregate employment level was not determined by the level of real wage but by the level of aggregate demand. The level of aggregate demand was composed of the demand for consumer goods by consumers (consumption function) and investment demand by entrepreneurs (investment function). Consumers' expenditure decisions were determined by the level of income, its distribution between wages, profits and interest income, and expectations about the future. Thus a change in the money wage altered the income distribution as between wages and profits and influenced action depending on whether the change was thought to be temporary or not. But consumption was by and large a stable function of income. Investment demand was much more sensitive to expectations because an investment decision required the entrepreneur to take a view about the yield of his planned investment and consequently about the course of wages, prices, productivity and the rate of obsolescence over a long period in the future, there being no reliable information and no rational way of calculating the odds of the various likely outcomes. Keynes explicitly ruled out the possibility of using probability calculus for coping with this long run uncertainty because he thought the future was in some basic sense unknowable.[6] Thus the aggregate demand level was a function of wages and employment (i.e. income) and of expectations concerning the future course of the economy. Aggregate supply was on the other hand given by the behaviour of prime costs of output as more workers were employed in the short run with a given level of capital stock. The diminishing marginal productivity of labour made this an upward sloping curve. It was at the intersection of aggregate demand and aggregate supply curves that the employment level was determined. Given a level of money wage rate, the slope of the aggregate supply curve at the point of equilibrium determined the price level.[7]

Aggregate employment was thus determined by the intersection of a relatively stable Aggregate Supply Curve (which shifted as wages changed) and a much more volatile Aggregate Demand Curve. Both aggregate demand and aggregate supply were defined in nominal terms or in terms of nominal values divided by the money wage unit. Once the level of employment was determined, the price was known and the real wage determined as a consequence. The demand for labour thus depended on expectations concerning future demands for output and hence future levels of employment.

Adjacent to the theory of employment were of course Keynes' theories of interest and money. In the *Treatise*, Keynes had spoken of the degree of bearishness of lenders of money/holders of bank deposits. He now spoke of liquidity preference. In a money economy with an uncertain future, money was often the only safe asset to carry forward from one period to the next. Any other asset would have to be exchanged for money (sold) before its owner could purchase other goods with it. But the nominal price of these assets would be subject to fluctuation and hence uncertainty. They would be illiquid to a greater or lesser degree. The nominal price of money being unity, it is liquid like nothing else. To give up the use of money the individual will always demand a price. Money commands a liquidity premium and this is the rate of interest.

This theory of money (again only briefly sketched) is in contradiction of the classical dichotomy. In the classical dichotomy only the relative price of goods matter in real transactions and nominal prices are irrelevant. The nominal price of money is irrelevant, only its real price, its purchasing power in terms of goods matters. Thus the price of money is the purchasing power of goods foregone. The cost of holding money from one period to the next is the change in purchasing power over that interval. The rate of interest has to do not with money but with time preference and the productivity of durable capital goods. Here again it is the real rate of interest which measures the return from purchasing a durable good which yields income in the future rather than purchasing a currently consumable good. The real rate of interest is the nominal rate less the loss of purchasing power of money over the duration.

Thus the classical dichotomy is very much at issue. If the classical dichotomy holds, then the demand and supply of all goods — money, labour, durable as well as non-durable commodities — are functions of relative prices and nothing else. The demand and supply of labour depends on real wages alone. The demand for money is a function of price levels and not of interest rates. On this count, Keynes' theory denies the classical dichotomy.

The second aspect is the role of expectations. In Keynes' theory, expectations operate in a way to hinder perfect market clearing, excess supply may persist as an equilibrium phenomenon due to adverse expectations.

In neoclassical economics, the uncertainty concerning the future cannot play a systematic role as a hindrance to the equilibrating mechanism. Economic theorists find ways of overcoming the uncertainty via futures markets, insurance or by incorporating knowledge that markets always equilibrate in their expectations-generating mechanism. This latter is the theory of rational expectations which is a recent innovation and to which we shall return.

Denial of the classical dichotomy and the role of uncertainty in the context of a monetary economy are then the two strands around which basic disagreement exists between Keynes and classical economists. This is not however the way in which the question was seen in the years following the publication of the *General Theory*. Almost immediately upon its publication, the *General Theory* was translated by Hicks in his *Mr Keynes and The Classics* which minimised the difference between Keynesian and classical theory. While Keynes argued that his was the *general theory* of which the classical theory was a special case, Hicks' formulation reversed the roles by making Keynes' proposition depend upon certain assumptions about the slopes and elasticities of a few basic equations. Partisans of Keynes also found that only by simplifying his theory could they win the battle for Keynesian economics in both the economics profession and in the policy field. Hicks' simplification and the subsequent exposition and elaboration by Hansen, Samuelson and Modigliani established the Keynesian model as it was taught in classrooms and adopted in treasuries around the world.[8] It took thirty years before this 'reductionist' approach was exposed as a vulgarisation of Keynes. Since however it is the Hicks version that was debated, we ought to look at it in some detail.

Hicks began by ignoring the nominal magnitudes of aggregate demand and aggregate supply. The price level could be taken as fixed and hence one could talk in terms of real output, real income, real consumption etc. Indeed with price being taken as constant, things were labelled as income, output etc. without the prefix real/nominal which made for some ambiguity. Hicks then boiled down Keynes' system to two equilibrium loci. The goods market equilibrium was characterised by the consumption function, the investment function and an equation saying output was determined by expenditure which appeared as the national income identity.

$$C = C(Y), 1 > C'(Y) > 0, C''(Y) \lessgtr 0 \qquad (17)$$

$$I = I(r, *), \ I'(r) < 0 \qquad (18)$$

$$C + I = Y \qquad (19)$$

These three equations can be condensed into a single equation – the *IS* curve – which gives the locus of values of income (*Y*) and interest rate (*r*) for which the output expenditure equilibrium holds. Thus

$$I(r, *) = Y - C(Y) \equiv S(Y) \qquad (IS)$$

$S(Y)$ is the savings function. The *IS* curve is downward sloping since $S'(Y) > O$ and $I'(r) < O$. The volatility of the aggregate demand was allowed for by adding the role of expectations via an unspecified variable which we denote simply as *. Nothing very much was said about the expectations mechanism.

The *IS* curve described the goods market equilibrium. The money market equilibrium was described by a demand for money equation in which Keynes' distinction between the transactions motive, the pre-cautionary motive and the speculative motive was collapsed into a two part distinction following Keynes' exposition in Chapter 15 of the *General Theory*. Thus the total demand for money is given by

$$M^D = L_1(Y) + L_2(r, r^e) \quad L_1' > O, L_{2r}' < O \qquad (20)$$

L_1 being the transactions and the precautionary demand for money, L_2 the speculative demand. The speculative demand was related as in the *Treatise* theory of bearishness in terms of the relative preference for bonds as against money. (It was the expectations concerning the rate of interest relative to its normal level that determined for Keynes the speculative demand. Ideally one should write $L_2(r, \bar{r}^e)$ $\bar{r}^e$ being expected normal interest rate.) $L_1(Y)$ could be thought of as the Cambridge cash balance term kY.

Combining (20) with the assumption that the supply of money was controlled by the monetary authorities and hence exogenous, Hicks derived the *LM* curve

$$\bar{M} \equiv M^D = L_1(Y) + L_2(r, r^e) \Rightarrow$$

$$L_2(r, r^e) = L(\bar{M}, Y) \qquad (LM)$$

Since $L(\bar{M}, Y) = \bar{M} - L_1(Y)$, the slope of *LM* curve is positive and the curve shifts as $\bar{M}$ changes. In subsequent developments r^e was ignored.

The fudging of the price problem meant that it was not clear whether (20) gave one the nominal demand for money or the real demand for money. But in terms of the different kinds of deposits Keynes spoke of in the *Treatise* (and distinctions which today would be denoted as M_1, M_2 or M_3 etc), it is not at all clear if all of M^D can be exogenously controlled by the monetary authorities. The specification of the role of price level and its rate of change in the money demand function, and the controllability of money supply are very important questions in the present debate.

The intersection of the *IS* and *LM* curves determined the equilibrium level of income and interest rate. It was then argued that there were a number of factors which predisposed that the equilibrium level of income would be an underemployment one. These factors were singly or severally responsible for the level being where it was. Keynesians argued as to why monetary policy through the interest rate mechanism will not work (the wage cutting explanation having already been rejected as we saw above).

The actual *IS, LM* equilibrium gives Y below Y_f at the full employment level. If the authorities tried to cut the rate of interest by increasing the money supply this would not help because the *IS* curve is very steep since investment is supposed to be interest-inelastic. Even at zero rate of interest, the *IS, LM* intersection is at $Y < Y_f$ (Figure 2.3).

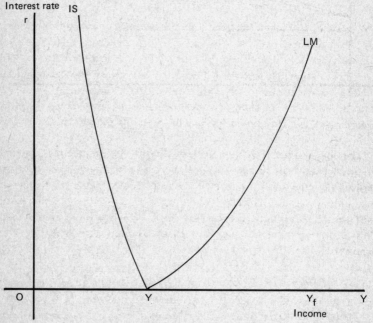

Figure 2.3: An Inelastic IS Curve makes $Y < Y_f$ at $r = 0$

The interest rate consistent with Y_f given the shape of the *IS* curve is lower than the minimum psychological level that the money market will tolerate. The *LM* curve becomes horizontal — infinitely elastic at a level above the required rate of interest. No increase in the money supply can nudge the rate down (Fig. 2.4).

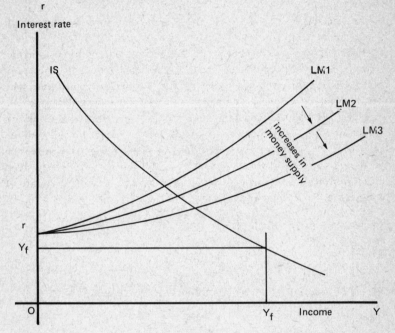

Figure 2.4: LM Curve perfectly elastic at $\bar{r} > r_f$ (required for Y_f)

The low interest elasticity of investment and high interest elasticity of the demand for money could in the extreme version be stylised as a vertical *IS* curve or a horizontal *LM* curve. The lesson for policy was that only exogenous injection of government expenditure could bodily shift the *IS* curve sufficiently to the right to produce full employment. This is done by simple rewriting (19) to accommodate government expenditure

$$C + I + G = Y \tag{19a}$$

$$I(r, *) = S(Y) - G \tag{ISa}$$

Fig. 2.5 illustrates this solution but also points to the difficulty inherent

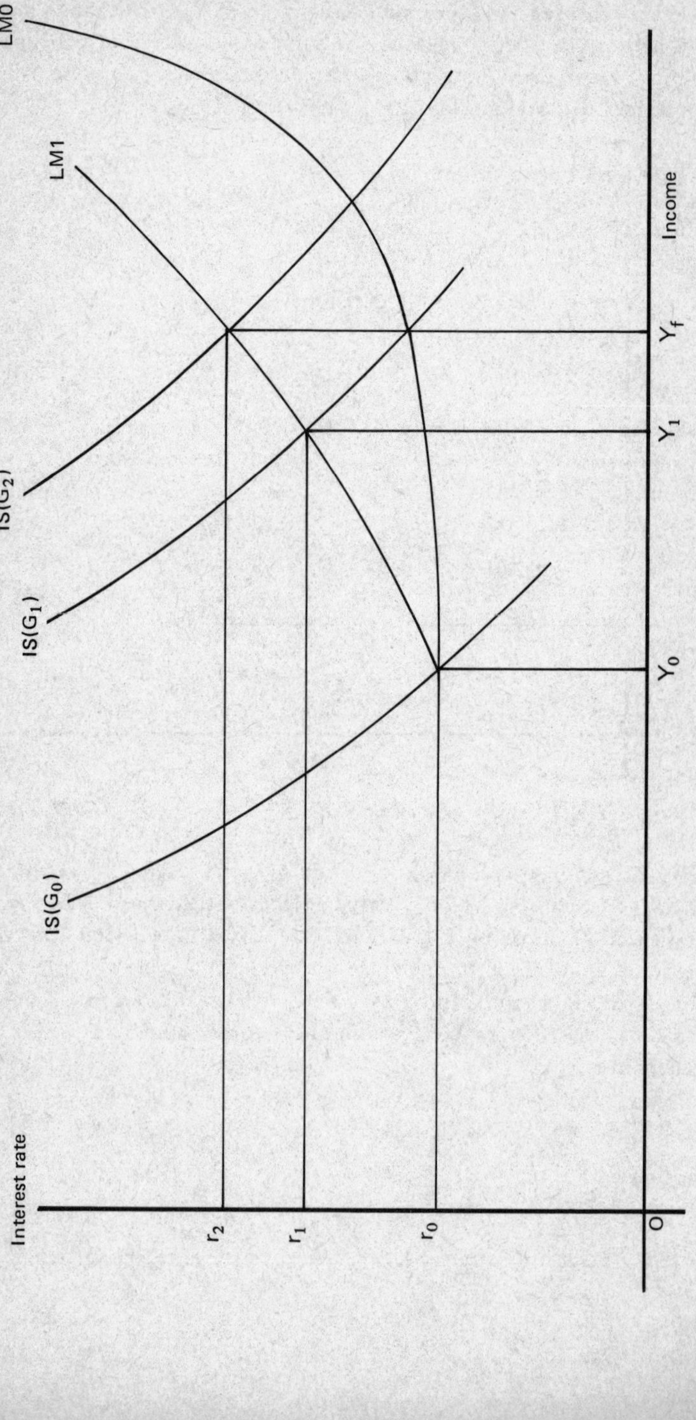

Figure 2.5: Full Employment Equilibrium with a Fiscal Stimulus

in the argument, a difficulty which provided the crack through which the opposition to Keynesian policies began to undermine its foundations. At IS with $G = G_0$, income is Y_0 and the LM curve is taken to be horizontal up to that point so the interest rate is r_0. Now to get Y_f, a fiscal injection is needed. If the LM curve is horizontal over much of its length (LM), then, given $G = G_1$, $IS(G_1)$ will secure $Y = Y_f$ with the interest rate unchanged. The market will absorb the additional government debt which would finance the G_1. If however, the LM curve is upward sloping beyond Y_0 then $IS(G_1)$ will mean $Y_1 < Y_f$ and $r_1 > r_0$. A further injection will be needed up to $G = G_2$ which will raise interest rates to r_2. The steeper the LM curve, the greater would be the size of additional government expenditure necessary to 'buy' an extra increase in output (employment) and the sharper the rise in interest rates.

Once it was seen that the LM curve could not be infinitely elastic over its entire range, the monetary (interest rate) consequences of fiscal policy could no longer be ignored. Living in the interwar period (and, at various points in the *General Theory*, explicitly deploying the special circumstances of the period as a backdrop to drive his points home), Keynes had been persuaded that oversaving and the control of investment were going to be major problems in the future if society was going to ensure full employment (*General Theory*, Chapter 24). He had been so persuasive that governments of the UK and USA were committed after 1945 to a policy of driving interest rates to the lowest value compatible with the liquidity preference schedule. Hugh Dalton's name is associated with this policy in the UK and in the US it took the shape of the Federal Reserve System supporting the government bond market.

The destruction of consumer and producer durables during the war, the availability of major inventions whose markets remained to be exploited and the overhang of wartime savings meant a boom rather than a slump following the end of the war. In the short run, savings were drawn down to finance consumer durable purchases and investment activities in the US. In Europe, the need was for massive reconstruction activity and oversaving was hardly the problem. Even after the first postwar recession of 1948–49 in the US, the Korean War boom soon put pressure on interest rates.

These economic events signalled a simultaneous end to the cheap money strategy in 1951, in the UK via the accession of a Conservative government and in the US with the 'accord' between the Treasury and the Federal Reserve Board. This was the period of 'the Rediscovery of Money' as Howard Ellis called it in his classic article. This rediscovery did not bring a wholesale questioning of the Keynesian model; it only added to the armoury of government economic policy the instrument of the rate which functioned as the rediscount rate.

The economics profession agreed that Hicks' formulation of the Keynesian model was pedagogically a sound representation and further work proceeded on the refinement and measurement of the underlying relationships. Various qualifications were entered to the Keynesian formulation.

First, Haberler revived an argument of Pigou's which was later refined by Patinkin, to the effect that consumption is a function not only of current income Y but also of the stock of real balances. A sustained fall in the price level during a depression could so enhance the real value of the liquid balances that some would be spent on consumption. This means that over time the IS curve could drift upward and full employment could be restored automatically. Thus a situation such as one depicted in Fig. 2.3 could be modified to one in Fig. 2.6. As the price fell from P_0 to P_1, the IS curve would shift and a new equilibrium at Y_f would be established. So we now could write the consumption function as

$$C = C\,(Y,\, M/P) \tag{17a}$$

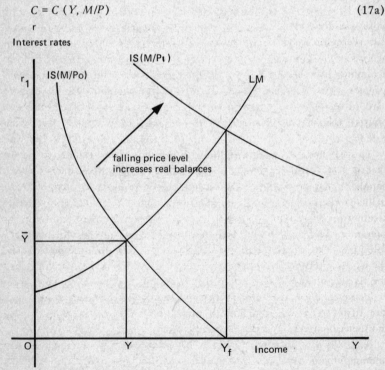

Figure 2.6: Real Balance Effect to the Rescue

Second, Tobin pointed out that Keynes' theory of money was based on too narrow a focus on money and bonds as the only two assets. The existence of a spectrum of assets modifies the absolute need for liquidity preference. Baumol showed at the same time however that the transactions demand would be interest elastic. This somewhat softened the belief in the liquidity trap.

Third, various attempts were made to rationalise the upsurge in consumer spending in the postwar period. Kuznets established that the consumption-income ratio far from declining as income rose stayed roughly constant. If this was so, then underemployment was not a secular threat but only a cyclical problem. Duesenbery, Modigliani and Brumberg and Friedman in different ways modified the Keynesian consumption function by down-grading the primacy of current income and emphasising relative, lifetime and permanent income, and the role of wealth etc.[9]

Despite these amendments, the Keynesian model remained intact in academic research and among policy makers. Its formulation and measurement provided the major outlet for the new discipline of econometrics. Starting with Lawrence Klein's pioneering Cowles Commission monograph *Economic Fluctuations in the United States, 1921–1941*, much work was done in econometric model building, not least by Klein himself. But there remained one worry which grew more serious as the fifties progressed. While full employment seemed assured and more rapid economic growth an attainable if not an achieved goal, inflation seemed a major worry. It seemed that full employment and price stability may be hard to reconcile in policy. What was more (at least to academic economists), there seemed to be no theory of inflation within the Keynesian paradigm.

This Keynesian paradigm by now had become established to the extent that it had reached a *modus vivendi*, an 'accord' with the neoclassical paradigm that preceded it. Keynes had never seriously challenged (Marshallian) micro-economic theory but only the automatic full employment assumption underlying it. Now it seemed with Keynesian policies to guarantee full employment, Walrasian micro-economics could come into full play. This then was the neoclassical/neoKeynesian synthesis.[10] The theory of inflation that was now added to the Keynesian paradigm had the flavour of neoclassical micro-economics but had the macro-economic/econometric form that much Keynesian economic theorising took in the late fifties. This was the Phillips Curve. The Phillips Curve is now an indispensable element in the monetarist story.

A.W. Phillips came to examine the relationship between wages and unemployment against a background of previous work on the trend of wages and prices over several centuries by his colleague E.H. Phelps-Brown and an influential work *The Great Inflation* by A.J. Brown. They had related wage *levels* to levels of productivity and extended this to looking at the connection between prices and wages. Phillips fundamentally revolutionised this area of research *first* by looking at the rate of change of wages rather than their levels, and *second* by providing ingenious econometric estimates of the underlying economic relationship. The emphasis on the rate of change of wages made the connection with rate of change of price level (inflation) much more direct. The econometric implementation gave it an instant appeal in a profession which was just taking to econometrics on a much wider scale than had been the case hitherto.

Phillips examined the data for fifty-two years preceding the First World War 1861–1913, and derived a nonlinear relationship between the percentage change in money wage rates and the percentage of the labour force unemployed. He carefully measured percentage change in money wage rates by centered first differences and then plotted the data for the rate of change of money wage rate so measured ($\dot{w}_t = (W_{t+1} - W_{t-1}) / 2W_t$) against unemployment for each of the fifty two years. He hypothesised a relationship between unemployment as measuring the pressure of demand in the labour market and money wage as the price employers would pay for hiring labour. Appropriate to the nineteenth century economy to which the data referred, he pictured this as a process whereby employers bid for labour and as labour supply became scarce they increasingly bid labour away from each other by offering higher money wages. Thus for Phillips the employer was the active agent in the labour market and the worker, as yet only lightly unionised, was the passive element who went wherever he got the highest wage.

This relationship was estimated by Phillips in two stages. First he averaged his data down to six points in such a way that he would remove the effects of short run changes in unemployment and so that each average observation captured the up and down of the same phase of the cycle. [See for an explanation of the Phillips procedure Desai (1975) and Gersovitz (1980). For a contrary view see Gilbert (1976).] The resulting equation was

$$\dot{w} + a = bU^{-c} \tag{21}$$

This equation was drawn as the celebrated Phillips Curve. This curve showed that as unemployment declined towards zero, the rate of change of money wage rates became very large tending towards infinity. As unemployment increased, $\dot{w}$ reached a floor equal to $-a$. Thus there was a

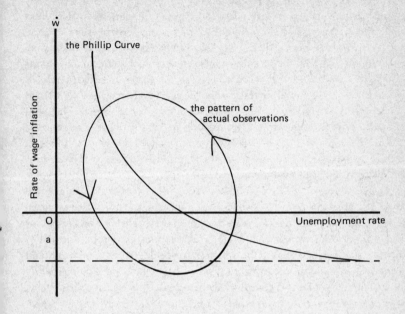

Figure 2.7: The Phillips Curve

limit to how rapidly money wages could fall but no limit to how fast they could rise (Fig. 2.7).

Having estimated his relationship for his six averaged points, Phillips proceeded to show that each of the six trade cycles (of 8 years in average length) traced a counter-clockwise loop around his curve. This indicated that while equation (21) gave the 'long-run' relationship between $\dot{w}$ and U, for any particular year one had to look at whether U was falling ($\dot{U} < 0$) or rising ($\dot{U} > 0$), to predict whether wages were going to be above the Phillips curve ($\Delta \dot{w} > 0$) or below ($\Delta \dot{w} < 0$). Once he had explained to his satisfaction the long-run equilibrium relationship and the short-run dynamics of wages and unemployment, Phillips proceeded to examine how well his equation explained subsequent observations on wages. He did not estimate a new relationship for each period and test for significant differences with that fitted in the 1861–1913 period. He merely plotted actual data for 1914–47 and 1948–57 against the equation for the 1861–1913 period and noted that mostly the observations fitted around the curve and that for most short cycles there was a counter-clockwise loop pattern with some exceptions in the 1948–57 sample.

Phillips was a pioneer in economectrics and in control theory. His early training as an engineer led him to adopt formulations which were somewhat advanced for the economists of his day. At the same time he managed to make his methods look so simple that others thought they were almost *ad hoc*. Economists however took the spirit of his results though not the details. His relationship was non-linear in its parameters as well as in its variables and he resorted to his averaging technique to make it amenable to estimation. Subsequent authors drop the averaging and immediately recast his original formulation making it linear in parameters but not in variables. This made estimation by well known econometric techniques possible. The replication of the result for different time periods and different countries was launched.

In many ways, Phillips' contribution had arrived at an opportune moment. Economists were looking for a macro-economic theory of inflation. Phillips had found an *empirical*, stable relationship that seemed to hold over nearly one hundred years. This relationship related unemployment — a crucial variable in the Keynesian world — to money wages and seemed to rationalise a downward rigidity of money wages which many had assumed was part and parcel of Keynes' model. As we have seen above, Keynes' views on money wages were a bit more complicated than merely assuming downward rigidity, but here was empirical confirmation of a theorist's assumption. By the mid fifties, in the US as well as the UK, there were moves to examine the trend of wage settlements and to look at the connections between wages, prices and productivity. (See Dow (1964) for UK attempts to control inflation in the fifties.) Phillips' study provided a quantitative answer to the inflation problem; by maintaining full employment, i.e. a low level of U, inflationary pressures were generated in the labour market and a high $\dot{w}$ led to a high rate of price inflation $\dot{p}$.

In the UK Lipsey (1960) immediately tamed the Phillips Curve by taking a linear approximation and estimating a Phillips relationship for each of three time periods 1882–1913, 1924–47, 1948–59. His relationship was

$$\dot{w}_t = \alpha_0 + \alpha_1 U_t^{-1} + \alpha_2 U_t^{-2} + \alpha_3 \dot{U}_t + \alpha_4 \dot{p}_t + \epsilon_{1t} \tag{22}$$

Equation (22) is linear in parameters α_i and non-linear in the variables U. The terms U^{-1}, U^{-2} approximate U^{-c} in equation (21). Lipsey added $\dot{U}_t$ to take care of the counter-clockwise loop and he added the rate of inflation $\dot{p}_t$ following some remarks Phillips made in his original 1958 article. To make it conform to the least squares method, an error term ϵ_{1t} was added to the equation. This formulation fitted the data reasonably well and again while Lipsey did not test whether the α_i were the same across the three periods, an impression was created that here again was another 'constant' of economics.

In the US, Samuelson and Solow (1960) siezed upon the Phillips Curve as a tool for fashioning an anti-inflation policy. While they did not carry out any estimation for US data, they posited a Phillips Curve roughly of the same shape for the US as for the UK and they interpreted prices and wages by relating prices to labour cost. Thus we could have the following two-equation model

$$\dot{w}_t = \alpha_0 + \alpha_1 U_t^{-1} + \alpha_2 \dot{p}_t \tag{23}$$

$$\dot{p}_t = \dot{w}_t - \dot{q}_t \tag{24}$$

Here $\dot{q}$ is the growth rate of labour productivity. Thus equation (23) is the Phillips Curve simplified and equation (24) relates the increase in prices to increases in the unit labour cost. Putting (23) and (24) together, we get a direct relationship between inflation $(\dot{p})$ and unemployment (U). This looks very much like the Phillips Curve and was drawn as in Fig. 2.8.

$$\dot{p}_t = \left(\alpha_0 + \alpha_1 U_t^{-1}\right) \big/ (1 - \alpha_2) \tag{25}$$

Unlike Phillips' case, either equation (22) or (23) was assumed to hold for each time period. It was then an easy matter to look upon (23) as a stable relationship which summarised the objective situation facing an economy. One could have low inflation and high unemployment or vice versa. To achieve price stability or at least a low rate of inflation, a certain level of unemployment was desirable. Thus policy could be directed towards achieving that level of unemployment.

The Phillips Curve seemed to most economists in the early sixties to provide the missing element in the Keynesian model. Now there was a theory of inflation which could be integrated into the IS–LM framework and the Keynesian edifice was complete. To have provided a theory as well as an econometric relationship was Phillips' acknowledged achievement. His work had immediate policy implications. Full employment and price stability seemed within the economic policy-maker's grasp.

It is paradoxical therefore that it is entirely around the Phillips Curve that the battle between monetarists and Keynesians raged in the sixties and seventies. The neoclassical synthesis came apart and there came to be distinct camps in macro-economic theory and policy represented by the neoclassical/monetarist school and the Keynesian school respectively. But before we take up the story of the monetarist attack on the Phillips Curve, we need to backtrack a little and look at Friedman's revival of the Quantity Theory of Money.

The Revival of the Quantity Theory of Money

As we saw above, the quantity theory was in eclipse even before the *General Theory.* But the triumph of the Keynesian model completely obliterated it from classroom teaching, except in a caricature form. The quantity theory of money, one was told, was an identity, nothing more. By defining velocity circularly one could always establish a Fisher or Marshall type equation but it had no theoretical content. While in the *Treatise* Keynes carefully laid down the (full employment) conditions under which the quantity theory would come into its own (See p. 32 above), the Keynesian school completely ignored the quantity theory at all levels. Monetary policy was an ineffective instrument in obtaining high employment and its role was to be essentially passive — to manage government debt financing unobtrusively. Even when significant concessions had been made on the nature of the consumption function and a sophisticated multi-asset model of the financial markets admitted in theory, the primacy of fiscal policy and the passivity of monetary policy were never questioned.

It is in this context that Friedman's attempts to revive the quantity theory have to be viewed. The theory could not be revived as if nothing had changed in economic theory since the days of Fisher and Marshall. Keynes had provided a theory of aggregate output and employment and this had changed the nature and scope of monetary theory. Friedman developed the quantity theory as an alternative to the Keynesian liquidity preference relationship. By taking Hicks' formulation of the money demand curve as a point of departure, Friedman developed the quantity theory as a theory of demand for money. Thus he says in his 'The Quantity Theory of Money: A Restatement': 'The quantity theory of money is in the first instance a theory of the *demand* for money. It is not a theory of output, or of money income, or of the price level.' (Friedman (1969) p. 52)

While in the 1980s this seems an obvious statement, this was a profound change in the way the quantity theory was viewed. For Fisher it was a theory of the aggregate price level and its purpose was to provide the missing equation in a Walrasian system. But Keynes had clearly established the demand for money at the aggregate level as a meaningful and important macro-economic relationship. In a sense Friedman abandoned the Fisherian version of the quantity theory in favour of the Marshallian cash balance formulation.

The 'Restatement' of 1956 also discussed money as an asset and integrated the demand for money into a theory of the demand for capital. It argued against Keynes' proposition that the opportunity cost of holding money was the rate of interest foregone on bonds. It argued that the opportunity cost of money was the rate of change of consumer prices. In terms of the *Treatise*, Friedman plumped for the consumption standard rather than the cash transaction standard or the cash balance standard.

Thus the 1956 version of the quantity theory combines the Marshallian version with the Walrasian classical dichotomy to provide an alternative to the Keynesian money demand function. In a simple form Friedman proposed a demand for money function of the following kind

$$M^d \Big/ P = f(r, \dot{p}, y, \phi, \tau) \tag{26}$$

P is the price level, r is the rate of interest standing in for a vector of yields on different assets which are money substitutes, $\dot{p}$ is the rate of inflation as before, y is real income, ϕ is the ratio of non-human wealth to human wealth and τ stands for variables reflecting tastes and preferences of wealth holders whose demand for money is being embodied in (26).

In its form as equation (26), the demand for money function is comparable to equation (20) but now it is explicit that we should be speaking of the demand for real balances and that apart from r and y, we should include $\dot{p}$, the rate of inflation. (There would be no dispute about the inclusion of ϕ and τ in (20).) The crucial new element in a quantity theoretic demand for money is that it is homogeneous of degree zero in income and the price level.

While nothing explicit was said at this stage about the interest elasticity of the demand for real balances, it was implied that a liquidity trap — a phase of the demand for money schedule at which the demand became infinitely interest elastic — was not a part of the new theory. Neither did Friedman accept any distinction between the transactions and the speculative demand for money, nor yet the distinction between the individual and the business demand for money function. They were both captured by (26).

By redefining the quantity theory in terms of a demand for money function, Friedman brought it into line with modern macro-economics, but made it a vehicle for his attack on the Keynesian model. Thus it was due to the *General Theory* and its influence that the emphasis in the quantity theory had now shifted onto an aggregate macro relationship. The importance of money was in terms of its ability to relate nominal income and price changes to changes in the (aggregate) stock of money. But whereas the Keynesian macro theory of the demand for money had made money a passive agent in income determination, Friedman made it an active ingredient.

This was done in two ways. The first step was to assert that the demand for money function was *empirically* stable: not in the sense of a fixed or rigid constancy of the income velocity of money but an empirical stability in an econometric sense. Friedman also added that the persuasiveness of his argument depended crucially on the function being represented parsimoniously, i.e. one needed only a small number of variables to specify an empirically stable relationship. This crucial step shifted the macro-economic argument into the empirical, statistical and econometric arena. In one sense macro-economic theory has been getting increasingly meshed with econometric/statistical theory ever since the coincidence of the *General Theory* with the revolution in national income accounting (the Kuznets Revolution) and the revolution in the use of econometric techniques (the Tinbergen-Frisch Revolution). But while early use of econometrics was to model business cycles or, later, to provide operationally usable models for fiscal policy makers, Friedman's innovation was to appeal to econometrics as a way of settling the choice between rival theories.

But at this stage, all this was still in the future. The second step in the innovation was to use the demand for money as a theory of income determination. This is done by asserting that the supply of money is *autonomously* determined. This may mean that it is exogenous and fixed by policy or that it is a function of variables which do not enter the demand for money function nor are in any way determined by the demand for money. Readers will recall that Fisher's conditions on the components of his equation M, V, P and T involved a similar restriction, e.g. V could not be a function of M, P, T etc. If an autonomously determined supply of money interacted with a stable demand for money, one then had to have a theory of how the variables in equation (26), apart from M^D, were now determined by that equation. Thus, similar in structure to the (LM) equations, we have

$$\bar{M} = M^D = Pf\,(r,\,\dot{p},\,\dot{y},) \qquad\qquad (27)$$

This is then the modern version of the quantity theory as a theory of demand for money.

Now in the Keynesian model, the exogeneity of the supply of money gave a locus between r and y on the LM curve which intersected with the IS curve to determine r and y. Implicit, however, was a notion that effective demand forces determined real income given the level of autonomous demand G and the idea that expenditure automatically got translated into output (the $45°$ line of the Samuelson Keynesian cross). Prices in this world were fixed. If they became endogenous via the Phillips Curve, it was still said that $\dot{p}$ and y were still largely determined by G. Then the LM curve determined the level of interest rate as a function of the supply of money.

If this set of implicit steps was to be made explicit, what it means is that the IS–LM model becomes *recursive*. The level of income is determined by G unaffected by r (zero interest elasticity of the IS curve) and then r is determined by the position of the LM schedule which depends on $\bar{M}$.

Friedman explicitly states that to obtain a theory of income determination from the quantity theory, he has to choose one of the variables as determined and the rest as being fixed outside the system. Friedman first writes (26) and (27) as

$$(Py) \equiv Y = Y(r, \dot{p}, y, \phi, \tau)\, \bar{M} \qquad\qquad (QT)$$

We call this equation (QT) to correspond to the (LM) equation as the quantity theoretic rival to the Keynesian equation. Y nominal income is then proportional to $\bar{M}$ if the arguments of the function $Y - r, \dot{p}, y$ can be said to be determined elsewhere in the system. But this is not as straightforward as it sounds. One could say that the rate of interest is determined by real factors — 'by productivity, thrift and the like' and that real income is also fixed by other 'supply side' factors — capital stock, labour force, technology etc. But even then $\bar{M}$ determines Y only if prices are stable i.e. $\dot{p} = O$; which then means that (QT) only determines the price level P which is required to be constant. But then this is hardly a theory of how important money is in determining income.

Friedman is explicitly aware of this dilemma. As he says

> Even under the most favorable conditions, for example, that the demand for money is quite inelastic with respect to the variables in [*f*], equation [(27)] gives at most a theory of money income: it then says that changes in money income *mirror* changes in the nominal quantity of money. But it tells us nothing about how much of any change in Y is reflected in real output and how much in prices.

To infer this requires bringing in outside information, as, for example, that the real output is at its feasible maximum, in which case any increase in money would produce the same or larger percentage increase in prices; and so on.

Friedman (1969) p. 62.

We have italicised the word 'mirror' to bring out how the ambiguity of the English language is often a methodological device. Does 'mirror' mean cause or can it be said to leave open the direction of causality between Y and M and assert only correlation? Such ambiguous use of language is a Marshallian legacy shamelessly indulged in by all sides, Keynes no less than Friedman. It is only the requirements of econometric modelling which have forced some precision into this area.

The 1956 'Restatement' of the quantity theory thus represents the first step towards a rehabilitation of the old doctrine. But there are several modern (Keynesian) aspects to it. First Friedman recast it as a demand for money function rather than as assertion, via the constancy of velocity, about money and prices. But to counter the Keynesian model, this was clearly not enough. As often happens in scientific controversies, the dominant theory defines the ground on which the battle is to be fought by any rival challenger. To counter Keynesian theory, Friedman had to have a theory of income determination. It is quite clear from the above quotation that as yet such a theory was not completely formulated. But Friedman was successful in taking the attack into the econometric/empirical area. Thus in the discussion following the quotation above, he shifts the argument about the quantity theory to an empirical one of the stability of the demand for money function. He states three grounds on which a modern quantity theorist would differ from a Keynesian '. . . (i) the stability and importance of the demand function for money; (ii) the independence of the factors affecting demand and supply [of money]; and (iii) the form of the demand [for money] function or related functions.' (Friedman (1969), p. 62)

Not much need be said at this stage about (iii) except as we said above, it rules out a liquidity trap. As far as (ii) is concerned, the *IS–LM* version of Keynesianism accepted the exogeneity of M. There is however a longer standing debate since the days of the argument over the Banking Act of 1844 as to whether the supply of money is or is not demand determined. This argument was revived by the Radcliffe Report in the UK in 1959 and is still an important plank of the anti-monetarist stand. But it was (i) that was the debated issue in the next ten years and this was partly because Friedman kept the battle there by a bold stroke. In developing (i) in the 'Restatement', he said, 'The quantity theorist accepts the empirical hypothesis that the demand for money is highly stable — *more stable than functions such as the consumption function that are offered as alternative key relations'* (Friedman (1969) p. 62). We have italicised the second half of the sentence because it is the assertion of the greater stability of the demand for money function compared to the consumption function that was to be the next stage in the debate.

Friedman had been working over a number of years on a history of the monetary aspects of the US economy in collaboration with Anna Schwartz. While this was not to come out till 1963 in book form, they had already constructed the long series on money stock. Friedman's next building block in his attempt to rival Keynesian theory was to estimate a demand for money function. This was published in the *Journal of Political Economy*, August 1959 as 'The Demand for Money: Some Theoretical and Empirical Results'. This article combined National Bureau methods of cyclical measurements and the econometric method of using regression analysis. It is on the latter that we shall concentrate.

Friedman formulated equation (26) above explicitly for secular data (long term averages arrived at after removing cyclical fluctuations) as

$$M/NP^* = \gamma \, (Y^*/NP^*)^{\,\delta} \tag{28}$$

N is population, M is money stock (both actual values). Y^* is the value of permanent income following the hypothesis advanced in Friedman's 'A Theory of the Consumption Function' and is in effect a moving average, using fixed weights, of past actual incomes. P^* was, similarly, the permanent price level against a weighted moving average of past actual price levels.

So we have in (28) that the per capita demand for real money balances is a function solely of the per capita real permanent income. The most notable omission is the interest rate when we compare (28) to (26). This particular omission constitutes a prior restriction on the derivative attached to interest rates in (26), i.e. that $\partial f/\partial r = O$: the demand for real balances is interest inelastic. This restriction was not tested at this stage by Friedman and in all subsequent work has been rejected.[11]

One defence of the omission of the interest rate would be that (28) defines a secular relationship and that short-run variations around the long run would be determined by the rate of interest (compare Phillips' explanation of the 'loops' around the Phillips Curve. Note however that Phillips' method of averaging was not the National Bureau method of moving averages.) Friedman takes this stance in his 1966 article and adds that in his work with Anna Schwartz they took the interest elasticity to be -0.15. Thus we have the assertion that the demand for real money balances is not interest inelastic in the sense of zero elasticity but that the function has a very low elasticity: the curve is not vertical but pretty steep. This parallels a similar restriction on the interest elasticity of investment in the Keynesian model: it is taken to be either zero (vertical *IS* curve) or very small (steep *IS* curve).

Friedman obtained for his observations of cyclical averages, the following fitted equation

$$M/NP^* = 0.00323 \ (Y^*/NP^*)^{1.81} \tag{28a}$$

Having obtained this relationship for cyclical averages, he then examined the fit of the actual velocity of circulation to the velocity computed from (28a). The fit improves as one goes from individual cycles to averages over many cycles. (Compare Chart II to Chart III on pp. 128–9 of Friedman (1969)) Some of these deviations are explained by looking at the two missing variables – the rate of interest and the rate of inflation. (See Chart IV, Friedman (1969) pp. 132–3)

From this study, two important conclusions were drawn by Friedman. *First*, that given the stability of the long run (or permanent) income velocity, any short run variations in the stock of money would rapidly translate into changes in measured (rather than permanent) income. Once this has happened, permanent income being a weighted average of measured income, the demand for money would rise permanently and further rises in income will not be sustainable without further increases in the money stock. This meant that the impact multiplier of a change in M on Y is greater than the long-run multiplier. *Second*, that monetary policy acted on income directly through changes in the money stock rather than indirectly via the rate of interest through investment to income. These two conclusions implied that money multipliers were larger in the short run than investment multipliers and that 'the transmission mechanism' of the monetary policy was much simpler (hence more effective?) than that of fiscal policy.

While Friedman's revival of the quantity theory made money an active determinant of national income, his policy conclusions were, in line with his general social philosophy, anti-interventionist. These were outlined in his evidence, 'The Supply of Money and Changes in Prices and Output' which he gave in 1958 before the US Congress Joint Economic Committee.[12] In this, Friedman concentrated on the cyclical or short-run relationship between money and nominal income in contrast with the long-run or secular relationship emphasised in the parallel work, *The Demand for Money*, discussed above. Friedman's major points in the

'Supply of Money' paper can be summarised under three headings, causality, lags, and limits to fine-tuning. We shall throughout use Friedman's own words to present his case.

Causality

> The direction of influence between the money stock and income and prices is less clear-cut and more complex for the business cycle than for the longer movements . . . changes in money stock are a consequence as well as an independent cause of changes in income and prices, though once they occur they will in their turn produce still further effects on income and prices. This consideration blurs the relation between money and prices but does not reverse it . . . even during business cycles the money stock plays a largely independent role.

Lags

> The rate of change of the money supply shows well-marked cycles that match closely   those in economic activity in general and precede the latter by a long interval. On the average, the rate of change of the money supply has reached its peak nearly 16 months before the peak in general business and has reached its trough over 12 months before the trough in general business . . . . Moreover, the timing varies considerably from cycle to cycle. Since 1907, the shortest time span by which the money peak preceded the business cycle peak was thirteen months, the longest 24 months; the corresponding range at trough is 5 months to 21 months . . . from the point of view of policy directed at controlling a particular movement such as the current [1958] recession, the timing differences are disturbingly large . . . and of course, past experience is not exhaustive; the particular episode may establish a new limit in either direction.

Limits to Fine Tuning

> The variation in timing means that there is considerable leeway in the precise relation between changes in the stock of money and in prices over short periods of time — there are other factors at work that lead to these variations and mean that even if the stock of money were to change in a highly regular and consistent fashion, economic activity and prices would nonetheless fluctuate. When the money changes are large, they tend to dominate these other factors . . . But when the money changes are moderate, the other factors come into their own. If we knew enough about them and about the detailed effects of monetary changes, we might be able to counter these other effects by monetary measures. But this is utopian given our present level of knowledge. There are thus definite limits to the possibility of any fine control of the general level of prices by a fine adjustment of monetary change.[13]

(Friedman (1969) pp. 179–81).

The conclusion that he drew from these points was that it was best to have a rule for a fixed growth of money stock from 3 to 5% per annum and avoid any marked short-run variation in this rate. Any policy purporting to adapt money growth to variations in the economic activity ('the feedback rule') would be more destabilising than not. Thus 'political pressures to "do something" should be resisted since yielding to them would do more harm than good. (Friedman (1969) p. 187).

Thus in the two studies on the demand for and the supply of money at the end of the fifties, Friedman established a number of propositions which form the core of the revival of the quantity theory. These relate to the stability of the demand for money over the long run, the relatively greater stability of the money demand function compared to the consumption function and hence the larger the size of the money mulitplier compared to the fiscal multiplier, the long and variable lags in the short run between changes in money stock and changes in real income and prices, the independent nature of changes in money stock and its causal primacy *vis-à-vis* changes in income and prices, the limits to fine tuning due to the imprecision of lags, the desirability of a fixed money growth rule with no feedback mechanism.

Considerable controversy has surrounded each of these points and a large body of economic research can be cited on either side of each question. For our present purpose, we need to note that much of what was being asserted was empirical rather than theoretical. Friedman did not have, as yet, a fully fledged theory of the ways in which money affected output and prices. The empirical regularity of the relationship between money and nominal income was only strong in the secular context, the cyclical relationship being blurred and hedged by qualifications about the feedback from income to money. Even if Friedman's empirical assertions were to be admitted as true (and they were not), critics could still say that this did not amount to an explanation of how money affected economic activity. In the ranking order used by academic economists (and, I suspect, by researchers in other sciences) a theoretical model ranks much higher than 'mere' empirical evidence. Where was 'the transmission mechanism'?

Even from the point of view of a quantity theorist, the Friedman story was incomplete. The traditional basis for the support the quantity theory has received has been that excess money (debauched currency) causes inflation and attendant economic and political crises. Indeed to the fundamentalist quantity theorist, the *only* truth of the quantity theory was that money determines prices. For those who are in this camp, the state issues excess money frequently, if not, always, and the decline of civilisations and the end of Empires, if not the corruption of morals, can be traced to unsound money. (In this demonology, bankers and especially Jews also used to figure prominently in the past as villains in the debasement of money). To such people, Friedman's abandonment of the simple truths of the Fisherian quantity theory for the new sophistications about the demand for money was a diversion. Indeed it was not at all clear whether the restated quantity theory was the same as the old.[14]

The crucial link was the breakdown of any change in nominal income (caused by a prior change in money stock) between a change in real output and a change in price level. While there are hints about this in his 'Restatement', Friedman did not forge this link in his chain of arguments until his Presidential address to the American Economic Association in 1967. This link was provided by Friedman's re-interpretation of the Phillips Curve.

As we saw above, Phillips established a long-run relationship between the rate of change of money wages and the percentage of the labour force unemployed, with the added proviso that the short-run cyclical variation in $\dot{w}$ and U took the form of a counter-clockwise loop (Fig. 2.7). The Lipsey version of this relationship related the year to year variation in $\dot{w}$ and U to each other (Equation (22). In the further simplified version implicit in Samuelson-Solow (1960), the model became as in (23) and (24).

$$\dot{w}_t = \alpha_0 + \alpha_1 U_t^{-1} + \alpha_2 \dot{p}_t \tag{23}$$

$$\dot{p}_t = \dot{w}_t - \dot{q}_t \tag{24}$$

Now if we accept this as a true (even if highly simplified) picture of how inflation and unemployment relate to each other, it is easy to take a step further and say that the policy maker can choose a combination of values of $\dot{p}$ and U that he wishes to achieve, and trim his policy instrument accordingly. If this were true, given the short-run cyclical interpretation of the Phillips Curve, we have a counter-example to Friedman's proposition about the limits of fine tuning. The Phillips Curve also showed that one can 'buy' a little extra output (i.e. a small drop in unemployment) by conceding a small amount of inflation. Thus, a government could sustain a high employment policy with a small cost in inflation since the economy could be 'kept' at the chosen equilibrium by fine tuning.

Not only did this set of assertions show that intervention and fine tuning could be effective (which went against Friedman's social philosophy if not his monetary theory) but it also rationalised a state of permanent 'mild' inflation. Friedman's attack on the Phillips Curve has to be seen thus, not only as an isolated technical exercise, but as part of his attempt to construct a complete alternative to the Keynesian model. His attack struck at the heart of the neoKeynesian-neoclassical synthesis. He pointed out that the Phillips Curve in the form of equation (23) was inconsistent with neoclassical theory since the dependent variable was the rate of change of a nominal price — money wage — rather than that of a relative price. If the classical dichotomy held — and the neoKeynesians had not challenged this fundamental part of the neoclassical core — then the Phillips Curve was misspecified.

The Phillips Curve had been roughly justified as reflecting the way in which excess demand in the labour market led to a change in the price of labour but to be a consistent version of the excess demand–price change relationship in a Walrasian general equilibrium model, this price had to be a relative price not an absolute price. If the Phillips Curve reflected labour supply behaviour then Friedman was insisting that labour supply was a function of the real wage and not of the money wage. As readers will recall, Keynes had seen this as the basic question between his theory and classical theory (see pp. 45-6 above). Friedman thus saw that the reconciliation of the Phillips Curve with micro theory was impossible without, in some sense, abandoning the classical dichotomy.

Technically, Friedman's objection to the Phillips Curve centred around the size of α_2: the coefficient of $\dot{p}$ in the $\dot{w}$ equation. Friedman criticised Phillips for completely ignoring $\dot{p}$ in his specification of the relationship as in equation (20). Friedman took this to mean that Phillips either thought $\dot{p} = 0$, i.e. fixed prices, or that $\alpha_2 = 0$, i.e. a misspecification. Neoclassical theory requires $\alpha_2 = 1$ at least in the steady state.

While there is now new, hitherto unpublished, evidence that Phillips thought of his equation as a reduced form of (23) and (24), i.e. having solved out for $\dot{p}$ in terms of $\dot{w}$ and $\dot{q}$ (Perry (1980)), the point at issue is the size of α_2 in the Phillips Curve. Friedman agreed that if one tried a regression equation of $\dot{w}$ on U^{-1} and $\dot{p}$, the estimated α_2 coefficient was indeed less than one. But he explained this departure from neoclassical theory by introducing a distinction between *actual* and *expected* rates of inflation. Friedman saw the Phillips Curve as a wage bargaining relationship (reflecting labour supply behaviour) but with the proviso that since the wage income referred to a future time period prices were unknown over this period. Thus the workers could at best only take into account the expected rate of inflation in the wage bargain. Thus we have instead of (23)

$$\dot{w} = \alpha_0 + \alpha_1 U^{-1} + \alpha_2 \dot{p}^e \tag{23a}$$

Now added to this was Friedman's view of the way in which workers formed price expectations. For this process, Friedman adopted an adaptive framework whereby $\dot{p}^e$ was a weighted average of previous $\dot{p}$. This paralleled Friedman's definition of permanent income Y^* and the permanent price level P^* as we saw in the discussion of the demand for money above. (See p. 65 and Friedman (1969) p. 124) This is best written as

$$\dot{p}^e = \lambda \sum_{i=0}^{\infty} (1-\lambda)^i \dot{p}_{t-i}, \quad 0 < \lambda < 1 \tag{29}$$

$(1-\lambda)$ is the weight attached to actual inflation which decays as one goes back from the current period into the distant past. When $\lambda = 1$, $\dot{p}^e = \dot{p}$, i.e. inflation is fully anticipated. When $\lambda = O$ expected inflation bears no relation to the history of actual inflation rates.

Combining (29) and (23a) we get

$$\dot{w}_t = \alpha_0\lambda + \alpha_1 U_t^{-1} + \alpha_1(1-\lambda)U_{t-1}^{-1} + \alpha_2\lambda\dot{p}_t + (1-\lambda)\dot{w}_{t-1} \qquad (30)$$

Now equation (30) rationalises the observed coefficient of $\dot{p}_t$ in a specification such as (22) or (23). Thus the Lipsey specification omits the lagged value of U^{-1} and of $\dot{w}$. The coefficient of $\dot{p}$ is now a combination of the speed of adaptive expectation λ as well as the extent to which inflationary expectations are incorporated into the wage bargain α_2. If $\alpha_2 < 1$, then $(1 - \alpha_2)$ is a measure of the degree of money illusion as defined within the neoclassical paradigm.

But a more far reaching consequence of α_2 being 1 is that while (30) describes the short-run (disequilibrium) configuration of the relationship between $\dot{w}$ and U, the long-run steady state relationship is made very different. Thus, in the steady state, let inflationary expectations catch up with actual inflation $\dot{p} = \dot{p}^e$. Combining (24) with (23a), we get when $\alpha_2 = 1$.

$$U^* = \alpha_1\Big/(\alpha_0 - \dot{q})$$

U^* is the natural rate of unemployment of the steady state (equilibrium) level given when inflationary expectations have caught up with actual inflation. Thus if there is no money illusion ($\alpha_2 = 1$) and no gap between actual and expected inflation ($\dot{p} = \dot{p}^e$), the Phillips Curve becomes vertical at the level U^*.

Thus any observed trade-off between $\dot{w}$ (or $\dot{p}$) and U is entirely a short-run transitory phenomenon, a consequence of the failure of inflationary expectations to catch up with actual inflation. Once this gap has been eliminated, there is no trade-off. The neoclassical relationship which relates real wage growth to the excess demand for labour is thus re-established if $\alpha_2 = 1$.

Friedman's next step was to use the short-run Phillips Curve along with the adaptive expectations mechanism to generate a theory of income and prices. By positing a downward sloping relationship between $\dot{w}$ (or $\dot{p}$) and U and a vertical long run relationship, he was able to provide the missing element in his theory of the link between money and prices. Thus it is in the context of the 1956 'Restatement' that his presidential address of 1967 has to be seen.

Start the economy at $U_t = U^*$. Now suppose the (monetary) authorities wish to lower the level of unemployment. They do this by pursuing an expansionary policy. Grant for the time being that this is done by expanding the money supply. Then, employers would bid for extra labour and money wages would be bid up. At this stage, nothing has happened to change the price level (since money acts on prices with a lag). So we observe $\dot{w} > 0$, $\dot{U} < 0$ as the short-run Phillips Curve predicts. But once $\dot{w}$ feeds through to price increases via equation (24), $\dot{p}$ is up when the next wage bargain comes about. Workers thus lose the real wage gain of the previous period and, *if nothing further happens*, U goes back to U^*.

In the context of Fig. 2.9 we start at E. Assume there is no growth in labour productivity: $\dot{q} = 0$. Then the economy moves to A where $U = U_1 < U^*$ and $\dot{w} = \dot{w}_1 > 0$. But if $\dot{p} = \dot{w}_1$ by equation (23a) then $\dot{p}^e$ would adjust upward to the extent that $\lambda \dot{w}_1$ and the Phillips Curve would shift up by that amount. At this stage, the real wage declines and workers give up the jobs they had and unemployment goes back to U^*. If however the government wishes to maintain U at U_1, then a further increase in money supply will be called for to finance the extra rise in money wages equal

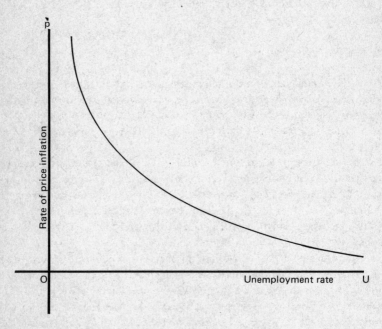

Figure 2.8: Inflation — Unemployment Relationship

to the distance AC in Fig. 2.9. This takes the $\dot{w}$ to $\dot{w}_2$. Notice that given the shape of the Phillips Curve, AC is bigger than AU_1 i.e. the rate of wage inflation accelerates.

Once again the Phillips Curve will shift up in the next period since now the new rate of inflation $\dot{p}_2$ equals $\dot{w}_2$ which exceeds $\dot{w}_1 = \dot{p}_1$. So the next period $\dot{w}_3$ is higher still and so on. At successive rounds, actual inflation climbs up but expected inflation is also climbing up. Thus, a process of hyperinflation can be explained by combining a neoclassical Phillips Curve with an adaptive expectations process.

But note that while an attempt to keep U below U^* (via monetary expansion) leads to inflation, there is also some extra output gained in the short run, since the extra employment, equal to (U^*-U_1) times the labour force, will not be unproductive. Thus, Friedman's view of the effects of monetary expansion parallel those of Hume at this stage of the cycle. Extra money leads to (or is required to generate) extra employment and output. It also leads to a rise in wages. If this fall in U were to be permanent, then there is some net addition to real output through monetary expansion. Once you grant this, the long-run proportionality between the rise in M and the rise in P, so central to the quantity theory, cannot hold.

Thus for the quantity theory to hold there has to be some loss in real output before the economy converges back to equilibrium. (It *has to be* in the sense that the theory requires that the economy trace out such a pattern to validate the theory. There is no objective necessity since the theory can after all be wrong). Friedman does this by saying (much as Hayek did in *Prices and Production*) that there are limits to this process of monetary expansion. The sequence of $\dot{w}_t$ gets larger with each t as does $\dot{p}_t$ with $\dot{p}_t^e$ scrambling to keep up with it. Sooner or later the government cannot or will not expand the money supply any more in order to sustain U_1. In the contraction phase, the economy over-reacts since $\dot{p}^e$ is slow to adjust downwards. So $U > U^*$ in the contractionary phase as money supply growth decelerates. This loss of output due to $U > U^*$ cannot be avoided since there will persist a gap between $\dot{p}$ and $\dot{p}^e$ by the logic of the model. A picture will emerge such as in Fig. 2.10.

In Fig. 2.10 we have filled in the points along the left hand side E, A, C. The economy hits some ceiling level of inflation and then turns around. It is difficult to predict the extent to which unemployment would rise above U^* and also difficult to say how long the process of adjustment would take before the economy can return to E. (These points are very much at issue in the recent course of the UK economy as it reacts to a monetarist policy. We shall return to this question later.) The economy

describes a *clockwise* loop around the vertical long-run equilibrium level U^*.

The adjustment path being a loop around U^* implies that the temporary increase in real output caused by monetary expansion is matched by the loss of output during the contraction. The *long-run influence of money on real output is thus zero. All monetary expansion ultimately dissolves into price increase.* Thus at the end of the sequence of short cycle expansion and contraction, the economy returns to its equilibrium. The neoclassical dichotomy holds in the sense that changes in the *nominal* money stock do not and cannot cause any change in real output (or employment).

With this re-interpretation of the Phillips Curve, Friedman had found the missing element in his theory of the relationship between money and income. The 'transmission mechanism' from money to prices was the wage bargaining process, the link between wages and prices and the generation of inflationary expectations. These three elements rationalised the regression results for the Phillips Curve, re-established the neoclassical specification in terms of relative prices, explained the process of sustained inflation and finally gave Friedman a theory of the long-run break-down between inflation and real output growth.

In a sense, this re-interpretation of the Phillips Curve enables Friedman to bring back into academic respectability the theory that had ruled in the days before the publication of the *General Theory*. The theory that Keynes had combated and overcome, the Walras-Pigou theory of market equilibrium became once again a serious area of investigation. This theory had never been supplanted in micro-economics; now it began the take-over of macro-economics. The next ten years, following Friedman's presidential address in 1967, were to see the theoretical battle joined between Keynesian and neoclassical theories. The battle was also fought on the econometric terrain as we shall see below. It was in this period that a neoclassical macro-economic theory emerged taking full advantage of the new mathematical general equilibrium theory (the Arrow-Debreu Revolution) and the new developments in econometrics and in time series analysis.

Before we go into that, let us look again at Friedman's theory. The course of the economy along the clockwise loop as in Fig. 2.10 reconciles the money–nominal income relationship in the short run with the money–price link of the quantity theory in the long run. It does this by maintaining that unemployment is determined *independently* of the happenings in the wage–price nexus. Thus unemployment is determined by real factors–capital stock, labour supply, technology etc. and is determined

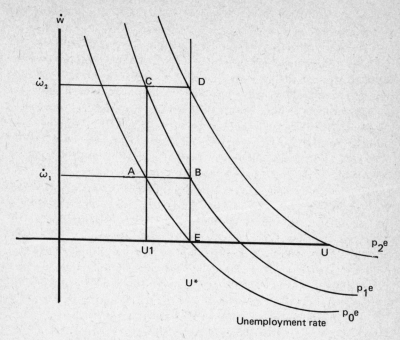

Figure 2.9: The Inflationary Process Along the Phillips Curve

prior to the wage–price determination. To some extent the neoKeynesian synthesis had assumed that unemployment was controllable by government policy. Thus the neoKeynesian, as well, took U to be determined by forces other than W and P. (It will be recalled that this is not the way Keynes in the *General Theory* described the determination of employment. See pp. 44–8 above and note 7 at the end of this chapter. But there was no attention paid to this issue in the subsequent debate). So the only difference between the Friedman and the neoKeynesian view was about the degree of money illusion, i.e. the size of α_2 and nothing more fundamental in the Friedman analysis was challenged on theoretical grounds.

Two rather contradictory events determined the subsequent course of the debate. By now, of course, monetarism had emerged in the literature as a topic of discussion. Comparisons were made between the Keynesian Revolution and the Monetarist Counter-Revolution (Johnson (1971), Friedman (1970)). But despite its greater spread, the battle of the Phillips Curve was not at this stage (1971) won by Friedman. Many econometric attempts to test for the hypothesis that $\alpha_2 = 1$ ended by concluding that

α_2 was less than one.[15] It seemed that the long run Phillips Curve though steeper than the short run was still not vertical. There was something to be gained from running an expansionary policy.

While the empirical evidence seemed to check the neoclassical resurgence, all was not well with the neoKeynesian synthesis. In the late sixties and early seventies the rate of inflation began to increase in all developed capitalist economies. The war in Vietnam and the attendant upsurge in US military spending and balance of payments deficits, the strains imposed by the fixed exchange rate system and by the key currency role of sterling on the British economy, the transmission of dollar deficits into the Euro-dollar markets, the strengthened position of the workers after two decades of high employment, the student rebellions in the US, France, the UK and Germany in 1968 — all these factors converged in the years 1968–1971 to increase inflation to a point where the Bretton Woods system had to be abandoned. At the technical level, complaints were heard that the Phillips Curve (the neoKeynesian version) had broken down or had shifted and was no longer usable as a policy tool. There did not seem to be a stable trade-off available that the policy maker could use. Attempts to bring down the rate of inflation by deflationary measures succeeded only in increasing the level of unemployment. Attempts to move along the Phillips Curve seemed to be frustrated by (upward) shifts in the curve itself.

The failure of the Phillips Curve as a policy tool coincided with a general failure of econometric models to predict the recession caused by the OPEC oil price rise of 1973. In the USA, Keynesian policies were slow to be officially adopted, contrary to their acceptance in Western Europe. They finally triumphed with the Kennedy-Johnson tax cut of 1964. Within less than ten years, the promise of Keynesian econometric models to provide a recipe for full employment with price stability was increasingly being questioned. In the UK there was a successful dash for full employment during the Heath-Barber expansion of 1973 as we have seen in the Introduction but the consequential collapse of the speculative boom and the hyperinflation of 1974–5 succeeded in discrediting this expansion.

The next development in this debate came in an unexpected way and, if its proponents are to be believed, its implications go far beyond monetarism and towards a new nonKeynesian or classical macro-economics fully consistent with micro-economic theory, by rewriting both macro-economics and micro-economics in a dynamic stochastic language and dropping the deterministic static framework of the old economics (Lucas and Sargent (1979)), Lucas (1980)). Its beginnings and early development are due to the work of Robert E. Lucas and of a small groups of economists — Thomas Sargent, Christopher Sims, Neil Wallace, Bennet McCallum and

Robert Barro. This development is associated with the theory of rational expectations. The whole topic of new classical macro-economics is beyond the scope of this book but we shall look at it in as much as it abuts on the questions raised by the debate between monetarists and Keynesians. Many of the issues raised by the theory of rational expectations are explicitly statistical and econometric and their full explanation will only emerge after we have discussed the methodology of estimation and testing in the next chapter.

The starting point of Lucas' new theory was Friedman's neoclassical Phillips Curve as given in equation (24). He took the view that it was inappropriate to couple the wage bargaining equation for which a plausible optimising micro-economic behaviour could be supplied as a foundation with an adaptive expectations framework. The adaptive framework may be a convenient rule of thumb but it had no rational foundation. It could be shown for instance that in a period of accelerating inflation, i.e. where $\dot{p}_t > \dot{p}_{t-1}$ for all t, the expected inflation rate will always lag behind actual inflation, i.e. people will be perpetually making mistaken forecasts and not learning from past mistakes. This can be easily shown in our framework of equations (23), (24) and (25). Take $\dot{q}_t = 0$ to simplify. Begin with $U_o = U^*$ and posit again an expansionary policy which brings U_o to U_1. Assume also that until this period there has been no inflation: $\dot{p}_{t-i} = 0$ for all i up to $i = 0$. Therefore with $U = U_1$ we have

$$\dot{w}_1 = (\alpha_0 + \alpha_1 U_1^{-1}) \big/ (1 - \lambda) \qquad (30a)$$

where the price inflation is in consequence

$$\dot{p}_1 = \dot{w}_1 \qquad (31a)$$

$$\dot{p}_1^e = \lambda \dot{p}_1 \qquad (32a)$$

In the next period, we shall have

$$\dot{p}_2^e = \lambda \dot{p}_2 + \lambda(1-\lambda) \dot{p}_1 \qquad (32a)$$

and so if we take it that U is kept at U_1 subsequently by suitable fiscal stimulus

$$\dot{w}_2 = (\alpha_0 + \alpha_1 \big/ U_1) + \dot{p}_2^e \qquad (30b)$$

$$\dot{p}_2 = \dot{w}_2 = (\alpha_0 + \alpha_1 \big/ U_1) + \dot{p}_2^e \qquad (31b)$$

This sequence of equations for $\dot{w}_t$, $\dot{p}_t$ and $\dot{p}_t^e$ will be repeated for all periods with the only modification that $\dot{p}_t^e$ will carry additional lagged terms in each period. Now it will be clear that for any period the difference between $\dot{p}^e$ and $\dot{p}$ will remain nonzero

$$(\dot{p}_t - \dot{p}_t^e) = (1 - \lambda)\,\dot{p}_t - \sum_{i=1}^{\infty}\,(1 - \lambda)^i\,\dot{p}_{t-i} \tag{33}$$

as can be seen from (31b) and (32b). This difference does not disappear once we have departed from $U = U^*$. On the downturn, the same difference may persist with the opposite sign.

Lucas took the view that an expectations generating mechanism with such a property of being constantly wrong was inappropriate in a world of rational maximising individuals (as is assumed by most economic theories). An expectations generating mechanism had to have the minimal property that it would generate unbiased forecasts, i.e. there would be no systematic error in the forecasts.

This does not mean that expectations are never wrong; that would be a very deterministic nonstatistical view of the theory, totally contrary to its nature. What it implies is that agents who act on the basis of expectations of any variable would try and use all the information they find it economical to use to generate forecasts of that particular variable. Since they are capable of observing how markets work to determine economic magnitudes, say, prices (remember we are in a neoclassical micro-theoretic context), individual agents would be able to mimic in their subjective expectations-generating process the way the market determines actual prices. Thus in a statistical sense the probability distribution of the subjective expectations of the variables and the objective distribution of the variables will have the same mean or mathematical expectation.[16] It is in this sense that the expectations will be unbiased or rational.

Lucas' theory, like that of Friedman, evolved over a number of years partly in his attempts to explain the divergence between the short-run Phillips Curve trade off and the long-run neoclassical result of a vertical Phillips Curve. But it was in the course of deriving an equation such as (23) from micro-theory that an alternative interpretation of the wage inflation–unemployment relationship emerged. At this stage, in his work with Leonard Rapping in 1969 and 1970, the use of micro-economic theory was confined to derive a labour supply relationship starting from individual consumer choice between consumption and leisure. Having derived a normal labour supply curve in terms of permanent (or normal) real wages, Lucas and Rapping modelled the difference between the observed supply of labour and the normal supply of labour as a function of the deviation of actual wages from permanent wages. By generating permanent wages in an adaptive framework as a moving average of previous actual wages, they were able to derive a specification of the Phillips Curve which reversed the dependent and independent variables. Let us look at this in some detail since it is crucial for subsequent discussion.

Lucas and Rapping get from their micro-theory a labour supply equation

$$ln(L/N)_t = \beta_0 + \beta_1 ln \ (W/P)_t - \beta_2 ln(W/P)_t^*$$

$$+ \beta_3 \ (r_t - ln \ (P_t^*/P_t)) - \beta_4 ln \ {}^a t/N_t \tag{34}$$

N is the labour force or total households in the economy and L is the labour supply. (W/P) is the real wage rate and an asterisk, as before, indicates the permanent or normal value of a variable, so $(W/P)^*$ is the permanent real wage. Now (P^*/P) indicates expected rate of inflation and r is the nominal rate of interest so the difference is the expected real rate of interest. Lastly a is the real value of assets, i.e. the real balances if money is the only asset.

Now (34) can be made to yield normal labour supply by putting $(W/P) = (W/P)^* = (W/P)_{t-1}^*$ and $P_t^* = P_{t-1}^* = P_t$. So we have normal labour supply as a function of normal prices and wages.

$$ln \ (L^*/N)_t = \beta_0 + \beta_1 ln \ (W/P)_{t-1}^* - \beta_2 ln \ (W/P)_t^*$$

$$+ \beta_3 \ (r_t - ln \ (P_t^*/P_{t-1}^*)) - \beta_4 ln \ ({}^a t/N_t)) \tag{35}$$

Combining (34) and (35) we have

$$ln \ (L^*/L)_t = \beta_1 \ [ln \ (W/P)_{t-1}^* - ln \ (W/P)_t] + \beta_3 ln \ (P_{t-1}^*/P_t) \tag{36}$$

Now the left hand side of (36) gives us the ratio of actual labour supply to normal labour supply. Taking the observed rate of unemployment as a proxy for this ratio and using adaptive expectations for W^* and P^*, Lucas and Rapping get (in our previous notation):

$$\Delta U_t = \beta_1 \ (\dot{w}-\dot{p}) - \beta_3 \dot{p} - \lambda U_{t-1} \tag{37}$$

where $\dot{w} = \Delta ln W_t$ etc and λ is, as before, the speed of adaptive adjustment. It is clear that equation (37) is a rewriting of Lipsey's equation (22) above where we take $\dot{U}_t$ as $U_t - U_{t-1}$ and take $\alpha_1 U$ instead of $\alpha_1 U^{-1}$.

Equation (37) will give the same natural rate of unemployment as equation (23) and we require $\beta_3 = 0$ for full rationality.

Note that (37) provides now a very different theory of the Phillips Curve. For Phillips and Lipsey as well as for Friedman, the Phillips Curve explained inflation as being caused by unemployment (proxying the excess demand for labour). Lucas and Rapping see real wage inflation as actually causing unemployment. Unemployment is now a proxy for short-run changes in labour supply and hence in output. So the Phillips Curve becomes a theory of aggregate output variations in the short run.

The empirical results obtained by Lucas and Rapping (1969) showed that the hypothesis $\beta_3 = 0$ could be rejected for some episodes in US history especially the inter-war period. This is parallel to other attempts in the area to test for $a_2 = 1$, as we have said above. So at this stage, Lucas made a radical switch in theorising about inflation and unemployment by rejecting not so much the hypothesis that $\beta_3 = 0$ but by rejecting the adaptive expectations franework that is required in going from (36) to (37). He asked fundamental questions about the consistency of adaptive expectations with the micro-economic theory of rational maximising behaviour. Thus, he maintained the assumption of no money illusion and the entire corpus of micro-theory and jettisoned the auxiliary hypothesis of adaptive expectations.

In the context of the Lucas-Rapping model this is best seen by examining equation (36). Why should there be a *persistent* gap between actual and expected values of W or P as the adaptive expectations hypothesis implies? Lucas castigated the persistence of such a gap as *a priori* evidence of the failure of rationality. The gap between W and W^* or P and P^* could only be random not systematic; they behaved like random variables, familiar in statistical work, which have zero means and finite variances. The expectation of a variable has to correspond to its mathematical expectation; this is the essence of rational expectations.

Once we take this view of the nature of expectations then it is clear that there can be no systematic deviation of L from L^*; the course of actual unemployment around the equilibrium, natural rate is purely random. This has the implication that there cannot be persistent involuntary unemployment as an equilibrium phenomenon.

This view of expectations-formation brings into full play the statistical theory which underlies much of empirical econometric work as we shall see in the subsequent chapters. But it immediately opens the way for general equilibrium theory to come into macro-economics. This general equilibrium theory starts with the twin propositions that individuals are rational maximising agents and that all markets clear to yield an equilibrium price vector at which there can be no persistent excess demand or excess supply (see p. 42 above). The fundamental point on which Keynes had challenged classical theory was thus reaffirmed as a maintained hypothesis, as prior theory which all empirical work had to take as a starting point. Lucas consciously went on to reformulate the basic propositions of this neoclassical theory in modern econometric/general equilibrium theoretic terms. This switch from adaptive to rational expectations is thus pivotal in the emergence of the new classical macro-economics.

The theory of rational expectations requires us to state precisely the date at which expectations are held, the date of the variable about which expectations are held and the information upon which the expectation is based. It is in the information set that the market clearing assumption plays the crucial role. Thus while in adaptive expectations individuals only look at past values of a variable to generate expectations about the future, in rational-expectation theory it is recognised that endogenous variables such as prices for which expectations are to be generated are solutions of a market clearing process. Besides, the prices and quantities of different commodities are interrelated through the general equilibrium character of the economic system. This amounts to making the breathtaking assumption that individuals can implicitly or explicitly solve large models of the economy speedily if not instantaneously to use available information to generate expectation.

In terms of the first two considerations mentioned above — the date as of which the expectation is held and the date for which it is held — we can describe equation (36) in alternative ways. Write (36) as

$$ln\,(L/L^*) = \beta_1\,[lnW - lnW^*_{t-1}] + (\beta_1 + \beta_3)\,[lnP_t - lnP^*_{t-1}] \quad (36a)$$

Here lnL^* is still the trend value of labour supply but lnW^*_{t-1} and P^*_t can no longer be thought of as normal or permanent values. We define lnW^*_{t-1} (and similarly for P^*_{t-1}) as the expected value of lnW_t held as of period $t-1$ or formally

$$lnW^*_{t-1} = E_{t-1}\,(lnW_t \mid \Omega_{t-1}) \quad (38a)$$

Equation (38a) says that lnW^*_{t-1} is the conditional expectation of lnW_t as of $t-1$, i.e. conditional upon the information set Ω_{t-1}. In Ω are included values of variables such as current and lagged values L, P, W as well as the form of the constituent equations. The complete model plus the known values of the variables thus enter Ω. Many critics of rational expectations have baulked at the idea that such huge amounts of information can be gathered and processed by individuals or that it need be gathered at all.[17] This is partly true in as much as one should really have an optimising theory of how much information is worth anyone's while to gather. But economists have always assumed perfect or complete information, perfect foresight and the like. In demand theory, one is asked to seriously assume that consumers maximise utility, defined over all goods and over all future time periods. Such assumptions are not descriptive pictures of the real world, they are parables convenient for analytical purposes. If one is to criticise the theory of rational expectations, it should be on the same grounds as one would criticise adaptive expectations or the Keynesian model.

An alternative version of (36) is to write it in terms of expectations of future prices and wages. With minimal change of notation, one can say

$$ln(L/L^*) = \beta_1 [lnW - lnW^*] + (\beta_1 + \beta_3) [lnP - lnP^*] \tag{36b}$$

where

$$lnW^* = E_t (lnW_{t+1} \mid \Omega_t) \tag{38b}$$

Equation (35b) says that lnW^* is the current expectation of future values of lnW, conditional upon current information. [18,19]

Many issues have arisen in connection with the rational-expectation approach in the new classical macro-economics.[20] While this is still an area for debate, let us put forward a small macro-economic model that is frequently encountered in the literature. This model contains an *IS* equation, an *LM* equation and an aggregate supply equation of the Lucas-Rapping variety:ﹴ

$$lny_t = a_0 + a_1 [r_t - E_{t-1} (lnP_{t+1} - lnP_t)] + v_{1t} \tag{39a}$$

$$ln (M/P)_t = b_0 + b_1 lny_t + b_2 r_t + v_{2t} \tag{39b}$$

$$lny_t = \beta_0 + \beta_1 (lnP_t - E_{t-1} lnP_t) + \beta_2 lny_{t-1} + v_{3t} \tag{39c}$$

The *IS* equation is derived by positing investment and consumption as being functions of the real rate of interest. The *LM* equation is demand for real balances and the aggregate supply equation is an adaptation of (36a). Here v_{1t}, v_{2t}, v_{3t} are random error terms. All expectations are held as of *t−1* about current and future variables. Except for the expected inflation terms, (39a) and (39b) terms are *IS*, *LM* equations as we noted

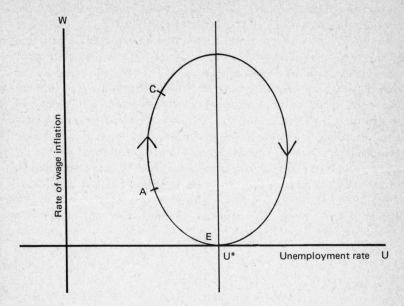

Figure 2.10: The adjustment Path of Wages and Unemployment

before. Equation (39c) can be derived from (36a) by solving out wages in terms of prices and unemployment and taking lny_t as a proxy for U_t. There is only one policy variable in the model and that is the stock of money.

In addition to equations (39a) to (39c), it is convenient to add a policy rule as a summary description of the policy formulation process. This is done by describing a path for lnM_t

$$lnM_t = \gamma_0 + \gamma_1 lnM_{t-1} + \gamma_2 lny_{t-1} + v_{4t} \tag{40}$$

Equation (40) says that current money supply reacts with feedback to money supply and previous output. Friedman's rule of a fixed growth rate can be described by putting $\gamma_2 = 0$ and $\gamma_1 = 1$ with γ_0 being the fixed growth rate. A Keynesian rule for stabilising output would be to set $\gamma_1 = 0$ and $\gamma_2 = -1$ with γ_0 being the target real output $ln\bar{y}$.

Now a most important argument of the Lucas-Sargent school has been about the ineffectiveness of policy. Perhaps more is made of this argument than it deserves. Its persuasiveness depends very much upon the nature of expectations, i.e. that we have $E_{t-1}lnP_t$ rather than $E_t lnP_{t+1}$, that they are backward rather than forward expectations, but since it is in line with the noninterventionist philosophy of the new macro-economics, we need to look at it.

Given (39a) to (39c), one can write down the reduced form of the system and, using this, generate $E_{t-1} ln P_t$. (For the formal treatment of this see Chapters 3 and 4). In generating $E_{t-1} ln P_t$, individuals are supposed to incorporate the policy rule (40). This means that the term $ln P_t - E_{t-1} ln P_t$ in the aggregate output equation will only involve non-systematic or random influences on the price level via the *IS–LM* curve and the policy rule. Indeed the policy rule and the *LM* curve can be combined to eliminate $ln M_t$ and its past values. Interacting this with the *IS* curve we can solve out r_t in terms of $ln y$ and $ln P$ and their expected values. This gives us a solution for $ln P_t$ in terms of $ln y_t$, $ln y_{t-1}$, $E_{t-1} ln P_{t+1}$, $E_{t-1} ln P_t$, $ln P_t$, $ln P_{t-1}$ etc. Since we only wish to indicate the nature of the solution here, let this condensed structural equation, obtained by solving (39a) to (39c), be

$$ ln P_t = \delta_0 + \delta_1 ln y_t + \delta_2 ln y_{t-1} + \delta_3 E_{t-1} (ln P_{t+1} - ln P_t) $$

$$ + \delta_4 ln P_{t-1} + \delta_5 ln P_{t-2} + u_t \tag{41} $$

where u_t is a composite error term made up of v_{1t}, v_{2t}, v_{4t} and their lagged values. Now the conditional expectation of $ln P_t$ from (41) is

$$ E_{t-1} ln P_t = \delta_0 + \delta_1 E_{t-1} ln y_t + \delta_2 ln y_{t-1} + \delta_3 E_{t-1} (ln P_{t+1} - ln P_t) $$

$$ + \delta_4 ln P_{t-1} + \delta_5 ln P_{t-2} \tag{41a} $$

Thus the only current term (output) is replaced by its expectation and the error term by its expectation which is zero. So

$$ (ln P_t - E_{t-1} ln P_t) = \delta_1 (ln y_t - E ln y_t) + u_t $$

Substituting this into (39c) we have

$$ ln y_t = \beta_0 + \beta_1 (ln y_t - E ln y_t) + \beta_2 ln y_{t-1} + v_{3t} + \beta_1 u_t \tag{42a} $$

So, since

$$ (ln y_t - E ln y_t) = (v_{3t} + \beta_1 u_t) / (1 - \beta_1) $$

we get

$$lny_t = Elny_t + \frac{v_{3t} + \beta_1 u_t}{(1 - \beta_1)} = \beta_0 + \beta_2 lny_{t-1} + \frac{v_{3t} + \beta_1 u_t}{(1 - \beta_1)} \qquad (42b)$$

Equation (42b) then says that if price expectations are generated rationally, taking full account of the systematic policy rule as well as the *IS–LM* model which generates the price-output curve (often called the aggregate demand curve), then the deviation of actual prices from expected prices which govern the aggregate supply will be purely random. Thus policy will have no systematic influence in determining aggregate output.[21]

Apart from the complex manipulations needed to derive (42b), its message is simple. The evolution of output (and hence unemployment since it is a proxy for output) over time is *independent* of monetary (or equivalently fiscal) policy. Thus, observed fluctuations in unemployment are random and hence there cannot be systematic involuntary unemployment. Individuals alter their labour supply temporarily if they interpret a current change in money wage as change in real wage; but soon they will revise their expectations and except for random errors, their labour supply will always be the equilibrium one. This says that all unemployment is voluntary except for a random error. Thus in the forty years since the *General Theory* was published, neoclassical economics has fought back, and refurbished itself with a new stochastic process alongside its old 'truths'!

In this world of market clearing Walrasian equilibrium, this error term plays a very crucial role. Thus, we know that macro-economic variables such as output, price level and nominal income trace out a cyclical pattern. Other series such as employment, labour productivity and real wages also move cyclically. Now a purely random error term is not sufficient to generate cycles; what is required is some moving average process of random errors. To overcome this longstanding problem with Walrasian theory (recall Hayek's statements in *Monetary Theory and the Trade Cycle* about the inadequacy of the Walrasian barter model to generate the observed cycles), Lucas in his 1976 paper suggested a theory of the manner in which limited information and/or misperception of signals generates cycles in a Walrasian model.

Lucas puts forward the idea that when there is a general rise in all prices, participants in various individual commodity markets, e.g. labour, perceive only the rise in their selling price, e.g. money wages. The signal that all prices have changed is delayed in arrival; so there is a mistaken

·response to this higher absolute price until it is discovered that relative prices have not risen. To sustain the higher response, a further rise in prices becomes necessary.

Thus, the classical assumption of perfect information has been modified in favour of limited information but perfect computing ability. As Lucas and Sargent (1979) put it

> Each agent is assumed to have limited information and to receive information about some prices more often than other prices. On the basis of their limited information — the lists they have of current and past absolute prices of various goods — agents are assumed to make the best possible estimate of all the relative prices that influence their supply and demand decisions.
>
> But because they do not have all the information necessary to compute perfectly the relative prices they care about, agents make errors in estimating the pertinent relative prices, errors that are unavoidable given their limited information. In particular, under certain conditions, agents tend temporarily to mistake a general increase in all absolute prices as an increase in the relative price of the good they are selling, leading them to increase their supply of that good over what they had previously planned. Since on average everyone is making the same mistake, aggregate output rises above what it would have been.
>
> (Lucas and Sargent (1979) p. 8).

Limited information and mistaken perception seem then like the latest in the series of ideas economists resort to marry an essentially static equilibrium theory with actual time series data. In an earlier time economists showed that a pattern of lags in the consumption, investment or inventory equations could generate cycles. But eventually it was pointed out that such a fixed pattern of lags lacked any rationale in a profit maximising world. A similar argument has been made about the Lucas assumptions. Why do not some individuals find it useful to overcome such limitations? On the basis of casual empirical observation, we know that financial markets and wholesale commodity markets use prodigious amounts of information and process them quickly to act on any opportunity for profitable arbitrage. Individuals in the labour market only worry about differentials when it comes to the annual wage negotiations. House prices are scanned only by those who are active buyers, and others may sit on an unrealised capital gain on the house they live in until other reasons compel them to move. So a theory of uniform misperception across all markets is clearly a great simplification.

This would not be a serious criticism if the theory generated empirical predictions which matched the observed cycle. Some claim has been made by the protagonists of the theory that they have explained the empirical business cycle. Thus, Lucas and Sargent say, 'The new theory can easily account for positive correlations between revisions to aggregate output and unexpected increases in money supply' (Lucas and Sargent (1979) p. 9). Many Keynesian economists, especially Tobin, have been sceptical of these claims (see Tobin's comments in the Journal of Money, Credit & Banking, November 1980). As we shall see below, a major effort to implement the classical macro-economic model which was made by Sargent (1976) has recently been subjected to an econometric test with adverse results. But this takes us into empirical matters which must wait till later chapters.

Perhaps the most fundamental criticism of the new classical macro-economic theory has come from those who have critically examined the general equilibrium framework of the approach.[22] At the heart of the Lucas–Sargent approach is the Arrow–Debreu model of competitive general equilibrium. In their work in the 1950s, Kenneth Arrow and Gerard Debreu established, in a mathematically rigorous fashion, the Adam Smith Invisible Hand proposition that we summarised on p. 42 above. Their work is mathematically demanding so we shall only convey its economic logic here.

To establish the Invisible Hand proposition on a logically sound basis, it is first necessary to define commodities (including goods and services) in a very general way. Thus the same physical good is a different commodity today than it will be tomorrow or in one place than it is in another. Once we index commodities by time and space as separate commodities, there still remains the problem of uncertainty. Individual's demand for goods will depend to some extent on which of the various possible outcomes would prevail in the future. Thus my demand for ice cream tomorrow will depend on whether it is a warm sunny day or whether it is drizzling and cold. More generally we know that in some commodity markets, there are futures contracts where action is contingent on certain outcomes. There are of course a large number of possible states that could prevail at each time/space combination and for each possible state there would be contingent demand and supply configurations.

Now if we could be sure that in the market for every possible commodity, i.e. in every time/space/state of nature combination, there will be market clearing of demand and supply at non-negative prices, then we can show that a competitive equilibrium will exist, i.e. the Invisible Hand will rule. But this requires a rather preposterous story to be swallowed if one is to use such a theory as a guide to practical policy rather than as a harmless pen and paper excercise. This is that there exist active markets in these contingent commodities — promises to buy and sell goods conditional on whether one or other event will occur at some future date — and that every individual can at once and simultaneously make all the transactions for actual and contingent commodities. This means that uncertainty in any meaningful sense can be ignored by this device of contingent markets.

Thus, for the competitive model to hold in a logically rigorous fashion, uncertainty has to be tamed. Indeed, Keynes' position was that the future in some sense being unknowable, there was only a limited possibility of rational calculation about future outcomes of current plans. But having said this, and having emphasised the importance of expectations, Keynes did not offer much by way of a theory of expectations (as Shackle has emphasised in his various books). The device of rational expectations is yet another way of taking care of the problem of uncertainty in such a way that no part of static micro-economic theory need be seriously questioned. Since every individual is supposed to know that markets clear and also that everyone else believes this too, they act together in such a way as to fulfil the expectations they formed. There are no obstacles to each seller of labour or of commodities being able to sell as much as he or she wishes. There is no prospect of the wage being too high, because if it is, the markets will instantaneously react by bidding down the price of labour until everyone is employed who wishes to be so.

To some extent all economic theorising makes unrealistic assumptions but economists also have the habit of giving the most practical advice drawn from the most abstract of models. Thus the existence of a competitive equilibrium in a highly mathematical model may seem a matter of but remote concern to practical politicians; but policies concerning employment subsidies or the price at which public housing should be provided hinge upon beliefs of politicians and their economic advisers concerning the efficacy of the market mechanism. At one level this belief may be no more than an ideological preference for private rather than government provision of goods and services, or at another level it may be a policy to alter the distribution of income in favour of profits or yet it may be a purely political bid to smash the power of trade unions; but the hard theoretic justification may involve propositions about speeds of adjustment, about the deviation of actual from equilibrium paths, or again the possiblity of a less than full employment equilibrium.

One strand of attack on the neoclassical model mocks its absurd assumption of a competitive economy when we live in the age of giant corporations, high concentration of production in the hands of a few large firms, the 'global reach' of multi-national corporations, the imperial residue that shapes international economic relations between the developed and the less developed world. Such would be the view of such a prescient economist as J.K. Galbraith. But mockery has limits as a technique of debate. Economic arguments have always been conducted simultaneously at a highly theoretic level, at the level of empirical observation and in the corridors of power. Keynes was able to win opinion over to his own side as much because of the book he wrote which was addressed mainly to his fellow economists, a book often opaque and at all times demanding, as he did because of his power to persuade Treasuries, Cabinets and Presidents.

So the new classical macro-economics needs to be examined on the grounds that it has chosen — of empirical validity, of its superiority in explaining observed facts. No such fully fledged new Keynesian macro-economics has emerged but Keynesians have mainly spent much time in a defensive attack on the monetarist models. Every major proposition put forward by the monetarists has been tested and, as the tests have revealed in many instances, the monetarist model has failed to pass the stringent statistical tests that it has undergone. At the popular level, it is still claimed that monetarism has offered a better explanation of inflation, that it has vanquished Keynesian policy analysis, that it has a superior theoretical and empirical record. But as we shall see these are controversial claims. Even the criteria by which one may evaluate such claims are open to dispute and have changed. What was thought an adequate criterion to show the validity of a theory in the late 1950s will no longer suffice in the early 1980s. Models, ways of estimating model parameters from data, and ways of discriminating between models have all undergone a continuous revolution in the last twenty-five years. It is essential therefore to look at the methodology of testing theories, and this we do in the next chapter.

Notes

1. See Marcello de Cecco *Money and Empire* for India's crucial position in the benefits Britain derived from the International Gold Standard.
2. See Keith Middlemass: *Politics in Industrial Society*, Chapters 3 to 5.
3. This was in his *Monetary Theory and the Trade Cycle* which appeared in German before *Prices and Production* but was translated in English only later. See Desai (1981b) for a discussion.
4. In this matter, there is no divergence between the classical and the neoclassical school, so I shall refer to them with either label.
5. While Keynes advanced this as a theoretical proposition, his theories always sprang from observing actual events in the economy. Thus Great Britain had seen some savage battles in the coalminers' struggle against wage cuts in the late twenties which for a short time escalated into the General Strike of 1926. In the late twenties and early thirties, in the UK as well as the USA, cuts in money wages failed to secure cuts in real wages which actually rose. Thus the resistance to cuts in money wages and the difficulty of cutting real wages by these means were propositions firmly grounded in experience.
6. This view of Keynes was connected with his early work of probability. The impossibility of rational calculation about the future has been relatively neg-

lected by modern Keynesian theorists. Only Shackle in his various works such as *Keynesian Kaleidics* and *Economics and Epistemics* among others has consistently held to this view. Recently Hyman Minsky in his *John Maynard Keynes* has developed this into a theory of financial crises.

7.   This is obviously a very sketchy summary. For detailed treatment, see Wein-traub (1957), (1960), Davidson and Smolensky (1964), Davidson (1972), (1978), Casarosa (1981).

8.   The bibliography is well known. See Liejohhufvud, A., *Keynesian Economics and the Economics of Keynes* (1968); Davidson, P., *Money and the Real World* (1972, 1978). While Hansen simplified the General Theory in his *A Guide to Keynes*, he also forsaw the limits to sustained growth in capitalist economies that ring more true today than when he propounded his theory of secular stagnation. In this way he developed the idea of the long run consequences of Keynes' theory differently from the neoKeynesian growth theorists of the fifties and sixties.

9.   One only has to read Chapters 8–10 of the *General Theory*, especially Keynes' list of the principal objective factors (pp. 91–5), and subjective factors (pp. 107–9), to see that a consumption function such as (17) was no more than a first appraoximation. It is also plain in Chapter 10 that the multiplier was for Keynes *variable* rather than constant and its variability is explicitly discussed.

10. Though Keynes was a liberal, interested in making capitalism work in a humane rational fashion, Keynesianism got identified with left wing politics especially in the US. The outset of the cold war and the climate of virulent anti-communism affected economists and the teaching of economics. Keynes' message concerning the social control of investment and the undesirability of unequal distribution of income and wealth were conveniently forgotten. It was politically safer to leave only a pump-priming role for fiscal policy, minimising 'state intervention'. This gave us a neoclassical synthesis in academic economics and it made for Butskellism in economic policy.

11. See the evidence in Laidler, 'The Rate of Interest and the Demand for Money – Some Empirical Evidence', December 1966. Friedman returned to this issue in 1966 in his 'Interest Rates and the Demand for Money' in the *Journal of Law and Economics*, October 1966 reproduced in Friedman (1969).

12. 'US Congress Joint Economic Committee Compendium: The Relationship of Price to Economic Stability and Growth', 85th Congress 2nd Session (US Government Printing Office, Washington D.C., 1958). Our citations will be from Friedman (1969) where this evidence is reprinted.

13. This did not imply that things would be better if one used fiscal policy. Fiscal policy lags were if anything longer than those of monetary policy according to Friedman.

14. For fundamentalist views, see Edwin Canan's preface to *The Paper Pound* (1916), Andrew Dixon White's paper '(Fiat) Money Inflation in France' (1876, 1959, 1980), Henry Hazlitt: 'The Failure of the "New Economics"' (1959). See also the Recommended Reading in the 1980 edition of White's pamphlet.

15. See for example Lucas and Rapping (1969), Parkin (1971), Solow (1969) and, for a summary of the evidence that $\alpha_2 < 1$, Friedman (1975).

16. It is absolutely vital to see that the word expectation is used here in two different senses. When we say *expected* prices we use expected in the sense of anticipated prices – prices thought likely to prevail tomorrow. When we say *expected* value of a random variable we are talking about the statistical concept defined as the first moment of a distribution. The latter need not be the same as the former unless we assume certain modelling strategies being

used by individuals to generate and revise subjective expectations of variables. See the comment by Franklin Fisher on Lucas (1972) in Eckstein (1972).

17. See Buiter (1980) for a detailed critique of rational expectation models.

18. While most readers will be familiar with the notion of mathematical expectation, a brief explanation may help some. The notion of expectations has to do with outcomes of random events and is associated with games of chance. Thus in drawing a card from a deck of playing cards we may assign probabilities to the 'event' that the card will be a spade (¼), or a queen (1/13) or a red card (½). If one was paid £10 for each high card (Jack, Queen, King, Ace) and £1 for each low card, then a card dealt out has the expectation of 16/52 (£10) + 36/52 (£1) = £3.78 reward for the player. In general if $f(x)$ is the probability density function of a continuous random variable then $\int x f(x) dx = E(x)$. Expectation of a random variable is its mean value. It is a linear operator in as much as the expectation of a square of a random variable is not the square of its expectations, i.e. $E(x^2) \neq (E(x))^2$. Notice in this connection that in (36a) or (36b) one is expected to have views about the logarithm of prices and wages rather than prices and wages themselves. This imposes the requirement that behavioural models contain these variables only in their logarithmic form.

19. For a contrast between the two different definitions of the expectations variable, see Minford and Peel (1980).

20. See, apart from Buiter (1980), the November 1980 special issue of the *Journal of Money Credit and Banking* on rational expectations and the papers therein by Tobin and Okun. The differences that emerge in that issue are both as between Keynesians and monetarists as well as among old economists as contrasted to younger ones. The model here is adapted from McCallum's paper in the JMCB. McCallum (1980).

21. This result is also subject to various qualifications. Obviously as one changes the specification of the *IS* or *LM* equations, there is a greater impact of policy on actual outcomes. Various specifications of this sort are listed in McCallum (1980). As we shall see later a crucial difference is made in these equations as to whether previous *levels* of variables enter into equations significantly or not. The invariance result is also modified if we have forward expectations as in (38b) rather than backward expectations as in (38a). See Minford and Peel (1980).

22. Hahn (1980a). See also his articles in *The Times*, April 28, 1981 and with Robert Nield in March 1980.

3. THE METHODOLOGY OF TESTING ECONOMIC THEORIES

Debates and controversies between rival schools of economic thinking are conducted at one or more of three distinct levels of discourse — the theoretical level, the empirical level and the policy level. At the *theoretical* level, it is the logical consistency and completeness of a theory relative to its rival that comprises the debating ground. Each theory claims to be more *general* than its rivals and seems to cast the rival theory as a special case of itself. This was Keynes' strategy in the *General Theory* and indeed the title itself embodies this claim. Keynes claimed that the neoclassical full employment equilibrium was a special case of his own theory which predicted mutliple equilibria one of which was the full employment equilibrium, the others being underemployment equilibria. The neoclassical answer which started with Hicks' 'Mr. Keynes and the Classics' of 1937 was to exactly reverse this. Hicks so formulated the neoclassical and the Keynesian model that the latter became a special case — the 'depression economics' variant of the neoclassical model. Subsequently even neoKeynesians in their desire to reconcile Walrasian micro-economic theory with Keynesian macro-economics, conceded this point by invoking fixity or sluggishness of wages and prices, either a low interest elasticity of investment or a high interest elasticity of money demand, a volatility of expectations and so on to justify Keynesian conclusions.

A second ploy at the theoretical level in the battle of theories is to invoke *simplicity* as a criterion for superiority of one theory over another. Thus if a theory can be encapsulated in a few key relationships and if even these are simple (i.e. linear) and the theory meets the other criterion of generality, then again this bolsters the claims of a theory. Of course simplicity in a theory is not a given; over time, a theory which is at the outset simple may get complicated. This may happen partly because once a new theory has established a beachhead in its battle with the older theory (by explaining some salient anomaly the other theory cannot cope with), then it seeks to extend its sway and provide explanations of minor as well as major phenomena. Such extension obviously brings in detail which complicates the theory. An example of this for the Keynesian theory was the introduction of inventory cycles or the extensions to the open economy.

But a more important reason for the complication of a simple theory is its defensive extension. This phenomenon, whereby a theory, when under attack, builds up a rationalisation of difficult problems as defensive outposts within its domain, Imre Lakatos has well illustrated in his fundamental work on the methodology of scientific research programmes.[1] As we shall see below, both Keynesianism and monetarism have resorted to this strategy.

Generality and simplicity are thus two main grounds on which theories can be evaluated relative to each other at the abstract level of discourse. But already contained within the problem of resolving the relative merits of rival theories is an implicit or explicit appeal to the next level of discourse. This is the *appeal to data and increasingly to the estimation of the parameters of models derived from theories and the use of formal hypotheses testing procedures.* Much of this chapter will be devoted to this issue since there are a number of points of methodological interest which must be explained before we can face up to the question of testing the claims of monetarism. Before we plunge into technicalities, however, something more needs to be said at a general level.

There is an asymmetry in Keynes' claim of generality *vis-a-vis* the neoclassical theory as against that of neoclassical theory with respect to Keynes. In order to uphold Keynes' claim, one needs to operate at the theoretical level and construct a general theory which furnishes the necessary (nonWalrasian) micro-economic theory which supports the non-Walrasian macro-economic theory. Keynes himself furnished only fragments of this nonWalrasian micro-economic theory, confining his attention to the more dramatic macro-economic results. The task of furnishing a nonWalrasian micro-economic theory to match Keynes' macro-economics is extremely difficult and has been relatively neglected.[2] On the other hand, the neoclassical attack on Keynes' theory as a special case has taken the argument on to an empirical level of discourse. Thus, wage rigidity, interest elasticity of investment, income elasticity of consumption, strength of the real balance effect have all been tested at an empirical level. This is because the neoclassical school is already equipped with a micro-economic theory and it has only to indicate the now obvious point that Keynesian macro-economics is not logically consistent with Walrasian micro-theory. Keynesians who accept Walrasian micro-economic theory can then only resort to empirical or institutional arguments to sustain a different (nonWalrasian) macro-economics. Thus it is no surprise that the neoclassical attack on Keynesian economics stayed on the empirical level for some time. Only after the empirical defences of the neoKeynesian synthesis were weakened, did the (Walrasian) micro-foundation of macro-economics begin to be constructed; but these were foundations for a Walrasian or classical macro-economics.

A third level of discourse is that of *policy*. At this level, public men — politicians, journalists, publicits, the intelligentsia in general — participate. Economists try to win 'the hearts and minds' of politicians who hold out some promise of wielding power some day and putting into practical effect the abstract notions of economists. This is where economics becomes more an art of persuasion than a science. While these three levels are being used simultaneously when theories battle, it is this third level which has the greatest pay off, and, from the point of view of ordinary citizens, it is when a theory wins at this level that it has consequences for them. Keynes, of course, was a past master at the art of persuasion. In fighting the battle against the neoclassical orthodoxy he constantly mixed up the theoretical and policy levels of discourse. (Keynes never did very much by way of empirical work in establishing his argument though he did make it possible for others to do so).

In the introductory chapter, we briefly outlined how in the UK at least, the policy battle for monetarism was engaged. At this level, theories get simplified and dramatised, simple slogans are made up, exaggerated claims are made and trite refutations are scored. Attempts made to raise the debate in newspapers to the theoretical level can always be frustrated by one side or other resorting to simple polemical tricks.[3]

We shall in this chapter and in much of this book confine ourselves to the empirical level of discourse. This does not mean that we can avoid controversy but hope that we can confine the area of controversy to one where disagreements can be given explicit forms. While we shall seek to simplify many technical matters these are unavoidable in the subsequent discussion. At each stage, additional references will be given for those who wish to pursue the matter further.

The central concern here is about the way in which one can evaluate the claim of a theory to explain observed facts. All theories make highly unrealistic assumptions. As descriptions of the world we live in, most theories are poor guides. But a claim is made that it is the empirical predictions made by a theory that should be tested. If the data support the empirical predictions then the theory passes the test, or, in Popper's terms, is not refuted by the data. So we shall need to look at the ways we can test the validity of predictions from data.

But at some stage we need to rank the predictive performance of a theory relative to another. We have to ask whether monetarist theories explain the world better than Keynesian theories and state the criteria for saying so. This is the problem of model selection. It is possible for example that both theories may pass the test.

The task of testing a theory thus involves three components: a theory which generates testable predictions (T); a (statistical) method for testing the prediction (M); and a body of data against which the prediction is tested (D).

There is a large literature on the methodology of statistical testing of hypotheses. By and large in this literature, the problem is seen as one of confronting hypotheses (H) arising from theory (T) with data (D). The method (M) is assumed to play a neutral role. If the data reject the hypotheses implied by the theory then 'scientific method' requires the researcher to cast out the theory and come up with another theory.

This approach though naive has strong appeal even today. One may label it the 'High Noon' approach to hypothesis testing. It visualises a duel between theory and facts, with the loser being vanquished if not killed. This approach was popularised from a simplified version of Popper's work on scientific method, in the early 1960s, by Lipsey, among others, under the name of positivism.

If the task of testing theories were so clear cut in its outcome, one would not be witnessing a controversy such as the present one between monetarism and Keynesianism which has now been raging for at least twenty years, if not longer. This approach, now called 'naive falsification-ism', is understood to be a simplistic view of the problem of scientific research. There are several ways of understanding this.[4]

First is the problem that in confronting theories with facts, the method of testing does not play a neutral role. There may be many methods available of varying complexity (as we shall see below) and the answer depends as much on the method used as on the hypothesis and the data being confronted. Through the twenty odd years of this debate, methods have grown increasingly sophisticated as a result of the debate itself.

Second is the problem that a theory does not generate just single hypotheses *seriatim*. A theory comes as a complete package with certain core propositions which are maintained *a priori* and are not testable (e.g. the classical dichotomy in neoclassical theory). Around this core, there is a protective belt of explanations arising from the core (e.g. the nature of equilibrium process in markets via the interaction of demand and supply curves). Then, there are actual hypotheses being exposed to formal testing procedure (e.g. Friedman's hypothesis that the coefficient of anticipated inflation in the Phillips Curve (α_2) is equal to unity).

The fact that a theory comes as a package — as a 'research programme', to use Lakatos' phrase — makes the dynamics of a controversy easier to understand. For as a single hypothesis gets rejected, there are several alternatives open to the research programme. It can question the method of testing, question the data base, reformulate a more elaborate explanation to explain away the rejection, or change the question being asked.

Let us illustrate this sequence in the way in which the debate about the Phillips Curve evolved. Thus, when the Lipsey formulation of the Phillips Curve showed that the coefficient of inflation — of $\dot{p}$ — was less than one, at a crude level this could be a rejection of the neoclassical labour theory whereby workers should be bargaining about real wages and not nominal wages. But then the relevant measure of inflation — actual rather than expected inflation — came to be questioned. Reformulating the Phillips Curve with expected inflation as a variable and adding an adaptive expectations process, the theorist obtains equation (30). Here the coefficient of $\dot{p}_t$ is now rationalised as $\alpha_2 \lambda$ rather than α_2. But then subsequent econometric work still failed to show $\alpha_2 = 1$ even allowing for $\lambda \leq 1$. (See, for an admission of this, Friedman: 'Unemployment versus Inflation: An Evaluation of the Phillips Curve' (1975), pp. 24–5). But then, rather than abandon the real wage Phillips Curve or abandon the hypothesis of no money illusion, the Lucas reformulation made this (rejected) hypothesis a maintained one, no longer directly testable. Lucas was able to question the suitability of adaptive expectations hypothesis and replace it by rational expectations. Thus the 'no money illusion', which is one of the core propositions of the classical dichotomy, was withdrawn from the arena of testable propositions. So, having questioned the method of testing by questioning the specification, having reformulated the hypothesis by allowing for expected inflation to be generated by an adaptive process, finally the replacement of adaptive by rational expectation changed the question. The coefficient of $\dot{p}^e$ was no longer at issue. The testable implications of rational expectations become different from the shape of the long run Phillips Curve.

This sequence of changes did not happen as part of any elaborate plan nor out of any departure from 'scientific' practice. The alternatives we have listed are all legitimate tactics in scientific debates. It illustrates the difficulty of settling a controversy. To some extent, in testing a theory one is shooting at a moving target. There is no once-and-for-all stand-up confrontation, a shoot-out of the 'High Noon' variety; theory battles and their outcome more closely resemble guerilla warfare — a messy, long drawn out confrontation during whose course friends and enemies change character and the outcome is seldom conclusive.

Third is the major problem that, by and large, propositions of economic theory relate to equilibrium configurations; these may be static equilibria or dynamic steady state equilibria. Economic theory is very reticent about the nature of economic events in disequilibrium. Thus Keynes even in his most radical attack on classical economic theory formulated his theory in equilibrium terms. The data that we seek to explain have a time dependent character. Prices, quantities, income, employment all have dates attached to them. Theory suggests that they should be in a certain equilibrium relationship to each other but if this is taken to mean that this equilibrium should exist at all times then the theory is obviously refuted by the data. Economists have thus employed the distinction between the short run and the long run, with equilibrium predictions only meant to hold in the long run. The long-run of economic theory is not however calendar time, it is not measured in years. It is the time over which all the adjustments to an initial perturbation are accomplished. It can be made a calendar time only if we add the proviso (impossible to fulfil in practice) that if nothing else changes in the meantime, *ceteris paribus*, it would take so many periods (months, years, decades) for the full adjustment to take place. The measurement of such adjustment lags and the testing of equilibrium predictions from actual data are tricky tasks involving theoretical and definitional problems as well as economic problems.

After these preliminary remarks, we now turn to the technical econometric details of measurement and testing of economic theories.

Suppose we have a theoretical proposition which asserts that a relationship exists between two variables, call them y and x. Now, y may be the price level and x, the stock of money. How do we confirm that such a proposition is valid? We first need to make the proposition somewhat more precise. Thus, we may say that

(A)   there exists an association between the movements of y and x over time; or

(B)   there is a causal relationship between y and x, with x the cause and y the effect.

Almost all problems of statistical inference as used in economics and econometrics arise from the task of separating statement *A* from statement *B*. Statement *A* asserts only that there is a *correlation* between *y* and *x*; statement *B* goes further and asserts that there is a *causal relation* between *y* and *x*. If correlation between *y* and *x* can be established, can we infer causation from this evidence? It is best to proceed with this answer in the way it evolved over time. (This may tax the patience of the specialist reader but it is still best to proceed in this fashion).

The technique of simple and multiple correlation has been known for a long time and constitutes a basic tool. Thus if we have a series of observations on *y* and *x* of the form $x_1, \ldots x_T$ and $y_1, \ldots y_T$ for time period 1 to *T*, we can compute the correlation between the contemporaneous values of y_t and x_t as

$$r_{y_t, x_t} = \sum_t (x_t - \bar{x})(y_t - \bar{y}) \Big/ \left[\sum_t (x_t - \bar{x})^2 \sum_t (y_t - \bar{y})^2 \right]^{1/2}$$

$$= cov\,(y_t\, x_t) \Big/ (\sqrt{var\, x_t\, var\, y_t}) \tag{43}$$

The correlation coefficient *r* is then the ratio of the covariance between *x* and *y* divided by the product of their standard deviations, or equivalently by the square root of the product of their variances. Having obtained a measure of the correlation, we then ask whether this correlation is systematic or could it have arisen by chance. So we set up a null hypothesis that the true correlation between *y* and *x* is zero, i.e. they are truly uncorrelated. This will be written as

$$Ho: \,{}^\rho y_t\, x_t = 0 \tag{44}$$

Setting up the null hypothesis in terms of the adverse of the assertion being made, i.e. an absence rather than presence of correlation allows us to work out the distribution of the possible values of *r*, the observed correlation, which may arise due to chance, even though the true correlation is zero. This is a function of the number of observations on *y* and *x* used in computing *r*. If our observed *r* lies outside the range of possible *r* values when $\rho = 0$ then we *reject* the null hypothesis that $\rho = o$ and thus provisionally (i.e. until a sample contradicts our results) assert that *y* and *x* *are* correlated. It is in the nature of statistical inference that we can only assert this absence of zero correlation probabilistically and not with certainty. Thus we may say, with 95% confidence, that we reject $\rho = 0$, i.e. we may not revise our view if in the next 100 cases we examine up to five turn out to contradict our assertion; or the same with the 99% level of confidence, etc.

In testing the null hypothesis of zero correlation between y_t and x_t, we have a *maintained hypothesis* that the relation between y and x is a linear relationship and r measures the strength of correlation between y and x under this maintained hypothesis. Of course, in a higher level test, one may wish to expose this particular maintained hypothesis to test.

Correlation is a linear symmetric relationship between the two variables. We may wish to extend the proposition (A) to one where we look at the relationship between current or future values of y and the present or past (lagged) value of x. Then, we have as in (43)

$$r_{y_{t+k'}, x_{t-j}} = \sum_t (y_{t-k} - \bar{y})(x_{t+j} - \bar{x}) \Big/ (\sqrt{\Sigma(y_{t+k} - \bar{y})^2 \Big/ (x_{t-j} - \bar{x})^2}$$

for $k \geq 0, j \geq 0$ \hfill (43a)

We may have situations in which the contemporaneous correlation may be small or zero but the lagged correlation may be quite high. The presence of a lag breaks the symmetry between x and y; since the variable occurring with a lag occurs prior to the other variable, a causal status may be conferred on x relative to y. This notion of causality which we shall examine below, has played an important part in the monetarist debate.

Recall now Friedman's work on the demand for money. At the simplest level, he asserts a correlation between the money stock in nominal or real terms and national income in money or real terms. Thus he says of secular behaviour,

> Secular changes in the real stock of money per capita are *highly correlated* with secular changes in real income per capita. For twenty cycles, measured from trough to trough and covering the period from 1870 to 1954, the simple correlation between the logarithm of the real stock of money per capita and the logarithm of real income per capita is 0.99 and the computed elasticity is 1.8.
> (Friedman (1969) p. 113, emphasis added).

This assertion of correlation would be acceptable without debate. After all, two variables y and x may move together because of the common influence of a third factor z and hence correlation says no more than that they are associated in their movements. Friedman is also making statements about long run averages and it is well known that such an averaging procedure may alter the behaviour of the original, unadjusted series by emphasising the trend or by generating cycles in the variable not discernible in the original data.[5] Lastly Friedman is correlating *levels* of M and Y or their price-deflated counterparts. It is well known that levels may be correlated but first differences of variables may not be. Thus a more stringent test of the correlation may be whether the change in $y - \Delta y$ is correlated with the change in $x - \Delta x$.

To assert something stronger than correlation, further steps have to be taken. By Friedman's own admission, the cyclical relationship between levels of money and income is much weaker than the secular relationship (op cit. p. 114-15). But in the supply of money study quoted above he does assert that though changes in money stock influence changes in real income and prices as well as being influenced by them, changes in the former *precede* changes in the latter variables. Thus he asserts that there is a correlation between *changes* in money stock *lagged* and the level of *current* nominal income. He showed this by examining the timing of turning points in changes in money and in the general business cycle and found this lag to be long and variable.

Friedman's evidence of long and variable lags was immediately challenged by John Kareken and Robert Solow who specifically examined the evidence in their study *Lags in Monetary Policy*. They first deny that Friedman's evidence of cyclical turning points constitutes causal evidence usable, as Friedman wished, to warn against the use of monetary policy for stabilisation purposes.

> The observed pattern of peaks and troughs in the general business cycle and in the money supply and its increments is compatible with many hypotheses about why events turned out just so . . . There's no evading the necessity of beginning with some kind of model which permits one, for better or worse, to estimate the *ceteris paribus* effects of monetary policy.
>
> (Kareken and Solow (1963) p. 16).

Another point that Kareken and Solow made also arose frequently in much of the subsequent debate. This was that a lead–lag relationship between the change in a variable and the level of another can be created artificially even when in the levels or in the changes there may be no such relation. Suppose that, apart from trends, the money supply and the level of activity move roughly simultaneously and that together they trace out fluctuations not too different from ordinary trigonometric oscillations. Then, as everyone knows, the rate of change in the stock of money will show an approximate quarter-cycle lead over business activity. (Kareken and Solow (1963) p. 17).

Kareken and Solow measured changes in M and in industrial production Q (as a proxy for real output) as centred first differences similar to Phillips' measure of change in money wages.

$$\Delta M_t = \tfrac{1}{2}\,[(M_{t+1} - M_t) + (M_t - M_{t1})] = \tfrac{1}{2}(M_{t+1} - M_{t+1})$$

They found the following correlation pattern

	1919–59	1919–38	1939–59
$\Delta M, \Delta Q$	0.3062	0.5712	0.2002
$\Delta M_{t-1}, \Delta Q$	0.2702	0.4850	0.1663
$\Delta M_{t+1}, \Delta Q$	0.2472	0.5213	0.1236

Thus correlations were low, much lower than Friedman's evidence indicated and the contemporaneous correlation was always the highest. Kareken and Solow then set up a Keynesian model of the transmission mechanism and in order to measure the lag structure they estimated a set of distributed lags. They made the now familiar distinction between an inside lag (a lag before the authorities recognise a problem and take action) and an outside lag (a lag before the economy responds to a policy move). They found short inside lags but long outside lags. They conclude

> though the full results of policy changes on the flow of expenditure may be a long time coming, nevertheless the chain of effects is spread out over a fairly wide interval. This means that *some* effect comes reasonably quickly and that the effects build up over time, so that some substantial stabilizing power results after a lapse of time of the order of six or nine months.
>
> (Kareken and Solow (1963) p. 2).

Kareken and Solow used multiple regression analysis rather than correlation for the measurement of distributed lags. Though their carefully arrived at results contradicted Friedman's findings, they are nonetheless less dramatic and more complex. As often happens in this case, no detailed answer was made of this critique by Friedman.[6] His dramatic assertion of long and variable lags has stuck by virtue of repetition, if nothing else. The next phase of the debate moved away from the question of the lags to the question of the relative size of the money multiplier and the investment multiplier. In looking at this, we need to examine some theory of the linear regression equation.

[Although correlation between a lagged money measure and current income was not taken to be evidence of causation at this stage (1963) subsequently Granger (1969) and Sims (1972) proposed a definition of causality which hinges crucially on such correlation patterns across lags. We shall come to this later. This is another piece of evidence of the way techniques change in the course of a debate.]

Friedman's assertion about the relative size of the money multiplier as compared to the investment multiplier was made in his study of the 'Demand for Money' as we saw above. In 1963 in their study for the Commission for Money and Credit, Friedman and Meiselman tested this proposition by using the tool of linear regression. At a simple level it amounts to making a stronger statement than correlation, more akin to causation. It posits a linear relationship with constant coefficients between y and x. Once however we move to this formulation, we have to state our assumptions carefully. The relationship between y and x is posited as

$$y_t = \beta_0 + \beta_1 x_t + u_t \tag{45}$$

Unlike correlation analysis, we now move to an asymmetric relationship. Now x is an independent variable, independent of the random error term u. The error term is assumed to have zero mean and constant variance. It is also assumed that u is uncorrelated with its own past values. We state this as

   (i) $E(u_t) = 0$ zero mean

   (ii) $E(u_t^2) = \sigma^2$ constant variance

   (iii) $E(u_t u_{t-s}) = 0$ for all $s \neq 0$, no autocorrelation

   (iv) $E(x_t u_t) = x_t E(u_t) = 0$ x fixed in repeated samples

We say that x is fixed in repeated sample because the linear regression analysis was first used in experimental subjects to describe the stimulus–response relationship. If one could vary the stimulus (x_t) for each of T cases $(t = 1, \ldots T)$ and measure the response y_t in each case, one can model the stimulus–response relationship as (45). In such cases it is possible to keep the set x_t fixed in repeated samples and for each sample measure the response y_t. The variation for the same x_t in y_t across experiments is then due to random variables over which the experimenter has no control, but these random variables, represented by the portmanteau variable u, are independent of the controlled stimulus administered. This is the origin of the fixed in repeated sample assumption.

If these assumptions are fulfilled then the estimate of β_0, β_1 and σ^2 derived by minimising Σu_t^2 are unbiased and minimum variance in the class of linear unbiased estimators. We can also measure the strength of the relationship by testing the null hypothesis that there is no relationship between y_t and x_t.

$$H_0 : \beta_1 = 0$$

If H_0 holds then the unconditional mean $E(y_t)$ is just as good an estimate of the likely value of the next drawing of the y variable from its distribution as the conditional mean $E(y_t | x_t)$ i.e. the presence of x in the information set does not improve our predictive power. To test H_0 we compute the coefficient of determination R^2 which is the squared value of r described above. The distribution $(R^2 / 1 - R^2)$ $[(T - k) / (k - 1)]$, when H_0 is true, is an F distribution so as in the case of simple correlation, if R^2 is high it will be evidence that H_0 can be rejected.[7]

The reason for going through this piece of elementary econometrics at some length is that the next stage of the Keynesian–monetarist ('Chicago School' as it was known in early 1960s) debate hinged on some elementary confusions about the linear regression model. We have made the experimental science background clear because it is obvious that (45), while computationally convenient, is not appropriate for economic investigation except in rare circumstances. This was known in econometrics since the pioneering work of Haavelmo in 1943. The problem we shall see hinges around the independence assumption regarding x and the non-autocorrelation assumption about u.

Recall that Friedman in his 1959 'Demand for Money' article had conjectured that the money multiplier may be more stable than the investment multiplier; Friedman and Meiselman (FM hereafter) now proceeded to test this by running a regression race between an equation derived from the LM curve embodying the money multiplier and one based on the IS curve embodying the Keynesian multiplier. Having carried out this race for US annual data for 1897–1958, they concluded:

> The results are strikingly one-sided. Except for the early years of the Great Depression, money (defined as currency plus commercial bank deposits) is more closely related to consumption than is autonomous expenditure (defined as the sum of net private investment expenditures plus the government deficit) . . . So far as these data go, the widespread belief that the investment multiplier is stabler than the monetary velocity is an invalid generalization from the experience of three or four years. It holds for neither later or earlier years.
>
> (FM (1963), p. 166).

The race that FM ran consisted of two linear regressions, consumption expenditure (C) on money stock (M) and on autonomous expenditure

$$C_t = \alpha_0 + \alpha_1 M_t + e_{1t} \tag{46a}$$

$$C_t = \alpha_0' + \alpha_1' A_t + e_{2t} \tag{46b}$$

A_t stands for autonomous expenditure. FM regarded the size of the R^2 of (46a) relative to that of (46b) as sufficient evidence for making their assertion that the money multiplier was more stable than the investment multiplier. For 1897–1958 as a whole they found $r_{CA} = 0.756$ and $r_{CM} = 0.985$. For every decade subsample, except that for 1929–39, r_{CM} exceeded r_{CA}. They saw this as evidence that:

> The income velocity of circulation of money is consistently and decidedly stabler than the investment multiplier except only during the early years of the Great Depression after 1929. There is throughout, including those years, a close and consistent relation between the stock of money and consumption or income and between year to year changes in the stock of money and in consumption or income. There is a much weaker and less consistent relation between autonomous expenditure and consumption with the same exception, and essentially no consistent relation between year to year changes in autonomous expenditures and consumption.
>
> (FM (1963) p. 186)

FM thus set up an explicit econometric criterion for ranking rival theories and concluded that the monetary version outperformed the Keynesian one on grounds of the variablity in the size of the correlation coefficient over time and the difference between the two correlation coefficients. The only way to describe the reaction of the profession to this piece of research is to say that 'all hell broke loose'. Three replies were promptly made to FM by Hester (1964), Ando and Modigliani (1965) and De Prano and Mayer (1965). A hundred pages of the September 1965 issue of the American Economic Review were devoted to this debate. We shall mainly confine ourselves to the Ando and Modigliani (AM) reply.

Ando and Modigliani pointed out that the method used by FM was, in our terms, non-neutral, i.e. the testing procedure was stacked deliberately to bias the results in favour of the money mulitplier. AM pointed out that the measured correlation coefficient is biased because of the way in which A_t was defined, i.e. A_t did not satisfy the assumption required for an independent variable with the result that the estimate α_1 and the associated r or R^2 were downward biased. This led to the charge that the consumption function implicit in (46b) was misspecified. Thus if personal consumption expenditure was related to disposable income (Y^d) and then via the income identity to personal savings one would have

$$C_t = c_0 + c_1 Y_t^d + e_{3t} \tag{47a}$$

$$C_t + S_t = Y_t^d \tag{47b}$$

$$C_t = c_0 \big/ (1-c_1) + [c_1 \big/ (1-c_1)] S_t + e_{3t} \big/ (1-c_1) \tag{47c}$$

Now S differs from A by various components such as corporate retained earnings and other small items which we denote as Z_t. So it turns out that FM implicitly specified their consumption function not as (47a) but as

$$C_t = c_0 + c_1 (Y_t^d + Z_t) + e_{3t} \qquad (48a)$$

But even with (46b) or (47c), the assumption of independence of A from e_2 or of S from e_3 does not hold. It is well known that in economics we are faced with a simultaneous (i.e. interdependent) equations system and the theory described in support of (45) is inappropriate when used for a simultaneous system. What it does allow us to do is compute the size of the error committed by misspecification. Thus we can show that the bias in the coefficient of α_1' or $c_1 / (1-c_1)$ will depend on the correlations r_{A, e_2} and r_{S, e_3} respectively. So the measured R^2 (or α_1') in (46b) will be downward biased. AM further showed that the inclusion of the war years 1942–6 depressed the R^2 for (46b) much more than that of (46a) because there were obvious limits to increasing consumer expenditure in wartime. Thus for 1929–58, the R^2 for (46b) was 0.49 including 1942–6 and 0.92 without, whereas for (46a) it was 0.94 and 0.98 respectively. Thus the difference narrows from 0.49/0.94 to 0.92/0.98.

These mistakes biased the FM results. As AM concluded

> We have thus shown that 'the strikingly one-sided' results of FM are largely accounted for by their 'strikingly one-sided procedure'. Once we rely on a less partisan approach, the income–expenditure model can readily meet the challenge on FM's own chosen ground, namely, the size of the correlation coefficient.
>
> (AM (1965) p. 714).

AM further point out that the correlation coefficient is sensitive to whether we define the dependent variable in terms of levels or first differences and hence the residual variance (σ^2) should be a better criterion than r or R^2. In the linear case with y and x in level form as in [(45)], σ^2 and R^2 correspond since $R^2 = (1-\sigma^2) / \mathrm{var}.\ y$. But if we change from y to Δy then var Δy being different from var y, we get a different R^2. Residual variance as a measure of predictive power need not change since in generating predictions of Δy we can take y_{-1} as known and hence predicting Δy amounts to predicting y conditional on y_{-1}.

AM thus drastically corrected the FM results and questioned the assertion of the greater stability of the money multiplier. Though the debate has never resumed on this ground with any intensity, the AM answer remains the valid one and has not been challenged. AM did however try in their article to answer the important question: if the correlation coefficient is not an appropriate criterion for ranking theories, how should one discriminate between theories? The answer they gave is important because it defines the next and very important layer in the hierarchy of techniques used for testing theories.

A theory such as the Friedman theory of the determination of nominal income circa 1963, involves statements about the slopes and size of certain relationships. Thus, as we saw in the previous chapter, Friedman posited low or zero interest elasticity of the demand for money in his 1959 paper. Though he subsequently defended himself by saying that the zero elasticity assumption held only in the long run and that the elasticity was low in the short run, the FM derivation of (46a) from the LM equation involved an *a priori restriction* that the interest elasticity was zero. This can be seen as follows. Let the demand for money be as before

$$M_t^d = a_0 + a_1\ Y_t + a_2\ r_t + u_t \tag{49a}$$

$$M_t^d = \bar{M}_t \tag{49b}$$

Then LM curve is

$$Y_t = a_0\big/a_1 + \bar{M}_t\big/a_1 - (a_2\big/a_1)r_t - u_t\big/a_1 \tag{49c}$$

Now comparing (49c) to (46a) we see that (apart from replacement of Y by C) that $a_2 = 0$ in (49c) will give us (46a) with $1/a_1 = \alpha_1$, $^{-a}0/a_1 = \alpha_0$ and $(-1/a_1)\ u_t = e_1$. Thus, for FM to claim that (46a) represents the money multiplier process involves the prior restriction that $a_2 = 0$. But FM nowhere *test* this restriction although it is crucial to the transmission mechanism they rely on for money stock changes to bring about income changes.

It can be shown that the omission of an interest rate term in (46b) involves a similar restriction on the IS curve. Thus FM model the Keynesian multiplier process as requiring a vertical IS curve. They set up a race between a world with a vertical IS curve and a world with a vertical LM curve. It is quite possible obviously that neither of these restrictions may be valid, i.e. that both investment demand and money demand may be interest elastic. Friedman's preference for stark, simple formulations implies a highly restrictive formulation with the restrictions themselves being untested. Despite the thirst of the policymaker and the public for simple answers, economic questions seldom yield such answers except when the theorist imposes untested invalid restrictions.

The method for testing restrictions in the context of a linear regression model can now be quickly described though we shall soon have to abandon (45) in favour of a simultaneous equations model. Let (45) be elaborated in terms of two variables x and z. Then

$$y_t = \beta_0 + \beta_1 x_t + \beta_2 z_t + v_t \tag{45a}$$

Thus if we impose on (45a) the restriction that $\beta_2 = 0$, we get (45). Equation (45) is then the restricted and (45a) the unrestricted equation. The principle of testing restrictions involves checking whether imposing the restriction involves significant loss of information and predictive power. Thus in this simple case we could estimate (45a) and test the null hypothesis that $\beta_2 = 0$. This can be done by straightforward t test comparing β_2 to its standard error. We could alternately compare the residual variance of (45) and (45a) and see whether σ_u^2 is significantly higher than σ_v^2. There exists a likelihood ratio test which handles this problem.[9] The idea is $H_0 : \beta_2 = 0$ corresponds to σ_u^2 / σ_v^2 being close to 1. The tests are parallel and equivalent.

When we come to the AM formulation of the problem we have quite correctly to abandon the single equation framework and move to a simultaneous equations framework. Simple correlation or regression analysis are no longer suitable tools for our task. We replace the dependent–independent variables division by an endogenous-exogenous one. Thus we have a model of, say, G equations in G unknown or endogenous variables and K exogenous variables. Besides the K exogenous variables, we may also have lagged values of some of the G endogenous variables appearing as explanatory variables in one or more equations.

Since formal presentations of these definitions can be found in the many textbooks available, we shall study these issues in the context of the model proposed by AM. Even the simple IS-LM model gets complicated once account is taken of national income components in detail. Thus let us begin with equation (47b)

$$S \equiv Y^d - C \equiv (Y-C) - (Y-Y^d) \equiv Z + X \tag{50}$$

Z and X (not to be confused with variables in equation (45a)) are respectively the difference between income and consumption and between income and disposable income. Some components of Z and X are autonomous, i.e. unaffected by the course of the consumption, income relationship and others are induced. Let the induced components be labelled Z^i, X^i and the autonomous components Z^a, X^a, Z^i and X^i can then be given auxiliary equations in terms of Y^d, C, Z^a, X^a and so on. The AM model then is

$$C = C(Y^d, r, C_{t-1}) + \epsilon_{1t} \tag{51}$$

$$Z^a = Z^a(r, C_{t-1}) + \epsilon_{2t} \tag{52}$$

$$M^d = L(Y, r, C_{t-1}) + \epsilon_{3t} \tag{53}$$

$$M^s = B(r, M^*) + \epsilon_{4t} \tag{54}$$

$$Z^i = Z^i(Z^a, X^a, Y^d, C, X^i) + \epsilon_{5t} \tag{55}$$

$$X^i = X^i(Z^a, X^a, Y^d, C, Z^i) + \epsilon_{6t} \tag{56}$$

$$C^f = C + Z^i \tag{57}$$

$$Y = C^f + Z^a \tag{58}$$

$$Y^d = C + Z^a + X^a + Z^i + X^i \tag{59}$$

We assume that the implicit functions C, Z^a, L, B, Z^i, X^i are all linear in the parameters. ϵ_1 to ϵ_6 are random errors. Equations (57) to (59) are accounting identities. The nine equations (51) to (59) determine nine *endogenous* variables, C, Z^a, M, r, C^f, Y, Y^d, Z^i and X^i. If we were to break down any of the variables into further components, we would have more equations. Thus we use only one interest rate and simplify the money supply relation , equation (54), by having only the single interest rate and M^* which is the maximum money supply that can be created given the size of demand deposits and the required reserve ratios. Apart from (54), equations (51) to (53) are standard consumption, investment and money demand equations. The *exogenous* variables are X^a and M^*.

Equations (51) to (59) define the set of *structural form* (SF) equations. A *reduced form* (RF) representation would express each of the nine endogenous variables as linear functions of only the three *predetermined* variables: two exogenous variables X^a and M^*, and the single lagged endogenous variable C_{t-1}.[10] To make the problem manageable we can condense the structural form equations into four by solving out equations (55) to (59) and substituting them into (51) to (54). This gives us a *condensed structural form equations* (CSFE) model whose coefficients are implicit functions of the parameters of (51) to (59). We get

$$C^f + \beta_{12} Z^a + \beta_{13} r = \gamma_{11} C_{t-1} + \gamma_{12} X_t^a + \epsilon'_{1t} \qquad (51a)$$

$$Z^a + \beta_{23} r = \gamma_{21} C_{t-1} + \epsilon'_{2t} \qquad (52a)$$

$$\beta_{31} C^f + \beta_{32} Z^a + \beta_{33} r + M = \gamma_{31} C_{t-1} + \epsilon'_{3t} \qquad (53a)$$

$$\beta_{43} r + M = \gamma_{43} M^* + \epsilon'_{4t} \qquad (54a)$$

We are now back to two equations (51a), (52a) from which an IS relationship could be derived and two equations (53a), (54a) from which an LM relationship could be derived. Notice that the FM procedure can be described precisely as follows: set $\beta_{13} = \gamma_{11} = \gamma_{12} = 0$ in (51a) and $\beta_{23} = \gamma_{21} = 0$ in (52a). Let A be Z^a, then we get equation (46b) with $-\beta_{12} = \alpha_1$ and $e_{2t} = \epsilon_{1t} - \beta_{12}\epsilon_{2t}$. In the money demand equations (53a), (54a), we again set $\beta_{33} = \gamma_{31} = 0$ and $\beta_{31} = \beta_{32}$. In the money supply equation $\beta_{43} = 0$ and $\gamma_{43} = 1$. We then get (46a) with $\alpha_1 = 1/\beta_{31}$ and $e_{1t} = (\epsilon_{3t} - \epsilon_{4t})/\beta_{31}$.

Thus, one way of testing whether the economy corresponds to FM's view of the money multiplier process is to test the restrictions $\beta_{33} = \gamma_{31} = 0$ and $\beta_{31} = \beta_{32}$. (Of these, it is only $\beta_{33} = 0$ which is the crucial restriction. The others may be dropped easily without affecting FM's theory.) One can also test the restrictions $\beta_{43} = 0$ and $\gamma_{43} = 1$. This involves in effect assuming that $M (= M^*)$ is exogenous to the model. Once we accept the restrictions $M = M^*$ and $\beta_{33} = 0$, then Y or $(C^f + Z^a)$ is determined by M alone and the only role of the IS equation is to determine r and the split between C^f and Z^a.

Alternatively the simplified version of Keynesianism proposed by FM requires $\beta_{13} = \beta_{23} = 0$. (Again the other restrictions on $\gamma_{11}, \gamma_{12}, \gamma_{21}$ are not crucial). Once we do this, then C^f (and therefore Y) is determined by Z^a alone and money, or the interest rate, plays no role in income determination. Then equations (53a) and (54a) determine r and M given Y and M^*.

The effect of either set of restrictions is to make the structure less interdependent and more recursive. To illustrate this, assume that $\beta_{23} = 0$, $\beta_{43} = 0$. Then $\beta_{13} = 0$ implies

$$C^f + \beta_{12} Z^a = \gamma_{11} C_{t-1} + \gamma_{12} X^a + \epsilon'_{1-t}$$

$$Z^a = \gamma_{21} C_{t-1} + \epsilon'_{2t}$$

$$\beta_{31} C^f + \beta_{32} Z^a + \beta_{33} r + M = \gamma_{31} C_{t-1} + \epsilon'_{3t}$$

$$M = \gamma_{43} M^* + \epsilon'_{4t}$$

The bottom two variables r and M^* do not appear in the top two equations but the top two variables do appear with non-zero coefficients in the bottom two equations. The block of first two equations is recursive with respect to the block of second two equations. This implies that the first two variables are determined independently of the last two but not *vice versa*. So one way to test the FM proposition is to test the recursiveness assumption or the exogeneity of C^f and Z^a in the money demand equation.

If $\beta_{33} = 0$ were true, then the situation is reversed and the money demand equation is recursive with respect to the consumption and investment equations. So FM's two equations arise from the recursive formulations of the basic IS–LM model. If these restrictions are rejected by the data as inappropriate, then this obviously means that the single equation assumption which requires the independence of the righthand side variables from the error term will no longer be valid. The results then are useless for ranking theories.

AM did not directly test the restrictions on equations (51a) – (54a). Instead they wrote down the reduced form equation for C^f under either of the two assumptions. Thus if money does not matter at all then C^f will be determined solely by Z^a, X^a and C_{t-1} since the first two equations are recursive with respect to the last two. We get

$$C^f = \delta_1 Z^a + \delta_2 X^a + \delta_3 C_{t-1} + u_c \tag{60a}$$

If the money equations were recursive, we get

$$C^f = \gamma_1 Z^a + \gamma_2 M^* + \gamma_3 C_{t-1} + u_m \tag{60b}$$

Notice that recursiveness imposes the restriction that M^* does not appear in (60a) nor X^a in (60b). In each case if we are willing to treat Z^a as independent of C^f, we have only predetermined variables on the right hand sides of (60a) and (60b) which then become analogous to the linear-regression equation (45a). Now to judge which of the two is correct, one can run a regression equation which is a hybrid of the two.

$$C_t^f = \pi_1 Z_t^a + \pi_2 M_t^* + \pi_3 X_t^a + \pi_4 C_{t-1} + v_{1t} \tag{61}$$

One way to test the two rival hypotheses is to see whether π_2 or π_3 equals zero. AM get

$$C_t^f = \underset{(0.17)}{0.62} Z_t^a + \underset{(0.09)}{0.21} M_t^* + \underset{(0.65)}{1.98} X_t^a + \underset{(0.11)}{0.38} C_{t-1} \tag{62}$$

Figures in parenthesis are standard errors and if we apply the t test we can reject the null hypotheses that $\pi_2 = 0$ or that $\pi_3 = 0$. So both the simple Keynesian and the simple monetary versions are rejected. Thus (61) is a linear combination of (60a) and (60b). This implies that the π_i estimates would be weighted averages of δ_i and γ_i with the weight being $\sigma_{v_1}^2$, $\sigma_{v_2}^2$ and their covariance. Thus for example

$$\pi_1 = \frac{\sigma_1 \sigma_{u_c}^2 + v_1 \sigma_{u_m}^2 - (\delta_1 + \gamma_1) \operatorname{cov}(u_c, u_m)}{\sigma_{u_c}^2 + \sigma_{u_m}^2 - 2 \operatorname{cov}(u_c, u_m)} \tag{63}$$

Now if the actual observed data come from a world in which fiscal policy is varied to determine income, and the money supply adjusts to accommodate income changes, then $\sigma_{u_c}^2 < \sigma_{u_m}^2$ and vice versa if money is used to control income and C^f adjusts passively. Using insights like this, AM find that the π_i estimates correspond much more to a regime where the fiscal multiplier dominates than where the money multiplier dominates. On the whole, they prefer the view that both IS and LM equations, both fiscal and monetary policy determine income and interest rates.

FM's paper purported to use econometric criteria to rank the two theories when confronted with data. We see that AM show how biased FM's procedure is. They take a highly restrictive model, do not test the restrictions and allow a misspecification of variables to influence the outcome of their tests. Testing a theory, or ranking two theories, turns out to be a much more complex task than mere comparison of R^2.

Not only do AM show that FM's conclusions are wrong but that the very question they ask is not helpful. In any case FM are setting up two strawmen and crowning one of them. No serious Keynesian economist has suggested that the IS curve was vertical nor should any monetarist suggest (Friedman himself does not) that the LM curve is vertical. So why then the attempt? One can only say that FM 'put monetarism on the map' as a serious challenge to Keynesian economics for ever more and in the battle for persuading policy makers it shook the complacency of the Keynesians in the US. Hereafter, more attention would be paid to incorporating money into macro-economic models. In a way, few people remember now how completely wrong FM results have been shown to be. As has happened before and since, this debate did not settle the issue; the losers did not lose, they chose to fight on another ground.[11]

The AM critique of FM methods is a convenient point at which to consider the nature of econometric building in general. At the end of their paper, they say

We conclude, therefore, that . . . there is little point in pursuing the game of testing one-equation-one-independent-variable models in search for the highest correlation, fascinating as the game might be. We need instead to buckle down to the unended and the unending labour of learning more about the *structure* of our economy. This applies in particular to the task of charting the complex and still ill-understood channels through which money and the tools of monetary policy affect economic activity.

(AM (1965), p. 716, emphasis added.)

AM were thus pointing out that single equation methods lead to spurious correlation and erroneous conclusions about the strength of an economic relation. Since the economy is an interdependent system, it is necessary to model the *structure* of the economy. This is done by specifying a many-equations model in which each equation captures some important behavioural relationship. It is only the entire structural model that captures the causal links — the transmission mechanism — from the set of policy variables to the set of endogenous variables. This is the classical econometric methodology pioneered by Haavelmo ((1943), (1944)) and by Koopmans in the Cowles Commission monographs numbers 10 and 14 ((1950), (1953)). When AM were writing, this was the accepted 'best scientific practice' and the NBER methodology of cycle measurements and single equation correlation maximising exercises were thought to be deficient.[12] In the next ten years after AM's paper, even this certainty about the best practice was challenged. The new monetarists not only criticised Keynesian theory but also the associated econometric methodology. They revived the old NBER, single equation methodology refurbishing it with new techniques associated with time series analysis. This controversy takes us into a technically demanding area but it is essential to understand this debate.

Let y be the set of endogenous variables (e.g. C^f, Z^a, r, M, Z^i, X^i, Y^d in the AM model) and x be the set of exogenous variables (e.g. X^a, M^* in the AM model). A general dynamic model can be written as

$$B_0 y_t + B_1 y_{t-1} \ldots + B_m y_{t-m} + C_0 x_t + C_1 x_{t-1} + C_2 x_{t-2}$$

$$\ldots C_n x_{t-n} = u_t \tag{64}$$

where B_i are matrices of size $G \times G$ with G the number of endogenous variables, and $i > 0$ for lagged endogenous variables; C_i are $G \times K$ matrices of exogenous variables of which there are n; u is the vector of random error terms. Various assumptions can be made about the distribution of the error terms especially about the pattern of correlation between current and past values of the error term. It would however be true to say that in 1965, not much attention was paid to the specification of the serial correlation pattern of the error term.

Equation system (64) can be compactly written as

$$B(L)y_t + C(L)x_t = u_t \tag{65}$$

where L is known as the lag operator and $B(L)$, $C(L)$ are polynomial matrices in L. In this scheme B_0 reflects the contemporaneous interdependence of the endogenous variables, the simultaneity of economic relations as in Marshall's famous 'scissors' diagram. The exogenous and lagged endogenous variables are meant to capture the impulse shocks and the propagation mechanism of these shocks through the economic system (Frisch (1933)).

Now (64) or (65) embodies the economist's view of the way the world works but what he observes are just cross correlations between the y and x variables and their lagged values. Also the notion of causality in (64), especially the simultaneity in B_0, raises problems since the cause-effect relationship is thought to be asymmetric, i.e. if a causes b, b does not cause a. The notion of everything occurring in the same moment – *simultaneously* – also met with objection from some econometricians who took the view that the true description of economic events had to be along a temporal sequence: current consumption cannot be a function of current income since you must have income *before* you can spend it (Wold (1949)).

The asymmetric notion of causality is captured by writing down the reduced form (RF) of the system

$$y_t = -B_0^{-1}\,(\bar{B}(L)y_{t-1} + C_0 x_t + \bar{C}(L)x_{t-1}) + B_0^{-1} u_t$$

$$= \pi_0 x_t + \pi_1(L)y_{t-1} + \pi_2(L)x_{t-1} + v_t \tag{66}$$

where $\bar{B}(L) = (B(L) - B_0)$, $\bar{C}(L) = (C(L) - C_0)$, and y_{t-1} and x_{t-1} are respectively the y and x vectors excluding the contemporaneous y_t and x_t. Now in (66) y_t is caused by current exogenous variables x_t, lagged exogenous variables x_{t-1} and lagged endogenous variables y_{t-1}. Of these three sets x_{t-1}, y_{t-1} are clearly prior in time and thus by definition asymmetric in their effect on y_t. The contemporaneous exogenous variables x_t occur simultaneously with the endogenous variables y_t but are defined to be independent of them. Some x_t may be truly exogenous – noneconomic variables such as rainfall – but others may be policy variables such as the money supply, and much controversy attaches even today to the notion of exogeneity.

The π_0, π_1, π_2 matrices capture the transmission mechanism, i.e. they tell us that the predetermined variables affect the endogenous variables directly through C_0, $\bar{C}(L)$, $\bar{B}(L)$ coefficients but indirectly through the way in which endogenous variables affect each other, i.e. through B_0. Thus $\pi_0 = -B_0^{-1} C_0$ captures the total effect, direct and indirect, of x_t on y_t.

But the structural form (65) and the reduced form (66) embody the *a priori* notions of economic theory about relationships between y and x. What we actually observe in the real world is a set of correlations which can be written as an *unrestricted reduced form* (URF)

$$y_t = P_0 x_t + P_1(L)y_{t-1} + P_2(L)x_{t-1} + \epsilon_t \tag{67}$$

In (67), we have a set of linear regression equations with lagged variables. The P_i capture the information in the data, i.e. they say something about the correlation whereas π_i tell us about causation. How can we be sure that the P_i information matches that in π_i?

We are back to the correlation–causation problem (and we shall return to it yet again). In the vigorous burst of econometric activity in the Cowles Commission in the 1940s, this problem was faced and a solution was proposed. The problem is known as the *identification problem*, which can be briefly described as follows. Many causal systems other than (65) may lead to the same URF (67). Since we can observe only (67), these causal systems would then be *observationally equivalent* to (65) and statistical information will not allow us to discriminate between (65) and its rivals. How can we be sure that there is a unique relationship between (67) and (65) as there is between (66) and (65)?

The answer in the latter case was in terms of prior restrictions imposed on the structural equations. These restrictions took the form of *zero* restrictions, which meant the absence of a certain variable from a particular equation, e.g. the absence of M from the C^f equation in AM's model or the absence of C^f from the money supply equation. Other types of restrictions are *homogenous* restrictions whereby two variables may have identical coefficients, e.g. C^f and Z^a may be restricted to have identical coefficients in the money demand equation. These two sets were sets of *linear* restrictions. *Nonlinear* restrictions which were not yet in vogue in 1965 would involve, for example, one parameter being a product of two others, as we shall see below. A further set of restrictions would be *prior* restrictions on the relative error variances of different equations. Thus the researcher would 'know' that the supply function is more stable than the demand function of a commodity, e.g. the error variance of the demand equation is some multiple of that of the supply equation.[13]

Of these three ways of identifying a structural system, the zero restriction method is the simplest and proved to be the most appealing. Large econometric models were built containing hundreds of equations, but since each equation had been to some extent developed separately it normally contained only a few variables, i.e. it excluded or set equal to zero the coefficients of many other variables. To some extent this was due to the fact that at the stage of specifying variables for a relationship and choosing among different specifications, the methods employed were those appropriate to single equation linear regression models such as (45). This led to the singling out of one variable as the dependent or the explained variable and other variables as independent, though it was recognised that some of the independent variables were not exogenous, i.e. were not unrelated to the error term. Such singling out made sense in terms of economic theory where variables could be labelled as causal *a priori* without the need for empirical validation. But though in theory the notion that *a* causes *b* is quite unambiguous, the causality criteria become much trickier, when *a* and *b* are time dependent variables.

In terms of zero restrictions, it is sufficient to have $(G-1)$ zero restrictions in each equation for it to be identified. Most equations in most models had more than the sufficient number of restrictions, so the equations were over-identified. But the question still remained as to how one knew that the zero restrictions — omission of certain variables — were valid. As we saw in the AM critique of FM, the restrictions on the interest rate coefficient of the IS and the LM curves were both rejected as inappropriate. Since the restrictions were *a priori*, they still had to be consistent with the observations.

If zero restrictions imposed on equations in a model are inappropriate, but not rigorously tested then, once again, we have reason to doubt if the estimated coefficients can be given a causal interpretation. If one took Walrasian general equilibrium theory as a starting point, then there would be precious few zero restrictions, since *all* the relative prices enter into *every* demand and supply equation.[14] T.C. Liu (1960) pointed out that most zero restrictions are probably inappropriate and 'truly' economic equations should have insufficient zero restrictions and therefore are technically under-identified. Under-identification implies that a unique structure cannot be associated with an observable reduced form, i.e. we cannot separate correlation and causation.[15]

Liu's ideas were too unorthodox and, if correct, would have inconveniently impeded the progress of econometrics at the time of its most rapid growth. They were more or less ignored until their recent revival in a separate development by Sims, Sargent and others (Sims (1977)). At the same time Wold was arguing that simultaneity was misspecification, i.e. that variables could only influence each other after a passage of time. What appeared to be simultaneous occurrence was in fact a consequence of the data being only available over long intervals. Thus if one had daily or weekly data, then the lag of consumers' expenditure behind the earning of income would be obvious, but with quarterly or annual data this lag would be obliterated. Wold's idea was that economic models were recursive with the B_0 matrix triangular or even diagonal.[16] A triangular B_0 matrix means that endogenous variables can be ordered in a hierarchy of causal influence: y_2 affecting y_1 but not vice versa, y_3 affecting y_1 and y_2 but not vice versa and so on. A diagonal matrix means that there is no interdependence among contemporaneous values of the endogenous variables. The causal structure is then transparent.

If Liu were correct, one would abandon any search for causality and operate only with the unrestricted reduced form (67) which will at least summarise the information on correlation. The only snag here would be to make sure of the number of lagged ys and current and lagged xs, which in theory can be as many $mG + (n + 1)K$ in the context of equation (65), since the longest lag among endogenous variables is m. A model with ten equations and with the highest order lag of six on both y and x variables, and ten exogenous variables would have 130 independent variables in each equation. Since most samples in economics are much smaller than that, the Liu strategy can be implemented only for small models. But if that problem did not arise, Liu's assertion allows us to use regression analysis on a single equation to estimate the equations in (67).[17] This would justify single equation equations in the face of criticism such as AM's.

Wold's ideas, if correct, also allow one to use single equation techniques to estimate the parameters of (65). If B_0 was triangular, and if one could be sure that the error terms u_t were not correlated across equations (i.e. $[E(uu') = \Sigma]$ was diagonal), then we are back to a world of single equations and simple techniques are again admissible.

The ideas of Liu and Wold were philosophical theories of the nature of causation, but, as justification of the use of single equation techniques, they were rather esoteric. The Cowles Commission view of simultaneous equation structural model estimation prevailed. The best method of estimating (65) (once the sufficiency of the number of restrictions had been checked) was to treat it as a system. The technique of *maximum likelihood* required assuming some probability distribution for the u_t and then maximising the joint likelihood of the u_t's with respect to the parameters in the $B(L)$, $C(L)$ matrices. In the mid-sixties, this was computationally infeasible and impossible for large models. In theory, it was known that the zero restrictions in (65) could be tested by estimating the restricted reduced form (66) and the unrestricted reduced form (67) and comparing the ratio of their likelihood values. If the restrictions were invalid, then the likelihood of (66) being a summary measure of the goodness of fit of the entire system of equations, would be much lower than that of (67). It can be shown that twice the logarithm of the ratio of the likelihoods is distributed as χ^2 with as many degrees as the number of restrictions, so we compare the estimated χ^2 with the critical χ^2 value to test the null hypothesis that the restrictions are invalid.[18]

The difficulty of implementing maximum likelihood estimation led to a search for simpler methods, methods which were analogous to single equation methods. Of course, no such method, simple as it was, could extract as much information from the data set as the maximum likelihood method. The technique of *instrumental variables*, suggested originally by Reirsøl (1943), was popularised by Theil in his *two stage least squares* method. Since this is analogous to a single equation method we can return to equation (45) and the conditions for least squares estimates to be optimal.

Recall that equation (45) was a single independent variable equation

$$y_t = \beta_0 + \beta_1 x_t + u_t \tag{45}$$

For many independent variables we could write in matrix terms

$$y_t = x_t \beta + u_t \tag{45a}$$

where, if there were K independent variables, x_t would be a 1 x K vector and β would be a K x 1 vector. By minimising $u'u$, one can derive *best linear unbiased estimates* for β and σ_u^2 as

$$\hat{\beta} = (x'x)^{-1} x'y$$

and

$$\hat{\sigma}_u^2 = \sum_t \hat{u}_t^2 \Big/ (T-K)$$

For these estimates of $\hat{\beta}$ to be best linear unbiased ones and for the test statistics to be valid, as we saw before, the assumptions of the classical regression model must be satisfied. These are

(i) $E(u_t) = 0$ $\qquad\qquad$ for all t

(ii) $E(u_t^2) = \sigma_u^2$ $\qquad\qquad$ for all t

(iii) $E(u_t u_{t-s}) = 0$ $\qquad\qquad$ for all t and s

(iv) $E(x'u) = x'E(u) = 0$

The last mentioned assumption is the crucial one in the technique of instrumental variables. It is really valid only for x's being fixed in repeated samples. For stochastic independent variables, we replace it by

(iva) $\underset{T \to \infty}{\operatorname{plim}} \; T^{-1}\,(x'u) = 0$

This says that x's and u must be uncorrelated in the limit as the sample size gets larger, while the OLS properties are not dependent on sample size. Once we have stochastic regressors (x's), the condition required for the estimates to have the desired properties and the properties of the estimators themselves become functions of sample size. Thus the *unbiasedness* property of OLS estimators, $E(\hat{\beta}) = \beta$, is replaced by a *consistency* property, i.e. in the limit, as sample size gets larger, the probability that β is not equal to β goes to zero. This is written as

$\underset{T \to \infty}{\operatorname{plim}} \; \beta_T = \beta$

(To keep the stochastic regressor case distinct from the fixed regressor case we label the stochastic estimators β. β_T is the estimate of β from T observations)

This technical detour allows us to return to the problem of estimating simultaneous equations, without either invoking the Liu or Wold assertions, or plunging into systems-wide, maximum-likelihood estimation. Take any equation from (64), say the first. It is

$$y_{1t} = -\Sigma \beta_{01j} y_{jt} + \sum_k \sum_j \beta_{k1j}\, y_{jt-k} + \sum_i C_{01j} x_{it} + \sum_k \sum_i C_{k1i} x_{it-k} + u_{1t}$$

$$\text{(64a)}$$

Equation (64a) looks rather complicated but many of the right hand coefficients will be zero in any actual model. To see this, let us look at the Z^a equation of the AM model. Here we have seven endogenous variables (reduced to four by substitution of the identities), two exogenous variables and only one lagged endogenous variable. Thus each endogenous variable can have in principle at most six coefficients. Of these the Z^a equation has two non-zero and one zero coefficients

$$Z_t^a = \beta_{23}\, r_t + \gamma_{21}\, C_{t-1} + e_{2t} \qquad (52a)$$

In (52a), r_t is endogenous and hence it will not be uncorrelated with e_{2t}. So we replace r_t by an instrument — a single variable or a combination of variables which satisfy two conditions — the instrument must be highly correlated with r_t and independent of the error term e_{2t}. This may be satisfied for example by some rate of interest, chosen by the monetary authority, which determines r_t but is independent of the error term in the Z^a equation. Alternatively we could use as an instrument the URF *estimate* of r_t, i.e. by regressing r_t on the predetermined variables in the model: X^a, M^*, C_{t-1}. This is the two stage least squares technique which will also satisfy the same properties as the instrumental variables technique estimator (Sargan (1958)).

The instrumental variables estimation technique, being a single equation rather than a systems technique, led to a neglect of the question of testing restrictions. This was especially true if there were across-equation restrictions. While claiming to deal with simultaneous equations bias, the method led to the neglect of attention to the model *as a system*. While large econometric models continued to be estimated, there was much *ad hoc* practice tolerated in their estimation. In systems with over-identified equations, the URF contained so many regressors that the estimate of each variable was almost perfectly correlated with the original variable itself. It was practically like performing OLS twice.

By the end of the 1960s there were still claims that the links between money and income were more stable and had larger multipliers, or that money acted on income more quickly and with greater effect etc. The St. Louis model built by Andersen and Jordan from a simple URF regression of income on monetary and fiscal policy variables, concluded in favour of monetary policy being a quicker, more powerful instrument, judging from the size of the URF coefficients attached to the monetary variables.[19] While this caused a flurry of excitement and a spate of claims and counter-claims, the objection to the St. Louis model was the same as that to the FM claims. The econometric response, apart from evaluating the veracity of these claims, was to insist that only by building structural models, embodying prior restrictions on the equations and by estimating the structural equation parameters, could one hope to learn anything about the

economic mechanism, about how policy changes affected economic outcomes. The structural equations were assumed to capture the fundamental
economic behaviour (though without overcoming the micro–macro divide).
By specifying policy instruments among the exogenous variables, it was
hoped to learn about ways of stabilising the economy. Econometrics was
agreed at this time to have three aims: to learn about how much of
observed behaviour could be predicted by prior theory and in turn how
theory could be improved in the light of experience; to learn about the
impact of policy variables on endogenous variables especially about the
length of lags over which such impact was felt to help minimise economic
fluctuations, and to help forecast the course of economic variables.

It was over the last of these three aims that doubts persisted about
econometric model building, since naive autoregressive equations continued to outperform large models in forecasting. But at the same time,
new developments in fitting such autoregressive models were clarifying
some issues and beginning to challenge traditional econometric practice. To begin with these time series techniques clarified the spurious
correlation problem.

To understand the problem of spurious correlation as analysed by time
series analysts, we have to understand the nature of the random error
term u_t in the regression equation (45). Of the four conditions attached to
the linear regression model, we have already seen that condition (iv) may
not be fulfilled. This may be either due to the stochastic nature of x
in which case we can see if the condition (iva) is satisfied, but usually it
is due to simultaneous equations bias, as AM showed in the case of the FM
specification of the investment multiplier.

The time series analysts not only emphasised the stochastic nature of
the variable, they also questioned assumption (iii) about the autocorrelation
structure of the error term. Rather than thinking about the experimental
situation where a variable y is made up of a systematic component $x\beta$ and
an uncontrollable random component, they thought of variables as being
generated by combinations of variables which are each in themselves
random. Variables such as y and x are generated by moving average,
autoregressive combinations of random error processes, and if this is
not taken into account when studying them, spurious correlation could
result. Serial correlation is any process that makes errors dependent
on their own past or future values, which means $E(u_t u_{t-s}) \neq 0$. This
invalidates the usual χ^2 tests using the residual variance since this can
no longer be a sum of squares of *independently* normally distributed
variables.

Serial correlation can be of two types: an *auto-regressive* process and a *moving average* process. They are represented as

(AR 1) $\quad u_t = \rho_1 u_{t-1} + \epsilon_t \qquad E(\epsilon_t) = 0, E(\epsilon_t^2) = \sigma_\epsilon^2, E(\epsilon_t \epsilon_{t-s}) = 0$

(MA 1) $\quad u_t = \gamma_0 \epsilon_t + \gamma_1 \epsilon_{t-1}$

In each case we have confined ourselves to only first order lags. In (AR1), u_t is a first order autoregressive series apart from a purely random error ϵ_t, which is known as *white noise*. In (MA 1), the error u is a weighted total of current and past errors ϵ. The presence of serial correlation means that we can no longer treat u_t as a white noise but must extract the information contained in the history of u_t, leaving only a white noise error ϵ_t. R^2 etc. can then be measured in terms of ϵ_t.

Now if in equation (45) we have an (AR1) process for u_t, we can transform it by substituting $(1-\rho_1 L)u_t = \epsilon_t$ into it and get

$$y_t - \rho_1 y_{t-1} = \beta_0 (1-\rho_1) + \beta_1 x_t - \beta_1 \rho_1 x_{t-1} + \epsilon_t \qquad (68)$$

Equation (68) now has a white noise error which will satisfy conditions (i) to (iv) attached to (45) above. The autoregressive process for the error term being now incorporated, we extract the information contained in the previous values of y_t and x_t via the autoregressive parameter ρ_1. An alternate way of viewing (68) is that we have a new pair of variables y_t and x_t and an equation analogous to (45)

$$\tilde{y}_t = \beta_0 + \beta_1 \tilde{x}_t + \epsilon_t \qquad (68a)$$

where $\tilde{y}_t = (1-\rho_1 L)y_t, \tilde{x}_t = (1-\rho_1 L)x_t$. Now it stands to reason that the R^2 for (68a) would be different from that for (45), since if $\rho_1 = 1$, (68a) amounts to regressing with first differences rather than with levels.

The autoregressive and moving average processes can be generalised to higher order lags. For example we may posit a pth-order autoregressive process or a qth-order moving average process

$$(AR(p)) \quad u_t = \sum_{i=1}^{p} \rho_i u_{t-i} + \epsilon_t$$

$$(MA(q)) \quad u_t = \sum_{i=0}^{q} \gamma_i \epsilon_{t-i}$$

The idea of viewing any random variable as the sum of a systematic autoregressive component, based on its own past values, plus an error process, that is not explained by the previous history of the variable, is a powerful one. Statistical time series analysis has for a long time explored this approach to modelling time series and it is this approach that points to many pitfalls in the use of econometric techniques to data modelling.

The problem with econometric modelling as in equation (45) or equations (51a) – (54a) is that the variables Y, X or C^f, Z^a etc. are looked at in terms of their economic meaning but not as statistical series. As we said above, much economic theory is static or steady-state and the temptation is to treat economic time series as realisations of these static concepts. The only exception made is to add an error term which then is assumed to be normally distributed etc. Econometric modelling also puts much more faith in the role of prior theorising in specifying an equation and seeks to endow the coefficient estimates with an economic interpretation. Thus, as we saw in the FM/AM debate, it was the interpretation of the coefficients α_1, α_1' in equations (46a), (46b) that was the point at issue. Time series analysis on the other hand takes an agnostic view about economic theory but treats the series as the statistical realisation of an underlying data generation process. The aim is to extract as much information out of each series as possible that will help to forecast its future values and to leave as an unexplained residual a term that is a sum of white noise error processes. The simplest way to think about it is to see that the history of a series is captured by modelling it as an autoregressive process and the unexplained residual as a moving average process; hence the description of time series processes as autoregressive moving average processes (ARMA).

The problem of spurious correlation can now be taken up in the time series analysis framework. To model any time series as an ARMA process, it is first necessary to remove any trend in it, i.e. to make it stationary. Commonly trended series often show high correlation which is mistaken for a causal connection, and the removal of this trend is a first step. This can be done by differencing a series repeatedly until the remainder is a stationary time series. *Stationarity* requires that the series be non-explosive; as a difference equation it has to have stable roots.

Take for example our equation (45). Suppose y_t stands for the logarithm of the price level $(lnP_t \ (=p_t))$, and x_t for the logarithm of the money supply $(lnM_t \ (=m_t))$. Now p_t has had an upward trend through much of the previous fifty years. Indeed in the last ten years, even the rate of increase in p_t has had a trend. This means that p_t has a quadratic trend. So we first look at the first difference of p_t $\triangle p_t$ and see if it has trend in it. If so, we again difference it and look at $\Delta^2 p_t$. Suppose there is no trend in $\Delta^2 p_t$. Let z_{1t} be the stationary series.

$$\Delta^2 p_t = z_{1t} \tag{69}$$

Now the time series analyst would model z_{1t} as an ARMA process as follows

$$z_{1t} - \rho_1 z_{1t-1} - \rho_2 z_{1t-2} \cdots - \rho_n z_{1t-n} = e_{1t} - \gamma_1 e_{1t-1}$$

$$- \gamma_2 e_{1t-2} \cdots - \gamma_q e_{1t-q} \tag{70}$$

Equation (70) can be written as

$$\rho(L) z_{1t} = \gamma(L) e_{1t} \tag{70a}$$

and the p series as

$$\rho(L) \Delta^2 p_t = \gamma(L) e_{1t} \tag{69a}$$

Here z_{1t} is an nth order autoregressive process and e_{1t} is a qth order moving average process and p_{1t} is differenced twice. This is called an ARIMA (*autoregressive integrated moving average*) process of order (n, d, q) where d is the order of differencing necessary to induce stationarity.

Economic series tend to be rather smooth, they do not change abruptly in a see-saw fashion. This indicates a very high degree of serial correlation. Thus merely first differencing has often been found to be enough in many cases. Alternatively if a series has no trend, it still is often highly autoregressive with ρ_1 being near unity.

Granger and Newbold (1974) have demonstrated how regressing the levels of two series on each other can lead to high R^2 etc. even when the series have been generated as independent ARMA processes. Suppose Y and X are 'truly' independent, i.e. we can experimentally generate Y and X from random numbers which are by construction independent of each other. Suppose we take random numbers e_t and ϵ_t and generate Y_t and X_t as

$$Y_t = \rho_1 Y_{t-1} + e_t, \quad X_t = \rho_1' X_{t-1} + \epsilon_t \tag{71}$$

Here Y and X are (1, 0, 0) ARIMA processes. Now we can take samples of T observations on the Y, X pair and for each sample regress Y on X as in equation (45). If we then compute the correlation coefficient r, the variance of r across samples of T observations is given by

$$\text{var}\,(r) = T^{-1}\,(1 + \rho_1\,\rho_1')\,/\,(1 - \rho_1\,\rho_1') \qquad (72)$$

Now although the true β_1 should be zero and the true correlation coefficient ρ should be zero, if say $\rho_1 = \rho_1' = 0.9$ then on average we would get r of about 0.7. Now this seemingly high correlation between Y_t and X_t is produced purely due to the fact that each series is highly autoregressive or a moving average of random errors.[20]

If $\rho_1 = 1$ and $\rho_1' = 1$ then the Y_t, X_t processes are called *random walk processes*. Granger and Newbold created such Y, X series as independent random walks and again ran the levels regression as in (45). They found that although the true value of β_1 should be zero (as it would be if the regression equation were as in (68a)), in 75% of the cases $\hat{\beta}_1$ was found to have a t ratio of above 2 and hence the econometrician would consider this a highly significant relationship. This problem is compounded if the regression equation involves more than one independent variable. Suppose there is no true relationship between Y_t and X_{1t} to X_{5t}, but we still carry out the regression in levels. When the Y and X variables were generated as independent random walks by Granger and Newbold, they found that in the case of one independent variable, out of a hundred runs, five had an R^2 above 0.7 and on average the R^2 was 0.26. But with five independent variables, the R^2 was above 0.7 in 37% of the cases and its average value was 0.59.

Such spurious correlation is indicated by presence of serial correlation in the residuals of the fitted regression equation. So if the researcher carried out tests for the randomness of residuals, he would be able to diagnose the trouble. Thus the Durbin-Watson statistic diagnoses the presence of first order autoregression in residuals and other tests have been devised, as we shall see below, for higher order regressions.

While early econometric work concentrated on R^2 as the criterion for ranking theories, the Granger-Newbold work makes it clear that this can be treacherous. Thus over time we have witnessed not only the non-neutrality of technique as used in the debate but also the obsolescence of old criteria and the introduction of better practice.[21] Ideally this would mean that we ought to recompute the FM equations and check their results again to see whether they exhibit a low Durbin-Watson statistics as a sign of high serial correlation. But since the debate has moved on, we shall not look into this further.

The Granger-Newbold exercise has several salutory lessons to offer. We quote three extracts from their article.

Thus, a high value of R^2 should not, on the grounds of traditional tests, be regarded as evidence of a significant relationship between autocorrelated series.

If one's variables are random walks, or near random walks, and one includes in regression equations variables which should not in fact be included, then *it will be the rule* rather than the exception to find a spurious relationship. It is also clear that a high value for R^2 . . . combined with a low value of d [Durbin-Watson statistic] is *no indication of a true relationship*.

From our own studies we would conclude that if a regression equation relating economic variables is found to have strongly autocorrelated residuals, equivalent to a low Durbin-Watson value, the *only conclusion that can be reached is that the equation is misspecified*, whatever the value of R^2 observed.

(Granger and Newbold (1974), pp. 114, 117).

Econometric practice had been looking at the problem of autoregressive errors in its own fashion. Following Durbin and Watson's pioneering work, Sargan ((1959), (1964)) looked at the problem of estimating equations such as (45) along with a first order autoregressive process. This approach casts the problem as one of testing restrictions on the equation derived by combining a regression equation with an autoregressive process, i.e. an equation such as (68). Compare (68) with any other equation containing the same variables such as

$$y_t = a_0 + a_1 x_t + a_2 x_{t-1} + a_3 y_{t-1} + v_t \tag{68b}$$

Now in (68b) the coefficients a_i are unrestricted but in (68) they are restricted. If, in (68b), we imposed the *nonlinear* restriction that $a_1 . a_3 = -a_2$, then it is equivalent to (68). Sargan (1964) showed, in an econometric application to wage and price data, that a likelihood ratio test could be conducted by comparing the residual variance of (68) and (68b) and that $T \log (\hat{\sigma}_\varepsilon^2 / \hat{\sigma}_v^2)$ is distributed as χ^2 with one degree of freedom. Thus as we said before if the equation does not involve autoregression but merely longer lags, then the χ^2 test will tell us whether the restrictions are valid. If the computed χ^2 is below the critical value of χ^2 for the chosen level of confidence, then we take it that the observed equation is a combination of a static equation and a first order autoregressive process. If the restriction is rejected then we know that the dynamic structure needs to be further investigated. We examine again whether the residuals of the unrestricted equation are random or show any evidence of further autoregression.

The Sargan approach builds a bridge between static econometrics with some *ad hoc* treatment of dynamics and error processes and the time series approach. It allows a role for economic theory in choosing specifications but then it seeks to model the dynamics so as to distinguish between systematic dynamics and error dynamics. Thus (45) can be generalised to a dynamic equation y and x as

$$\beta(L)y_t = \delta(L)x_t + \gamma(L)u_t \tag{73a}$$

$$\rho(L)u_t = \epsilon_t \tag{73b}$$

Equation (73a) is a dynamic version of (45) where

$$\beta(L) = \sum_{i=0}^{I} \beta_i L^i, \ \delta(L) = \sum_{i=0}^{D} \delta_i L^i, \ \gamma(L) = \sum_{i=0}^{q} \gamma_i L^i \text{ and } \rho(L) = \sum_{i=0}^{P} \rho_1 L^i,$$

Here $\gamma(L)$ and $\rho(L)$ are the moving average and autoregressive processes representing stochastic dynamics; $\beta(L)$ represents the endogenous or systematic dynamics derived from prior theory which may also tell us something about $\delta(L)$, the dynamics of the way in which the exogenous variables affects y_t. We do not however observe these various dynamics neatly separated out. What we observe is a conflation of (73a) and (73b). Their *restricted transformed equation* is

$$\rho(L)\beta(L)y_t = \rho(L)\delta(L)X_t + \gamma(L)\epsilon_t \tag{74a}$$

The *unrestricted transformed equation* is

$$\psi(L)Y_t = \phi(L)X_t + \gamma(L)\epsilon_t \tag{74b}$$

The task of an econometric model builder is to factor out the observed dynamics $\psi(L)$ into the systematic (endogenous) dynamic component $\beta(L)$ and the error dynamics $\rho(L)$, and similarly for $\phi(L)$. The researcher starts with the best fitting equation for (74b) which determines the length of lags $\psi(L)$ and $\phi(L)$. Once the order of $\psi(L)$, for example, is determined to be, say, J then he has to try to allocate $J = P+I$ by determining the orders P and I of the lags. Mizon (1977) has shown that Sargan's 1964 procedure discussed above generalises to a sequential procedure by which this can be done. (See also Hendry and Mizon (1978)).

We have thus in (74a) and (74b) an econometric analog to the time series method of fitting ARIMA models. These techniques are still in a developmental stage but their usefulness can be readily demonstrated. To do this let us look at Hendry's examination of the price–money relationship in UK data. Hendry regressed the logarithm of the consumers' price level on the logarithm of personal sector holdings of money supply measure M_3. He also tried as an alternate, 'explanatory' variable, cumulative rainfall in the UK. In view of Granger and Newbold's warnings, the results are interesting. He got

$$p = 0.02 + 0.73\,m \qquad\qquad R^2 = 0.984$$
$$\;\;\;\;(0.03)\;(0.016) \qquad \text{Durbin-Watson} = 0.3 \qquad\qquad (75)$$

$$p = 10.9 - 3.2C + 0.39C^2 \qquad R^2 = 0.982$$
$$\;\;\;\;(0.55)\;(0.23)\;(0.02)\;\text{Durbin-Watson} = 0.1 \qquad\qquad (76)$$

Here $p = lnP$, $m = lnM$ and C is cumulative rainfall. The data are quarterly from February 1964 to February 1975. In both (75) and (76), the R^2 is high and the Durbin-Watson statistic is low, otherwise, the standard errors of the parameter estimates (in parentheses) are very low and one would conclude that the coefficients are highly significant. But it is a bit absurd to conclude that rainfall causes prices as much as money supply does, though a mere comparison of R^2 will tell us so.

Using the dynamic specification test described above, Hendry arrives at the autoregressive version of (75), as

$$p = 0.02 - 0.00m_t + 0.02m_{t-1} + 0.995p_{t-1}$$
$$\;\;\;(0.003)(0.097)\;\;\;(0.094)\;\;\;\;\;\;(0.057) \qquad\qquad (75a)$$

$$R^2 = 0.999 \qquad\qquad \text{Durbin-Watson} = 1.6$$

$$(1-0.94L)p = 21.1 - 7.2\,(1-0.94L)C + 10.78\,(1-0.94L)C^2$$
$$\;\;0.02) \qquad\qquad (3.6)\;(1.4)\;(0.02)\;\;\;\;\;\;\;(0.13)\;(0.02) \qquad (76a)$$

$$R^2 = 0.998 \qquad\qquad \text{Durbin-Watson} = 1.8$$

In both equations the autoregressive coefficient is pretty close to unity, 0.995 in (75a) and 0.94 in (76a). The autoregressive transformation also makes the coefficients of money stock nonsignificant, though rainfall performs better!

We see then that spurious correlation can occur but also that it can be diagnosed by looking at the residuals and remodelling the equation until we obtain white noise errors.[22] But this discussion of spurious correlation brings us back to the question of *correlation* as against *causation*. Having eliminated spurious correlation, when can we say that a variable x (money supply) causes a variable y (nominal income or price level)? The notions of cause and effect may be quite clear in economic theory or in experimental subjects. But once we try to extract causal patterns from data, all we have to go by are correlations between the current and the past value of variables. Do the patterns lead to any conclusion about causation?

Granger's Definitions of Causality

Clive Granger proposed a criterion for determining causality using time series techniques, but he completely ignored the role of economic theory in providing prior restrictions. He relied on the prediction error variance as the sole criterion for choosing among specifications. Relying solely on the pattern of correlations between a pair of variables Y_1 and Y_2 and their lagged values, he suggested a way of sorting out whether Y_1 caused Y_2 or Y_2 caused Y_1. Briefly put, his criterion was that if after extracting all the information from the own past values of a variable, if the addition of the other variable as a regressor would further reduce prediction error variance, then the latter variable is causal. Thus a variable is causal if it explains the residuals of another variable which cannot be explained by the history of that explained variable. 'Causal' means in this context 'containing information that helps better predict a variable'. This has to be made clear, for much futile controversy can result by different definitions of causality. Thus the Cowles commission definition of causality in terms of the validity of identifying restrictions on the reduced form of a system of equation emphasises the uniqueness of the transmission mechanism of changes in the set of predetermined variables to those in the endogenous variables. The Cowles definition is therefore in terms of the parameter estimates and the Granger definition is in terms of prediction error variances. Under certain sets of circumstances to be seen below, these two may come to the same conclusion but normally there will be conflict.[23]

With these brief remarks we can look at the Granger definition. Let $(\hat{Y}_{it} \,|\, \Omega_{t-k})$ be the predicted value of Y_{it} using the information set up to the period $t-k$. The information set contains past values of Y_i and Y_j if $k \geqslant 1$ and contemporaneous values of Y_j $(j \neq i)$ if $k = 0$ in Ω_{t-k}. The conditional prediction error is then $(\epsilon_{it} \,|\, \Omega_{t-k}) = (Y_{it} - \hat{Y}_{it} \,|\, \Omega_{t-k})$. The criterion for defining causality is the variance of ϵ_{it} denoted as σ_i^2.

The First Definition: Now the information set contained two separable pieces of information in past values of Y_i, the variable being predicted denoted as Ω_i and the information on current and past values of Y_j as Ω_j. So we can compute the error variance conditional upon using only past values of Y_i: $(\sigma_i^2 | \Omega_{i, t-1})$ and compare it to the variance conditional on using Y_i and Y_j: $(\sigma_i^2 | \Omega_{i, t-1}, \Omega_{j, t-1})$. Then Granger's first definition says

$$\ll Y_j \text{ causes } Y_i \text{ if } (\sigma_i^2 | \Omega_{i, t-1}, \Omega_{j, t-1}) < (\sigma_i^2 | \Omega_{i, t-1}) \gg$$

The first definition deals with causality along the line of Wold's definition of causal chains but since contemporaneous Y_j is not being used to predict Y_{it}, it corresponds to B_0 diagonal in (64).

The Second Definition: The alternative to *unidirectional causality* is *bidirectional causality* or *feedback* which is Granger's second definition of causality. This states that

$\ll$There is a feedback between Y_i and Y_j if

$$(\sigma_i^2 | \Omega_{i, t-1}, \Omega_{j, t-1}) < (\sigma_i^2 | \Omega i, t-1)$$

and

$$(\sigma_j^2 | \Omega_{i, t-1}, \Omega_{j, t-1}) < (\sigma_j^2 | \Omega_{j, t-1}) \gg$$

The second definition then provides for the case where Y_j helps predict Y_i and Y_i helps predict Y_j.

The Third Definition: To accommodate Wold's definition of recursiveness in terms of a triangular B_0, Granger proposes a third definition of causality. He calls this *instantaneous causality*. This involves using Y_{jt} in addition to all other information. Thus Granger's *third* definition of *causality* states that

$$\ll Y_j \text{ instantaneously causes } Y_i \text{ if}$$

$$(\sigma_i^2 | \Omega_{i, t-1}, \Omega_{jt}) < (\sigma_i^2 | \Omega i, t-1, \Omega_{j, t-1}) \gg$$

If using Y_{jt} thus further reduces the unexplained variance of Y_{it}, then Y_{jt} instantaneously causes Y_{it}.

The Fourth Definition: One way to summarise Granger on causality is to say that Y_j causes Y_i if previous Y_j explains present Y_i, i.e. Y_j leads Y_i. To link this notion of causality with the lead–lag pattern that is claimed between money and income (see Chapter 2) we need Granger's definition of a *causality lag*. This says that if information up to time $t-m$ helps reduce the variance but not at $t-m+1$ then m is the length of the causality lag. This then is Granger's fourth definition:

$\ll$ The causality lag between Y_j and Y_i is m if

$$(\sigma_i^2 \mid \Omega_{i,\ t-1}, \Omega_{j,\ t-m}) < (\sigma_i^2 \mid \Omega_{i,\ t-1}, \Omega_{j,\ t-m+1}) \gg$$

Thus information about Y_j more recent than m periods ago is irrelevant, and indeed, by increasing the predictive variance, counterproductive.

All these definitions apply only between Y_i and Y_j when they have been made stationary, i.e. where the trend has been removed. This condition is required for various technical definitions to go through but as Granger remarks, 'In the nonstationary case' the various measures of conditional prediction variance such as $(\sigma_i^2 \mid \Omega_{t-1})$, 'will depend on time t and, in general, the existence of causality may alter over time' (Granger (1969) p. 429. Thus time series analysts prefer to eliminate trends separately from each series before operating with them. While this avoids spurious correlation, in economics the size of the trend may be related across two (or more) variables. Indeed what would the theory of economic growth be worth if the trend in every economic variable was taken to be a feature not worth explaining! Indeed for economists the order of differencing required for making a series stationary i.e. the value of d in an ARIMA (p, d, q) process, itself has interesting information content.

Granger's causality definitions were not extended to the case which is the Cowles commission view of simultaneity and which could be called 'instantaneous feedback' combining the second and the third definitions. In this case Y_{it} explains Y_{jt} and *vice versa* and the asymmetry required for causality is lost. Granger's definition is also of limited use to the econometrician who is modelling many economic variables at once. While Granger discussed the multivariate case, his results in that case are not as sharp as in the bivariate case.

Notice that in the context of a two-variable model if Y_j current and past influences Y_i but not vice versa, then Y_j can be treated as an exogenous variable relative to Y_i. The danger is that both Y_i and Y_j may be caused by a third variable, say, Y_k but with different causality lags, in which case we would misread the evidence as causal when it was not.

The extension of the Granger definition to the multivariate case remains problematical. We shall look at some recent work by Sims which tries to exploit the notion of *exogeneity* in order to extend Granger's results to a multivariate context.

Granger's definitions may seem a bit esoteric when our main interest is in evaluating monetarism but it is at the very heart of the debate in the seventies. Indeed Granger's work was the key to a new econometric methodology proposed by the Lucas-Sargent-Sims groups of new classical macro-economists. Indeed it is fair to say now that while in the sixties there was disagreement about theories but none about testing procedures, the disagreement now extends to theories as well as to procedures for testing the predictions of rival theories. The Keynesians are by and large still interested in Cowles Commission type estimation of structural equation parameters though they are willing to incorporate the diagnostic devices proposed by time series analysts but only in the context of a simultaneous model. They put great emphasis on a prior theoretic framework within which to interpret the observed correlations. The new generation of classical macro-economists who have taken over the lead in this debate from the old style pragmatic monetarists question the very notion of a stable structure invariant under different policy regimes. They reject Keynesian economic theory as well as the econometric methodology that Keynesians use.

Such deep differences, though not unusual in the history of other sciences, still make it difficult for one to arrive at a consensus from common evidence. These deep differences were first seen in the debate about the money–income relationship at the beginning of the seventies. Recall Friedman's claim that changes in money stock consistently led nominal income in the sense that peaks in $\dot{M}$ (change in M) occurred about sixteen months before the peak in general business activity. There was the usual qualification about the variability of this lag of income (business conditions) behind $\dot{M}$ but this was an element in Friedman's claims about the importance of money as a determinant of income.[24]

Tobin in an article entitled 'Money and Income: Post Hoc Ergo Propter Hoc?' (1970) constructed two very simple models, one 'ultra-Keynesian' and the other a 'Friedman' model. He then derived entirely from *a priori* theory a relationship between change in money stock $\dot{M}$, the level of income Y and its rate of change $\dot{Y}$. In the ultra-Keynesian model, investment expenditure $\dot{K}$ was the exogenous variable which changed autonomously in a cyclical fashion (as a sine wave). In the Friedman model, the growth rate of money stock was taken to be the exogenous variable which changed cyclically. With this structure Tobin showed that in the 'ultra-Keynesian' model with monetary authorities accommodating the supply of money to the 'needs of trade' (fluctuations in investment and in the demand for money) one would observe the lag pattern that Friedman had noticed, i.e. rate of change in money would lead income by just under half a cycle. The Friedman model did not produce such predictions, indeed income growth led the growth of money stock which itself had only a short lead over income level. The level of money stock M lagged behind level of income.

Tobin's article contains a long and ingenious argument which we have only space to barely summarise. His method is to construct a theoretical model embodying a transmission mechanism to generate predictions about the lag structure in his variables. No estimation is needed and the argument is quite general. Thus for the Keynesian model he obtains as the condensed structural form equation

$$\dot{M}_t = a_0 \ (r) \ (1-\alpha) G_t + a_0 \ (r) \ (k\alpha - t) Y_t + a_1 \ \dot{Y}_t \tag{77}$$

Here α is the proportion of investment financed by bank loans; $a_0(r)$ is the interest effect on the asset demand for money with $\partial a_0 / \partial r < 0$; $k = s(1-t) + t$ where s is the savings propensity and t is the tax rate and thus k is the reciprocal of the multiplier of $(G+\dot{K})$; the influence of $\dot{K}$ on income and money demand are solved out into (77); G and t are assumed constant; a_1 is the transaction demand coefficient income in the money demand equation.

Taking r and hence $a_0(r)$ as constant along with the other parameters, the crucial coefficient is that attached to income. If $k\alpha < t$, then at high income levels, the government budget is in surplus and this has monetary consequences. Now if investment $\dot{K}$ is a sine curve say $\dot{K} = \bar{Y} + \gamma \sin t$, where $\bar{Y}$ and γ are constants for simplicity, then we know that (with G constant) $Y = \bar{Y} + k^{-1} \gamma \sin t$ and $\dot{Y} = k^{-1} \gamma \cos t$. Thus the movements in M would be a weighted sum of a sine wave and a cosine wave but with $a_1 > 0$ and $(k\alpha - t) < 0$. This produces the result that the relationship between $\dot{M}$ and $\dot{Y}$ is an ellipse. Abstracting from a cycle ($\dot{Y} = 0$), then the $\dot{M}$, Y relationship is negative. When $\dot{Y}$ is at its peak, $\dot{M}$ would be past its peak because of the negative effect of Y, indeed M will peak before Y. The peak in $\dot{M}$ will come just after Y is at its lowest (trough) but $\dot{Y}$ is positive. Similarly for the trough of $\dot{M}$.

For the Friedman model, Tobin adapts Friedman 1959 article with the demand for money related to permanent income in a double log relationship. If we abstract from the common trend in actual and permanent income we get

$$g_y = g_0 \, (\delta\omega)^{-1} \, \ddot{m} + \delta^{-1} \, \dot{m} - \beta \qquad (78)$$

Where β is the growth rate of income, δ the income elasticity of demand for money and ω is the weight for current income in permanent income. δ is about 1.8 and ω about 0.4 in Friedman's calculations. g_y and $\dot{m}$ denote growth rates of income and money. $\dot{Y}/Y$, $\dot{M}/M$, and $\ddot{m}$ is the time derivative of m.

If money growth is held steady at $\delta\beta$ then income will not fluctuate. But if $\dot{m}$ is generated by a sine wave, $\ddot{m}$ is a cosine wave but now g_y is a sum of a sine and cosine wave with positive coefficients. The relation between levels of money and income and hence also between g_y and $\dot{m}$ is positive. This gives the result that when $\dot{m}$ peaks $\ddot{m} = 0$, so g_y does not peak at that time, g_y peaks before $\dot{m}$ when $\ddot{m} > 0$ and $\dot{m} > 0$ but not at its peak: thus g_y leads $\dot{m}$.

At the conclusion of his article Tobin claims 'Every piece of observed evidence that Friedman reports on timing is consistent with the timing implications of the ultra-Keynesian model . . .' While neither his argument nor his conclusions were accepted by Friedman (1970), Tobin raises an interesting issue about extracting the causal relationship between two variables when their disequilibrium movements form an ellipse or a loop around the equilibrium relationship. This has obvious parallels with Phillips' method where he derived an equilibrium locus separately from the short run dynamics relationship which formed a loop around the Phillips curve. (See Gersovitz (1980) for a development of this aspect of Tobin and Phillips' work.)

Equations (77) and (78) can be adapted to discrete data as follows. Rearranging (77) gives

$$\Delta M_t = \beta_0 + (\beta_1 + \beta_2) \, Y_t - \beta_2 Y_{t-1} \quad (77a) \qquad (77a)$$

Here $\beta_1 = a_0(r) \, (k\alpha - t)$, $\beta_2 = a_1$ and $\beta_0 = a_0 \, (r) \, (1-\alpha)G$ where G is taken to be constant. In (78) by rewriting $\dot{x}$ by $\Delta \ln X$ and $\ddot{x}$ by $\Delta^2 \ln X$ we get

$$\Delta \ln Y_t = \gamma_0 + (\gamma_1 + \gamma_2) \, \Delta^2 \ln M_t - \gamma_2 \Delta \ln M_{t-1} \qquad (78a)$$

where $\gamma_0 = \beta$, $\gamma_1 = \delta^{-1}$ and $\gamma_2 = (\delta\omega)^{-1}$.

Now if we look at (77a) and (78a) as two ways of modelling the M-Y relationship, the log linearity of (78a) aside, we have two rival hypotheses. In (77) or (77a), Y 'causes' M and in (78) or (78a) M 'causes' Y. These are however not the notions of causality that Granger was advancing. Also in (77), Tobin himself treats $\dot{K}$, investment, as exogenous and hence by the

Cowles commission consideration, even if (77) were valid Y does not cause M but $\dot{K}$ causes Y and M. So in a sense Tobin points to a likely confusion in making conclusions about causality from lag patterns as well as implicitly to the limits of bivariate analysis.

From Granger's point of view, in neither (77a) nor (78a) has the autoregressive information contained in the dependent variable been taken into account, so causality cannot be inferred. Making the relationships symmetrically linear and stochastic we can pose Granger's problem as

$$\beta_{11}(L)M_t + \beta_{12}(L)Y_t \quad = e_{1t} \tag{79a}$$

$$\beta_{21}(L)M_t + \beta_{22}(L)Y_t \quad = e_{2t} \tag{79b}$$

where $\beta_{ij}(L)$ is a lag polynomial of the jth variable in the ith equation and can be expressed as

$$\beta_{ij}(L) = \sum_{k=0}^{k_{ij}} \beta_{ij,\,k}\, L^k Y_{ij},$$

and where e_{1t} and e_{2t} are white noise processes. M and Y are also assumed stationary so any trend should have been eliminated.

Sims on Granger Causality

By Granger's definition, M causes Y (but not vice versa) if $\beta_{11}(L) \neq 0$ and $\beta_{12}(L) = 0$. M instantaneously causes Y if, in addition, $\beta_{21,0}$, the coefficient of M_t in (79b) is nonzero. If $\beta_{11}(L) \neq 0$ and $\beta_{12,0} = 0$ but all the other $\beta_{12}(L) \neq 0$ then we have feedback. This adaptation of Granger's definition to a closed dynamic bivariate model was made by Sims (1972) who again took up the Friedman–Tobin debate of money–income causality. Using time series technique and US quarterly data for 1947-69 Sims arrived at the opposite of Tobin's conclusions. As he put it

> Application of this [causality] test to a two-variable system in a monetary aggregate and current dollar GNP with quarterly data shows clearly that causality does not run one way from GNP to money. The evidence agrees quite well with a null hypothesis that causality runs entirely from money to GNP, without feedback.
> (Sims (1972), p. 541).

Sims restates Granger's conditions by writing the equivalent moving average representation of (79a) and (79b). We can then say

$$M_t = a_{11}(L)e_{1t} + a_{12}(L)e_{2t} \tag{80a}$$

$$Y_t = a_{21}(L)e_{1t} + a_{22}(L)e_{2t} \tag{80b}$$

Now $a_{ij}(L)$ are not just lag coefficients attached to current and past values but also to future values of the variables, i.e.

$$a_{ij}(L)e_{jt} = \sum_{k=-\infty}^{\infty} a_{ijk}\, e_{jt-k}.$$

This is a two-sided, infinite-order, moving-average process. Under certain simple conditions (80a) and (80b) are equivalent to (79a) and (79b). Now Sims states the conditions for *Granger causality* as

≪ Y does *not* cause M (in Granger's sense) if and only if, in the moving-average representation above, either $a_{11}(L) = 0$ or $a_{12}(L) = 0.$ ≫

Recall from our discussion of Wold's ideas of recursiveness that either $a_{11}(L) = 0$ or $a_{12}(L) = 0$ will make the coefficient matrix triangular. Once $a_{12}(L) = 0$, for example, then M is given by $a_{11}(L)e_{1t}$ and Y in turn becomes a function of M by

$$Y_t = a_{21}(L)a_{11}(L)^{-1}M_t + a_{22}(L)e_{2t}$$

Sims then shows that this result can be reproduced by writing each variable as a function of the present, past and *future* values of the other variable.

$$M_t = \delta_{11}(L)Y_t + \delta_{12}(L^{-1})Y_t + u_{1t} \tag{81a}$$

$$Y_t = \delta_{21}(L)M_t + \delta_{22}(L^{-1})M_t + u_{2t} \tag{81b}$$

In (81a), (81b) we represent future values separately by the lag operator L^{-1} where $L^{-i}X_t = X_{t+i}$. Then Sims' definition of *Granger causality* becomes

≪ Y does not cause M if and only if $\delta_{21}(L) \neq 0$ but $\delta_{22}(L^{-1}) = 0$ ≫

Thus in a regression of Y on current and past values of M, we obtain residuals which are not only (as any least squares residuals should be) independent of the current and past values of M but also of the *future* values of M.

The test that the vector of coefficients of future M is zero can be an F-test, as in the regression case, provided the errors are not serially correlated. It is necessary therefore to transform the basic M and Y series by pre-filtering out any elements which might lead to this. Sims used the common filter $(1 - 1.5L + 0.562L^2)$. Thus lnM_t (m_t) was replaced by $m_t = (1 - 1.5L + 0.56L^2)$ m_t and similarly with lnY_t. (It should be recalled that when we first discussed the serial correlation problem above we transformed our y and x variables by applying a $(1-\rho L)$ filter; see equation (68a) above.)

Sims used monetary base M_0 (currency plus reserves) and M_1 currency plus demand deposits. For Y he used current GNP. The data were seasonally adjusted quarterly for 1947–1969. He regressed the logarithm of Y on past values (8 lags), past m (8 lags) and future m (4 lags) for each measure of m, and the reverse procedure for m on lnY. He found that future GNP values were significant in the m regression but future m values were not significant in the GNP regression.

Sims' test like Granger's is for a bivariate model but Sims succeeds in adapting Granger's test to the regression method and what is more he demonstrates his method by tackling the age-old money–income problem again. The notion of causality has to do with predictive information contained in the future values of a putative causal variable. By ruling out that future M can explain current Y, the researcher guards against the possible misrepresentation of the relationship whereby past Y causes current M, but this is reversed as current Y being caused by future M. By making current, past and future values of M independent of the least squares residuals of Y on current and past M, Sims uses the criterion of *exogeneity* as a test of *causality*.

Many problems arise here some of which will come up in what follows. A major problem is about the possibility that a common third variable may be affecting both M and Y. Thus an essentially autonomous investment determined by 'the animal spirits' of businessmen may be the active ingredient. If monetary policy is fully accommodating to the investment demand then could this not lead to a spurious $M–Y$ correlation? Sims discounts this possibility by saying essentially that this would happen only under a very restrictive set of circumstances.

The special assumptions required to make endogenous money appear exogenous in a bivariate system must make money essentially identical to a truly exogenous variable. Thus if money has in the sample been passively and quickly adjusted to match the animal spirits of bankers and businessmen, and if animal spirits is a truly exogenous variable affecting GNP with a distributed lag, then money might falsely appear to cause GNP. However if there is a substantial random error in the correspondence between animal spirits and money and that error has a pattern of serial correlation different from that of animal spirits itself, then the bivariate relation between money and GNP will appear to show bidirectional causality.

(Sims (1972), p. 543).

This would seem to argue that Tobin's argument in his *Post Hoc Ergo Propter Hoc* carries through because it is deterministic. Sims' answer, though technically correct, is not problem-free and this has something to do with an aspect of doing research which we have hitherto not mentioned. The available tests and techniques for detecting differences in serial correlation patterns of the sort Sims would require in the quotation above all rely on availability of large samples. These techniques have been fashioned for engineering and natural sciences where they have literally millions of observations. The power of these tests to detect small differences in correlation patterns is very much a function of sample size. In economic time series, a hundred observations is a large sample. Sims' own exercise was carried out with 92 observations. From these 92 observations 13 coefficients were extracted before testing the significance of future coefficients. Now in the sort of proposition Sims is asserting about the difficulty of fooling the test with a Tobin-type setup, many more serial correlation coefficients would have to be extracted and jointly tested. The argument can be briefly set up in a three equation model

$$Y_t = \beta(L)Z_t + \delta(L)u_{1t} \tag{82a}$$

$$M_t = \gamma(L)Z_t + \lambda(L)u_{2t} \tag{82b}$$

$$Z_t = \ell(L)\epsilon_t \tag{82c}$$

where Z is the 'animal spirits' (private investment) variable. We allow for Z to be generated by a purely moving average process $\theta(L)$ of say order q_2. The relationship of M to Z has a lagged adjustment component though this could be small, say $\gamma(L)$ is of order $q_z = 4$. We also have to allow for the serial correlation pattern in the residuals of the M, Z relation (to allow for the animal spirits of the policy makers presumably). Suppose this is of order q_M which may be quite high. Certainly $q_M = q_Z$ would be one of the hypotheses to be tested. Add to this the Y, Z relationship where $\beta(L)$, $\delta(L)$ are also of reasonably high order. The Sims assertion requires us to distinguish between the patterns of $\lambda(L)$ and $\theta(L)$. In short we must be able to discriminate between (81a) and the condensed form of (82a) –(82c) which would be

$$Y_t = \beta(L)\gamma(L)^{-1}M_t + \delta(L)u_{1t} - \beta(L)\gamma(L)^{-1}\lambda(L)u_{2t} \tag{82d}$$

Now if $\theta(L)\epsilon = \lambda(L)u_2$ then (82a) and (82d) are of course identical. But testing the null hypothesis $\theta(L)\epsilon = \lambda(L)u_2$ or that (82a) and (82d) are identical means of extracting a large number of parameters from a not very large sample. If further, in (82a) – (82c), there were more than one Z variable involved, as most economists believe there are in modelling the economy, the task is hopeless. So while Sims' proposition is true that we require $\theta(L)\epsilon = \lambda(L)u_2$ it is not as easily detectable in data as he seems to suggest. (See for a further discussion of this and a precise statement of conditions, Sims (1977).)

There are however two issues mixed up in this assertion. First is the objection that money may seem to cause income because while the 'true' causality was the other way, the policy maker uses a rule to control the fluctuations in money optimally by controlling income through a feedback process. If the policy maker had an objective function, say, to minimise the variance of money stock around some path and he knew that there was a stable demand function for money in terms of income, then he could so regulate income that the resulting money series would appear to be causing income by the Granger-Sims criterion. In a later development of his work Sims recognises this possibility but dismisses it as not a serious explanation for the result he obtained. His grounds for dismissing it are that the conditions required for that to be true are very stringent. These conditions are that if the structural equation (demand for money) is of the form, as before,

$$\beta_{11}(L) M_t + \beta_{12}(L) Y_t = u_{1t} \tag{79a}$$

where $\beta_{11}(0) = 1$, then the authorities will observe the variables Y, M after a delay of at most one period; the objective function is in terms of M alone and is quadratic in terms of minimising the variance of M; and the policy rule is then of the form

$$\beta_{21}(L)M_t + \beta_{22}(L) Y_t = u_{2t} \tag{79b}$$

with $\beta_{21}(0) = 0$ and $\beta_{22}(0) = 1$.

These conditions are restrictive according to Sims.[25] He definitely rules them out as an escape from his 1972 result since money supply could not have been in the objective function. But his analysis by being restricted to two variables perhaps generates these excessive restrictions. Thus it is true that reducing the variance of interest rates at which the government budget deficit could be financed was one of the principal objectives of monetary policy during this period. If the income–government deficit multiplier was quick and stable and if money supply increase was determined by the need to keep interest rates stable, there would be a money–

income relationship. How precisely this would lead to spurious correlation would be tricky to work out since as we saw above, once we add another variable to these bivariate systems they seem to lose their simplicity and tractability. At the conference at which Sims presented his paper, David Pierce expressed his belief that the course of monetary policy during the 1947-69 period made such a spurious correlation not unlikely.[26]

Another likely case is where there is a third variable not necessarily controllable by policy makers but which may simultaneously determine Y and M. This is similar to the case in (82a) – (82c). Again the technical conditions are fairly stringent and while Sims thinks them unlikely to be fulfilled in actual situations, at the same conference Robert Shiller thought that this was worrisome.[27]

Shiller also puts his finger on the combination of technique (uncontroversial) and judgement about what is unlikely (controversial) in Sims' work on causality. This is not cited to single out Sims but is symptomatic of all work in the area of economics and econometrics where even as techniques get sharper, judgement cannot be avoided.

> It is, at this point, when we try to decide which models are 'likely' and which 'unlikely', that Sims' paper becomes a paper on economic theory. Although Sims never explicitly discusses any particular application, he clearly thinks that genuine structural Granger–Sims causal orderings are 'likely' on *a priori* grounds, and he is willing to conclude that certain coefficient restrictions are *unlikely* without even discussing the particular model in question. He is probably quite right in applying his intuition to the likelihood of certain restrictions on economic models, but his conclusion may seem unconvincing or puzzling to many readers.
>
> (Shiller in Sims (1977), p. 165)

A much more basic objection to the Sims test, which to our knowledge has not been made, is that by requiring the knowledge of the 'future' values of a variable, the test can only answer the causality question *ex post*, indeed, many periods after the sample being studied. *Ex ante*, we do *not* know the future values of variables. This is so by definition but also by the philosophical position Keynes took about the nature of uncertainty and lack of knowledge. If, as of now, we wished to know if M causes Y (or say inflation), say for evaluating the correctness of current monetarist policies or for suggesting policies for the future, the Sims test is utterly useless since it cannot be performed. We cannot use past tests as guidance for future policies since the very adoption of a monetarist policy (based on a reading of Sims' causality tests) may produce a structural break. Indeed it is the question of the structural break under policy changes that formed the next stage of the critique by the new classical economists of the old econometric methods.

Thus, while the causality question was (and is) by no means settled with Sims' extension, the sharp differences between the two approaches became clearer when Lucas attempted to define what a structural relation was. Lucas' criticism was that econometric models estimated by conventional methods were unlikely to have captured truly structural relations which would remain *invariant* under exogenous shocks such as policy changes. Thus these models were useless for studying (simulating) the possible effects of different policy packages, e.g. the effect of choosing different inflation–unemployment trade-offs.

The essence of Lucas' argument is that a structural equation should capture fundamental economic behaviour of agents and to be called a structural equation it must remain invariant under different policy regimes. But Lucas argues that we know from the theory of dynamic optimisation under uncertainty that policy rules will influence behaviour, i.e. if policy changes in a known fashion then people will incorporate this new information and embody it in their behaviour. These, let us say, *deep* structural equations are not estimated by econometric model builders and their so called parameter estimates are not true behavioural constants but variable coefficients which change upon re-estimation as exogenous and policy circumstances change.

Lucas in his powerful attack on conventional econometric model building 'Econometric Policy Evaluation: A Critique' is concerned about the use of econometric models via simulations to make policy recommendations. In particular, he follows up his 1972 idea, discussed in Chapter 2 above, of questioning the desirability and the existence of any policy that says there are real output gains from an expansionary (inflationary) policy. This means that he is particularly critical of estimates of Phillips Curve trade-offs generated from solutions of large scale macro-econometric models. Since for him, neoclassical theory via the classical dichotomy denies that any nominal price inflation can have lasting real output effects, he suspects the economic theoretic foundations of the specifications of the macro-economic equations. But Lucas then goes beyond his concern with the wage–price specifications to a general attack on econometric model building.

Lucas concedes that large scale econometric models have had a good short term forecasting record but doubts whether this does not arise from *ad hoc* practices in estimation and subjective adjustment of parameters while forecasting. Such practices amount to estimation of a variable coefficient model where each successive re-estimation incorporates new information and modifies the coefficients. Thus far from being parameters, i.e. behavioural constants, the estimates are short-run descriptive summaries of the data points. This would not be a problem if the models were used only for forecasting but they are used to infer something about what might happen to the paths of endogenous variables under different policy rules. Thus one may generate the unemployment–inflation combinations under different fiscal–monetary policy rules. But such results are valid only if we are sure that the estimates of the coefficients of the equation will remain invariant under these different policy rules.

Lucas then argues that if we are to treat these econometric equations seriously as reflecting micro-economic behaviour then there is an obvious fallacy. Rational optimising behaviour implies that individuals will take into account all the information available, especially any announced changes in policy. They will alter their behaviour in the light of these new policies. If so the data they generate for the model builder will show a break with the old pattern each time there is a change in policy. Thus economic series will show frequent structural breaks, i.e. if one split the sample into, say, two separate parts and tested the null hypothesis that the two periods had the same stochastic properties, the data would tend to reject the null hypothesis. Tests of structural breaks thus become crucial diagnostic checks in the methodology of new classical macro-economists.

We can look briefly at the technical aspects of Lucas' argument before putting it into an overall perspective. First the general argument starts by describing 'the theory of economic policy' which is a way of combining a description of the policy maker's objective function with a description of the constraints in the form of an econometric model. The model is written as a generalised form of the simultaneous equation model in the form of a vector nonlinear difference equation

$$Y_{t+1} = f(Y_t, X_t, \epsilon_t) \tag{83}$$

As before Y are endogenous and X exogenous variables and ϵ is a vector of independent, identically distributed, random errors. Lucas takes f to be a true description of the economy. The model builder does not know f but must estimate it. He does this by thinking of a fixed parameter vector θ so that

$$f = F(Y, X, \theta, \epsilon) \quad \text{and so}$$

$$Y_{t+1} = F(Y_t, X_t, \theta, \epsilon) \tag{84}$$

Thus F may be linear with constant parameters θ as in the Cowles Commission structural models. The specification of long lags in Y and/or X does not make any difference to the description of the model as (84).

The policymaker then maximises a social objective (welfare) function

$$W = \sum_{t=0}^{\infty} \alpha(t) \, U(Y_t, X_t, \epsilon_t) \tag{85}$$

$\alpha(t)$ are discount factors and U is a utility function. Different policies can then be evaluated in terms of their contribution to W as we maximise (85) subject to (84).

Lucas' criterion amounts to saying that policies — alternative paths for some components of X_t cannot be taken to leave θ unaffected. One should endogenise as much of the impact of policy changes on F as possible. Even for forecasting, success comes only by treating θ not as fixed but evolving through time i.e. on successive re-estimation θ is allowed to change. Policy can be endogenised by estimating

$$X_t = G(Y_t, \lambda, \eta_t) \tag{86}$$

where λ is a fixed parameter vector and η a vector of random disturbances. So ultimately in the economy θ becomes a function of λ. A policy change is then a change in λ. If policy changes are unannounced or revealed only slowly, then there will be a lot of noise — high variance — in the data. This will lead successive estimates of θ to behave in a somewhat random fashion. If changes in λ are fully anticipated then $\theta(\lambda)$ may be quite easy to forecast.

In essence, Lucas' scheme can be best understood by saying that practical model builders are forced to adopt a varying θ implicitly, i.e.[28]

$$\theta_{t+1} = \theta_t + \xi_{t+1} \tag{87}$$

Equation (87) then describes the drift in θ over time except for random errors ξ in an adaptive–regression fashion. Thus by ignoring (86) model builders are forced to adopt practices that amount to treating (84) and (87) as a joint system but they do it unsystematically. What they should be doing however is taking (84) and (86) plus some modelling of how λ changes

$$\lambda_{t+1} = H(\lambda_t, Z_t, \zeta_t) \tag{88}$$

where Z_t, a subset of X_t, is a set of 'deeply exogenous' or 'super exogenous' variables (to use the term of Engle, Hendry & Richard (1981)). Hopefully H is a stable function summarising the process of policy making and policy change. There would also need to be conditions about the interdependence of ζ and η and ξ and ϵ for true structural invariance. We hasten to add that Lucas does not write (88) explicitly but we interpret his argument this way.

Econometric model builders have always pushed the limits of their art so as to endogenise as many of the variables on which they have information. Thus what one generation of model builders treat as exogenous gets endogenised by the next generation. For example, government expenditure was treated as a single exogenous variable in earlier models with similar treatment for taxation. Now various components of government expenditure and taxation, not to mention components of the money supply and government debt, are treated as endogenous. So this part of Lucas' criticism is accepted by all sides.

Most econometric model builders would also openly express their dissatisfaction with the small size of the samples used for estimation and the limited amount of variation in such small samples. As time passes, more information becomes available — previous data get revised, new series are defined and collected. Model builders therefore start afresh with a longer list of endogenous variables (greater disaggregation, more endogenisation) and a somewhat larger sample. Never or hardly ever can the actual exercise of econometric model building be described by Lucas' parameterisation of (83) and (84). In *econometric theory*, one needs to start with assumptions of a known true model fully described at the outset, but in *practical econometrics* every result is seen and recognised as tentative. So econometricians are searching admittedly for new ways of characterising the unknown true function f and would never pretend that they had found F or θ.[29]

Why then Lucas' critique and what is its force? For one thing, he is mixing up levels of abstraction in his argument. His description in (83) and (84) is of the ideal model builder, and this backdrop is used in outlining the theory of economic policy. Also having obtained coefficient estimates, at each stage of model estimation, econometricians invoke tests of significance which *do* depend on the classical statistical theory of inference about constant parameters.

But Lucas not only describes the model builder of econometric theory, he also gives him a potency in policy matters which is questionable. Thus, if the model builder were actually *making* policy, he would need to be aware of many feedbacks. If the model builder had any hope that his policy simulations would be directly translated into actual policy, the strictures may hold perhaps. But in simulating the inflation–unemployment trade-off, let us say, or advocating a tax cut to encourage investment, the model builder is carrying out a pen and pencil exercise which he uses in the task of persuading the actual policymakers to put more weight on his preferred policy rather than on another. In terms of the three levels of discourse we outlined at the beginning of this chapter, policy simulations belong to the level of persuasion in the policy area. Economists and econometricians even at the highest level of being members of the Council of Economic Advisers in the USA or the Chief Economic Adviser to the Treasury in the UK provide only one input among many which determine what actual policies get made. Many layers of influence from lobbies and pressure groups within the party political system and from the government's perception of its electoral chances go into the policymaking process which we but barely comprehend. The idea that policy is made by maximising W subject to $f(Y_t, X_t, \epsilon_t)$, like the Walrasian auctioneer, is a convenient analytical fable but it is not descriptive of the policy making process. It is only by conflating these levels of discourse that Lucas succeeds in his argument.

There is no doubt much that model builders can learn about explicit endogenisation of policy processes, but what is at issue with Lucas is not merely a technical point that somehow more endogeneity is needed or again that, structurally, invariance needs a more rigorous definition. As in Shiller's remarks on Sims cited above, there is a mixture of the technical and the judgmental elements in Lucas' critique. Thus his derivation of the aggregate supply curve, which we described in Chapter 2 above and which is one of the main planks of his attack, is based on a theory of market clearing and information generation which is not uncontroversial. He begins by assuming 'rational agents, cleared markets, incomplete information'. But the point at issue between the monetarists and Keynesians is precisely whether markets, especially the market for labour, actually clear or not. By taking what is being debated, and hence should be subjected to tests, as a maintained hypothesis, Lucas makes his technical results conditional upon our acceptance of his theoretical basis. If everyone accepted that markets cleared, then the entire debate of the last fifty years, if not two hundred years, is futile. From that premise it follows that there is no involuntary unemployment, that fiscal expansion or any government intervention cannot generate net benefits; indeed government intervention is happily unnecessary in such a world.

So while the Lucas argument is a contribution, at the theoretical level, about the limitations of econometric modelling, it is also an exercise in the unending battle of persuasion — of the economics profession and the policy makers. He wishes to argue the case for non-intervention, for fiscal and monetary conservatism, just as a Keynesian may wish to argue the case for, say, a combination of fiscal–monetary policy and incomes policy.

Now at this level of discourse, the argument is about economic and political judgement and is not capable of being settled in the way a technical argument may be. Lucas at the outset of his article makes his predisposition clear by saying, 'The inference that permanent inflation will . . . induce a permanent income high . . . has undergone the mysterious transformation from *obvious fallacy* to cornerstone of the theory of economic policy' (Lucas (1976), p. 19). We have added the emphasis to show that, for Lucas, the inflation–unemployment trade off is the enemy. Indeed he traces the origin of this belief purely to econometric activity rather than economic theory, which in his view is exclusively Walrasian. But as we have seen there is a theoretical disagreement which goes right across micro-economics and macro-economics. This deep disagreement has led to disagreement even about techniques for evaluating empirical evidence about the very notion of causality. So taking Walrasian theory as agreed ground and eco - nometrics as the debated ground, Lucas is only demonstrating the use of a time honoured tactic in scientific debating. The validity of the rival schemes must be settled, if it can be at all, by looking at the evidence. The elegance, the logical consistency and even the widespread support for the neoclassical model within the economics profession are not sufficient for the argument to be won.

There is also a related issue which needs to be raised. If we accept Lucas' view that the econometrician is culpable for offering misleading advice and for the dire consequences of actual stagflation, we are still left without an explanation for the success of Keynesian policies in the 25 years following the Second World War. The record of economic growth, high employment and low inflation, in the absence of non-interventionist government policy and without the magical powers of Friedman's x-percent rule, remains to be explained within the Lucas-Sargent-Sims framework. Perhaps we should also have an evaluation of the episode of the Kennedy-Johnson tax cut of 1964 where Keynesian advice was formally offered and accepted. Even as far as the stagflation episode is concerned, which was the monetarists' first victory, one may be sceptical in readily accepting an explanation of hyperinflation which neglects the OPEC oil price rise. A Keynesian model would cite this factor plus the Vietnam war deficits, the existing degree of monopolistic elements in the commodity and labour markets, and the switch from the fixed to floating rate regimes after August 1971 as elements explaining stagflation. Against this is the explanation that stagflation was generated by domestic attempts to reap some output gains by exploiting the Phillips Curve trade-off frustrated by economic agents incorporating this information in their inflationary expectations. These models lead to different policies and as we shall see in

Chapter 5 below recent UK experience may be another testing ground for the rival models. In Chapter 4, we shall look at the empirical evidence on the various monetarist proportions, including the natural rate hypothesis.

Before we come to that, one further phase of the debate has to be described. The new classical macro-economics has specified macro-economic relationships based on a rational expectations theory such as the one described in Chapter 2. The estimation of these models raises many highly technical issues but in the course of advocacy of their theory, the new school has also carried the Lucas attack on conventional econometric methods much further. They have raised the question of the identifiability of conventional econometric models; they have questioned the role of prior theory in suggesting restrictions; and they have, in general, taken an agnostic position on the possibility of discovering much more than stable correlation patterns. Their work is technically advanced and demanding. The issues raised are also still very much in flux and many readers may wish to skip this section. It does however have a place in any book on monetarism because in its new version, monetarism affords a crucial role for rational expectations and this means that econometric estimation is no longer straightforward. We have however already described the ingredients which we shall need in this discussion. They are: identification conditions, serial correlation, instrumental variable estimation and the estimation and testing of models with restrictions.[30]

Let us recall the basic form of a simultaneous dynamic econometric model

$$B_0 Y_t + \sum_{i=1}^{n} B_i Y_{t-i} + C_0 X_t + \sum_{t=1}^{m} C_i X_{t-i} = u_t \qquad (89)$$

The identifiability of each equation in this system of G equations can be thought of in two ways. Firstly we check for the sufficiency of the number of zero and other homogeneous restrictions and these need to be more than or equal to $(G-1)$. Alternatively, we can ask whether for each equation there is an adequate number of instrumental variables. There will have to be at least one for each included endogenous variable, i.e. one for each Y_{jt} appearing with a non-zero coefficient in the appropriate row of B_0 apart from the one variable chosen to be the dependent variable. Now recall the requirements that the instrumental variable should be highly correlated with the endogenous variable it replaces and that it should (asymptotically) be independent of the error term of the equation in which it appears. Thus for the ith equation, for every $\beta_{ij,\,0}$

$\neq 0\,(i \neq j)$ we should have at least one instrument Z such that

$$\text{plim}\,\frac{1}{T}\,Z'Y_j \;\neq 0$$

$$\text{plim}\,\frac{1}{T}\,Z'u_i \;= 0$$

where plim is the probability limit as we have seen above. Now normally, there are many more zero restrictions on each equation than $(G-1)$, so there would be no problem in selecting among the predetermined variables X, lagged X and lagged Y for the instruments required. But if the error u_{it} are serially correlated with their own past values and the present and past values of the errors on the other equations, we cannot ensure that

$$\text{plim}\,\frac{1}{T}\,Y'_{jt-k}u_{it} = 0.$$

This means that lagged endogenous variables are not independent of the current error terms and so they do not behave like independent variables in a regression model. Thus serial correlation of errors reduces the set of admissible instruments. One can only use exogenous variables as instruments and even some of those may be misspecified as exogenous if Lucas' argument about the endogeneity of policy variables is admitted.

It is at this stage that the over-identification of an equation can be seen to be suspect. But the next stage of the argument is that even then, many of the zero restrictions imposed on the equations may be inappropriate in the light of the theory of rational expectations.

Let us take a small model of demand and supply for an agricultural product. Demand depends on current price and income. Supply depends on expected future price and last period's rainfall and the market clears. The assumption that the market clears and the assumption that expected price is the expectation of current price conditional upon all relevant information as of last period lead to the problem of identifiability. So we have

$$q_t^d \;=\; \beta_1 p_t + \beta_2 Y_t + u_{1t} \tag{90a}$$

$$q_t^s \;=\; \delta_1 p_t^e + \delta_2 R_{t-1} + u_{2t} \tag{90b}$$

$$q_t^d \;=\; q_t^s = q_t \tag{90c}$$

In (90a) – (90c) we have a three equation demand and supply model. We let the determination of expected price be adaptive in a simple way

$$p_t^e = (\gamma / [1-(1-\gamma)L]) \, p_{t-1} + v_t / [1-(1-\gamma)L] \qquad (90d)$$

Substituting (90d) and (90c) into (90b) we get

$$q_t = \gamma \delta_1 p_{t-1} + \delta_2 R_{t-1} - \delta_2 (1-\gamma) R_{t-2} + (1-\gamma) q_{t-1} + u_{2t}$$

$$- (1-\gamma) u_{2t-1} + \delta_1 v_t \qquad (90b')$$

The demand equation can be written as

$$p_t = \beta_1^{-1} q_t - \beta_1^{-1} \beta_2 Y_t - \beta_1^{-1} u_{1t} \qquad (90a')$$

In (90a'), (90b'), we have two endogenous variables, and five predetermined variables Y_t, R_{t-1}, R_{t-2}, q_{t-1}, p_{t-1}. Of these seven variables, only three appear in (90a') so we have four zero restrictions — on R_{t-1}, R_{t-2}, q_{t-1}, p_{t-1}. In (90b'), by the same token we have two zero restrictions p_t, Y_t.

This simple model satisfies the sufficiency condition of identification and in fact each equation is over-identified. (The necessary conditions are satisfied as long as any of the coefficients of these omitted variables is non-zero in the equation in which they do appear). This also matches the conventional practice for identification whereby some of the factors determining supply do not enter into the demand equation (R_{t-1}, R_{t-2}, etc.) and similarly some demand variables (Y_t, for example) do not enter the supply equation. We need instruments for q_t in (90a'), and (90b') contains no endogenous variables other than q_t. But for q_t we have four eligible instruments R_{t-1}, R_{t-2}, q_{t-1}, p_{t-1}. So far so good.

Notice however that the error in (90b') has a moving average component in u_{2t}. Suppose now that u_{1t} and u_{2t} were each highly serially correlated with their own past values and the other variables as well. To make matters simple, let

$$u_{1t} = \rho_{11} u_{1t-1} + \rho_{12} u_{2t-1} + e_{1t} \qquad (91a)$$

$$u_{2t} = \rho_{21} u_{1t-1} + \rho_{22} u_{2t-1} + e_{2t} \qquad (91b)$$

Now of course q_{t-1}, p_{t-1} are no longer eligible instruments since (q_{t-1} u_{1t}) will involve ($q_{t-1} u_{2t-1}$) which is non-zero in the probability limit and similarly for $p_{t-1} u_{1t}$. So we lose two eligible instruments. But we are still left with two instruments for q_t : R_{t-1} and R_{t-2}.

Imagine however that the expectations generating process is not adaptive and that (90d) is replaced by

$$p_t^e = E(p_t|\Omega_{t-1}) = E(p_t|R_{t-1}, p_{t-1}, q_{t-1}, Y_{t-1}) \qquad (90d')$$

So in generating p_t^e, agents will use the structural model (90a) – (90c) plus (90d') and the information on lagged variables. Now the reduced form of (90a) – (90c) tells the agents how the equilibrium price is generated by the market

$$p_t = \beta_1^{-1}(\beta_2 Y_t - \delta_2 R_{t-1} - \delta_1 p_t^e + u_{1t} - u_{2t}) \qquad (92a)$$

By (90d') $Ep_t = p_t^e$ we can put

$$p_t = [\beta_2 Y_t - \delta_2 R_{t-1} + (u_{1t} - u_{2t})]/(\beta_1 + \delta_1) \qquad (92b)$$

To generate p_t^e from (92b) information as of $t-1$ will be needed, which gives

$$p_t^e = \frac{\beta_2}{(\beta_1 + \delta_1)} E_{t-1} Y_t - \frac{\delta_2}{(\beta_1 + \delta_1)} R_{t-1} \qquad (92c)$$

If we put (92c) back our expression for p_t^e into (90b) we get

$$q_t = \frac{\delta_1 \beta_1}{(\beta_1 + \delta_1)} E_{t-1} Y_t + \frac{\delta_2 - \delta_1 \delta_2}{(\beta_1 + \delta_1)} R_{t-1} + u_{2t} \qquad (90b'')$$

and as before

$$p_t = \beta_1^{-1}(q_t + \beta_2 Y_t - u_{1t}) \qquad (90a')$$

Now take for instance plim $(R_{t-1} u_{1t})$ which will need to be zero if R_{t-1} is to be an instrument for q_t in (90a'). If rainfall last year was higher than normal, agents will have worked out via (92b) that prices this year would be lower. Thus R_{t-1} is correlated with the observed price p_t and hence with u_{1t} and so we lose R_{t-1} as an instrument.

Notice also how rational expectations leads, in (90b''), the coefficients in the supply equation now to involve parameters of the demand equations and also how these coefficients are nonlinear functions of the original parameters. Since β_1 appears in both (90b'') and (90a') we cannot estimate these equations separately any more. The four coefficients in (90a') and (90b'') are nonlinear functions of the structural parameters $\delta_1, \beta_1, \beta_2$ and δ_1. So we have to estimate the model by methods which incorporate these cross-equation nonlinear restrictions in the coefficients. As we shall see below only maximum likelihood methods enable us to do this definitely and also to generate test statistics for testing the validity of the nonlinear restrictions.

There is one further aspect which can be more easily illustrated in our small model than in larger models. The restricted reduced form (RRF) of the model with adaptive expectation is

$$q_t = \gamma \delta_1 p_{t-1} + \delta_2 R_{t-1} - \delta_2 (1-\gamma) R_{t-2} + (1-\gamma) q_{t-1} + u_{2t}$$

$$- (1-\gamma) u_{2t-1} + v_t \tag{93a}$$

$$p_t = -\beta_1^{-1} (\gamma \delta_1 p_{t-1} + \delta_2 R_{t-1} - \delta_2 (1-\gamma) R_{t-2} + (1-\gamma) q_{t-1})$$

$$+ \beta_1^{-1} \beta_2 Y_t - \beta_1^{-1} (u_{1t} + u_{2t} - (1-\gamma) u_{2t-1} + v_t) \tag{93b}$$

There are nine RRF coefficients which determine β_1, β_2, δ_1, δ_2 and γ thus giving us four over-identifying restrictions on the system as a whole.

Compare now the RRF of the rational expectation scheme

$$q_t = \frac{\delta_1 \beta_1}{(\beta_1 + \delta_1)} E_{t-1} Y_t + (\delta_2 - \frac{\delta_1 \delta_2}{(\beta_1 + \delta_1})) R_{t-1} + u_{2t} \tag{94a}$$

$$p_t = \frac{\delta_1}{(\beta_1 + \delta_1)} E_{t-1} Y_t + \beta_2 y_t - \beta_1^{-1} (\delta_2 - \frac{\delta_1 \delta_2}{(\beta_1 + \delta_1})) R_{t-1}$$

$$+ u_{1t} - \beta_1^{-1} u_{2t} \tag{94b}$$

The greater degree of complexity of (94a) – (94b) is quite obvious. Notice also that given the term EY_t, we need to generate conditional predictions of the exogenous variables as well as those of endogenous variables whose expectations appear in the equations.

The general approach to the estimation of rational expectations models has been given by Kenneth Wallis in his 1980 'Econometrica' paper. Wallis starts with a general model

$$BY_t + AY_t^* + CX_t = u_t \tag{95}$$

where $Y_t^* = E_{t-1}(Y_t | \Omega_{t-1})$ as before.

The matrices B, A and C are parameter matrices of size $G \times G$, $G \times G$ and $G \times K$. The other variables have been defined before. Although Y^* and Y are of the same size many variables will not appear in expectational form in the model and for those Y^* the appropriate coefficient in A would be zero.

Now from (95) and the definition of Y^* we have

$$Y_t^* = E(Y_t | \Omega_{t-1}) = -(B+A)^{-1} CE(X_t | \Omega_{t-1}) = -(B+A)^{-1} C\hat{X}_t \tag{96}$$

In (96), $\hat{X}_t$ is the optimal prediction of X_t given the information at $t-1$. Equation (96) is similar to (92c) above. Putting (96) back into (95), we get

$$BY_t - A(B+A)^{-1} C\hat{X}_t + CX_t = u_t \tag{97}$$

This gives us the RRF of the model as equation (98)

$$Y_t = B^{-1} A(B+A)^{-1} C\hat{X}_t - B^{-1} CX_t + B^{-1} u_t \tag{98}$$

We see then that the RRF incorporates the various cross-equation restrictions via the elements of $(B+A)^{-1}$. Now to generate $\hat{X}_t$ we add to (97) an ARIMA forecasting scheme for X_t

$$\phi(L)X_t = \theta(L)\epsilon_t \tag{99}$$

The estimation problem then is that of jointly estimating (97) and (99). An alternative is to first generate $\hat{X}_t$ by estimating (99) and then treating them as the variables $\hat{X}_t$ in (98), though this, as Wallis points out (Wallis (1980), p. 66) is somewhat less efficient.

The identifiability condition for the model in (95) is that the number of variables which appear as expectational variables say $H \leqslant G$ must not be more than the number of exogenous variables, i.e. $H \leqslant K$. This makes intrinsic sense since we use the X variables to generate the optimal predictors of the endogenous variables whose expected values appear in the structural form equations. So we must have at least one exogenous variable for each expectational variable. The similarity between this and the instrumental variables estimation requirement is obvious.[31]

Since rational expectations models frequently involve a large number of equations, we need to look at the multivariate generalisation of the Granger–Sims conditions of causality. This has been done in the context of a *complete dynamic simultaneous equations system* (CDSEM) by Geweke. Suppose we rewrite equation (98) as an unrestricted reduced form:

$$Y_t = J(L)X_t + v_t \tag{98a}$$

We make appropriate assumptions about the serial correlation pattern of v_t. We then write an alternative to (98a) including future values of x_t as

$$Y_t = J(L)X_t + K(L^-)X_t + v_t' \tag{98b}$$

Where $K(L^-)$ denotes coefficients on future lags of X, $K(L^-) = \Sigma K_i L^{-i}$ and of course $J(L)$ has matrices $J_i(L^i)$ for each period i and each J_i is $G \times K$.

It is easy now to state the Sims causality condition as the requirement that $K(L^-) = 0$. But a second way to state the same condition in terms of Granger causality is to write (99) in two alternate forms

$$X_t = F(L)X_t + e_t \tag{99a}$$

$$X_t = F(L)X_t + G(L)Y_t + e_t' \tag{99b}$$

where all the errors have zero mean and are assumed to be 'properly behaved'. For $K(L^-)$ to be zero in (98b), it is necessary and sufficient that $G(L)$ be zero in (99b). Under these conditions X is exogenous with respect to Y.[32]

Geweke has thus generalised the Granger–Sims conditions from the bivariate case to the multivariate case more frequently encountered in econometrics. But the notion of causality adopted here still relies on an asymmetry of correlation patterns. As we said before, the Cowles commission view of causality involves some notion of identifiability of structural parameters. So Geweke's extension still falls short of that.

Recently, in a hitherto unpublished paper, Robert Engle, David Hendry and Jean Francois Richard (1981) have suggested a reconciliation of this conflict by proposing a notion of exogeneity that encompasses the Granger causality condition as well as the structural parameter identifiability. The paper is technically demanding and here we intend only to give the flavour of the argument. (All technical detail is relegated to footnotes.)

The Granger condition is stated by Engle, Hendry and Richard in terms of the well known statistical result that the joint density between any two variables can be written as a product of a conditional density and a marginal density. Thus if X Granger-causes Y, then the joint density of Y, X (given initial values Y_0, X_0 and a parameter vector ϕ) can be written as the conditional density of Y_t given X_t, all the lagged values of

Y and X and the vector ϕ, times the density of X_t given X_{t-1}, Y_0 and ϕ. The point here is that the marginal density of X_t does not involve lagged Y.[33]

Now the interesting new element in Engle, Hendry and Richard's paper is the notion that the investigator may be interested only in some subset of the parameters — called the *parameters of interest*. He can then partition ϕ into θ and λ, say, where θ are the parameters of interest. We then add to the Granger causality condition the additional requirement that the conditional density of Y_t given X_t and lagged values of Y and X involve only the subset θ of parameters of interest and the λ vector then appears only in the marginal density of X_t.[34]

In a sense, Engle, Hendry and Richard have exploited the notion of recursiveness but made it much more rigorous. Thus in our example above of equations (95) and (99), we can estimate the parameters of interest B, A and C by maximising the joint likelihood of u_t treating the parameters of (99) as prior or recursive to these parameters since X is exogenous in the Engle, Hendry and Richard sense. This requires stringent conditions on lack of own and cross serial correlation between u_t and ϵ_t. If this were not the case then X_t would be correlated with u_t at some lag length, i.e. plim $\frac{1}{T} X_{t-s}$, $u_{t-\tau} \neq 0$ for some s, τ. Engle, Hendry and Richard thus bring attention to the serial correlation properties of the processes generating X_t and Y_t together with a concern for the possibility of obtaining appropriate parameter estimates of the structural form.

Their definitions also enable us to pose the Lucas problem of structural invariance properly. In terms of (84) and (86), θ are the *parameters of interest* and λ are the *auxiliary parameters*. For *structural invariance*, we need θ to be invariant to changes in the marginal density of X_t given X_{t-1} and λ. Engle, Hendry and Richard call the Z variables *super-exogenous* if Z satisfies the exogeneity conditions above *and* if the conditional model involving structural parameters θ is structurally invariant.

What super-exogeneity then implies is that we somehow develop our model so that the equations of interest as in (86) are *deep structural equations*, i.e. they incorporate all the endogenisation we are capable of, at the time that we are modelling. Such a requirement cannot obviously hold for all time, since, as we said above, new data are added, and as we learn more about the world, we endogenise a bit more, i.e. go for a deeper structure in successive periods. This is in the nature of the practice of econometrics.

We close this chapter by an overview of the main areas of debate in the methodology of testing theories. The role of zero restrictions arising from prior theory is one issue of debate. The rational expectations theorists who have taken over the monetarist mantle, are sceptical of restrictions arising from any macro-economic theory which does not have Walrasian micro-economic foundations. They seek to specify systems of equations based on their stochastic version of this theory. The resulting model shows many intra- and inter-equation restrictions on the parameters but very few zero restrictions (Sargent (1981)). This is because in Walrasian theory 'everything depends on everything else', and the rational expectations theory provides the statistical gloss on this. Walras' theory has, however, signally failed to explain the observed business cycle as Hayek observed fifty years ago. It is difficult at this moment to say whether the new classical macro-economists have produced a convincing estimated model of the business cycle. Much work is in progress and some success has been claimed (see for example Lucas and Sargent (1979)). The immense complexity of the equations generated by the new theory contrasts starkly with the one equation–one independent variable (i.e. simple and highly restrictive) models of Friedman. (See, for example, Sargent's discussion of the specification and estimation of supply and demand equations (26), (27), (8), (5) on pp. 238–40 in Sargent (1981), and that is only for a single industry.)

By contrast, existing macro-econometric models have incorporated much of the new time series analysis but they continue to use prior restrictions arising from Keynesian macro-economics and the Keynesians remain sceptical of the market clearing assumptions embodied in the Lucas–Sargent–Sims models. (See the contributions of Tobin and Okun in JMCB November 1980, Modigliani (1977), Solow (1980), and the contributions of Ando and Klein in Simms (1977).)

With the scepticism about the role of prior theory in aiding the identification of structural models, Sargent and Sims have advocated the use of statistical techniques which are best in summarising the dynamic correlation structure of the data series. Thus they take an agnostic view of the possibility of making causal inferences. A whole generation after Koopmans' critique of National Bureau methods in 'Measurement without Theory', the atheoretic search for stable correlation patterns has been brought back into fashion by the new monetarists (Sargent and Sims (1977), Sims (1980)). To some extent, of course, this despair is due to the fact that Walrasian theory must be either accepted to be true or not. It is practically impossible to validate the entire system empirically since it makes impossible informational demands. In the Arrow–Debreu version of the Walrasian theory, not only does one need information on the many contingent and actual commodity markets, but for the logically rigorous proof of the existence of equilibrium one must also accept the notion that all contracts for all future periods are settled in the single initial instance. Thus if we were to take the Arrow–Debreu theory as any guide to empirical specification one would have only one observation on each market to estimate demand and supply curves. Here is the fundamental under-identifiability of the Walrasian system. Adding stochastic specifications via rational expectations etc., still leaves one with too few observations and too many parameters. A true Walrasian therefore must acknowledge the impossibility of extracting causal information supporting his theory. So he must combine an *a priori* belief in the theory of general equilibrium as a picture of the way the economy works (all markets clear etc.) and then he must resort to correlation analysis for his empirical work. There is not much escape from this dilemma.

Of course, empirical claims are always being made in support of monetarism by economists and even policymakers. Thus the assertion frequently heard over the past five years from British Prime Ministers that reflation only leads to further unemployment or that unemployment results from inflationary wage demands are in the minds of these leaders solidly grounded in 'facts'. They are, of course, no such thing. They are empirically testable predictions of a particular theory, i.e. they derive from the interpretation monetarists put on the data. It is to the validity of these interpretations that we must now turn.

Notes

1. Imre Lakatos, 'The Methodology of Scientific Research Programmes', in Lakatos and Musgrave (eds), *Criticism and the Growth of Knowledge* (Cambridge 1970).
2. A beginning was made by Hahn (1964) and Clower (1964). Since then, there have been attempts to provide a fixed-price general-equilibrium argument by Barro and Grossman (1971), Dreze (1900), Malinvaud and Younes (1900), Malinvaud (1900), Benassy (1900). As far as the flex price argument is concerned only Hahn (1900), (1900), (1900) can be cited as even attempting this task. This quest is by no means over yet.
3. Two illustrations of this can be offered. An article by Patrick Minford in *The Times* of 4 February 1980, the reply by Frank Hahn and Robert Neild on 25 February 1980, the response of Milton Friedman (3 March 1980) and Patrick Minford (3 March 1980) and the ensuing correspondence is one such example. Frank Hahn returned to the battle on April 28 1981 again in *The Times* provoked by an article of Patrick Minford's on April 7 previous.
4. The best discussion of this, which I cannot hope to summarise adequately is in Lakatos, 'The Methodology of Scientific Research Programmes'. Discussions of Lakatos' work as well as that of Kahn is in Latsis (1900) and in Blaug (1981). The authors in these two books are however not practising econometricians and their views while of much interest are somewhat distant from

the battle we are surveying.

5. That cycles occur in moving averages of random variables but not in the original variables themselves was shown by E. Slutsky in his classic paper (1937). Using Slutsky's method, it can be shown that some of the averaging procedures used in the National Bureau method employed by Friedman also gives rise to artificial cycles. See R. Bird et al (1965).

6. See however, Friedman, 'The Lag in Effect of Monetary Policy', *Journal of Political Economy*, October 1961 reprinted in Friedman (1969). Friedman refers to Kareken and Solow in a footnote but does not meet their criticism. See, however, p. 253 in that book.

7. This subject is well covered in many econometrics textbooks. See for a recent exposition, Harvey (1981). T is the number of observations and k the number of parameters being estimated.

8. As the quotation makes clear FM also regressed ΔC on ΔM and ΔA and tried various lagged versions of the relationships. They also tried a multivariate version by adding M to equation (46b).

9. For a more detailed treatment, see Desai (1976), Harvey (1980) or Silvey (1970). We shall return to these issues in greater detail below.

10. These definitions of structural form, reduced form, exogeneity, endogeneity have become the subject of debate once again in the last few years. We return to this later.

11. It should be added that even the AM formulation, like most other macro models by taking a linear specification, imposes constant multipliers. Multipliers were for Keynes variable over the course of the cycle. An early attempt to capture variable multipliers has been made by Morishima and Saito in their model of the US economy. They specify a loglinear macro model which gives constant elasticities but variable slopes and hence variable multipliers. They come to the conclusion that both IS and LM curves are nonlinear, that the fiscal multiplier is higher than the money multiplier at less than full employment but that near full employment, the money multiplier is higher. [Morishima (1976)].

12. Earlier in the 1940s, a methodological battle had been fought when Koopmans in a famous review article 'Measurement without Theory' (Koopmans (1947)) had criticised the NBER method. A debate followed between Koopmans and Vining but the Cowles Commission methodology gained respectability. As we shall see below by 1975, the NBER method had been revived by Sims and others (see Sims (1977)).

13. Historically this was the first solution proposed to the identification problem by E.J. Working in his classic article 'What do Statistical Demand Curves Show?' (1928). See Desai (1976) for an introductory exposition and references.

14. This has always been known in demand analysis and applied econometric work has been possible only by choosing some sensible way of grouping commodities. See Deaton and Muellbauer (1980) for various separability, aggregation assumptions.

15. For further discussion of Liu's position, see Desai (1976) and references therein.

16. For Wold's ideas see Desai (1976).

17. There is some loss of efficiency–high variance of estimates–since there may be be information in the joint dependence structure of the errors ϵ which is ignored by carrying out single equation estimates.

18. This is much too condensed an exposition of this topic. In Chapter 4 below we shall give an example of the application of this procedure and also in some of what follows in this chapter we shall return to this question. For details

19. see Desai (1976), Harvey (1981).

19. L.O. Andersen and J. Jordan (1968). See also P. Cooper and C. Nelson (1975).

20. If ρ_1 and ρ'_1 are both less than one, then we can write them as infinite moving-average processes

$$Y_t = \Sigma_{i=0}^{\infty} \rho_1^i e_t - i \quad X_t = \Sigma_{i=1}^{\infty} \rho'^i_1 \, \epsilon_{t-i}$$

Thus a stationary (1, 0, 0) process with an autoregressive coefficient less than one is equivalent to a (0, 0, ∞) process.

21. It may be argued that the need to examine residuals and check for spurious correlation should have been obvious to the FM vintage econometricians and that the time series analysts are only reminding us of old truths. From such a point of view, the R^2 criterion is not made obsolete now by new knowledge but was slightly misguided at inception. It was always the wrong technique to use. But best practice technology in econometric research is a function of what is currently fashionable, computationally feasible and likely to be thought of as sophisticated. I dare say in the early sixties it was the AM criterion about misspecification and simultaneity errors of FM which were more telling than if some statistician had pointed out that these variables were highly serially correlated. See Hendry (1977) in Sims (1977).

22. Despite such warnings, the popular sport of correlating price level with money supply continues in public debate. For a recent example, see Tim Congdon's pro-monetarist dissertation in *The Times*, June 29 1981 and Gavyn Davies' demolition of his thesis in *The Times*, July 13 1981.

23. See the very interesting comments on different notions of causality by Arnold Zellner in the Sims (1977) volume. Zellner refers to an early paper by Bassmann where the philosophical and the statistical definitions of causality are confronted (Bassmann (1963)).

24. Of course, these various statements were couched in the felicitous ambiguity of the English language, making precision elusive.

25. Our presentation leaves out some of the technical details for which the original article should be consulted.

26. David Pierce in Sims (1977) pp. 159—62. Also at the conference, Albert Ando thought that sometimes money supply and at others interest rates or free reserves were controlled. Sims (1977) p. 210.

27. Robert Shiller in Sims (1977) pp. 163—6.

28. Lucas attaches errors η to the θ_{t+1} equation as well as to the X_t equation (86) above. We take it that this is an oversight, hence we use separate notation for the two error processes. This allows for the (unlikely) possibility that Lucas may need $\eta = \xi$.

29. Anyone following the various models associated with Laurence Klein from his 1950 Cowles monograph, *Economic Fluctuations in United States* to the present LINK model would see that this is obvious. Also one may look at different versions of the FMP model which started as a result of dissatisfaction with the monetary/financial side of the Brookings SSRC Quarterly Model and has steadily expanded to endogenise many aspects previously taken to be exogenous. In the UK, for example, the London Business School model began as a Keynesian model but evolved along (international) monetarist lines after forecasting problems in 1974 and 1975. (The FMP model is described in various journals over the last fifteen years. See for example, Ando, Modigliani and Rasche (1972) for its 1969 structure, Modigliani (1977) for a more recent bibliography. For the London Business School model, Ball et al. (1978)).

30. The references here are Sargent and Sims (1977), Wallis (1980), Sims (1980),

Geweke (1978), Hansen and Sargent (1980), Sargent (1981), Engle, Hendry and Richards (1981). The very important problem of uniqueness of solutions to rational expectations models is dealt with in Gourieroux, Laffont and Monfort (1979) but is too technical for our present purposes.

31. We do not prove the necessity of the identifiability condition here since Wallis' original treatment is crystal clear. The same goes for the details of the maximum likelihood procedure.

32. There are additional requirements about the stability of the various lag polynomials and serial correlation of errors which we have left unstated. See Geweke (1978).

33. Let Z represent Y and X together. Then the joint density of all Z_t is written as

$$D(Z \mid Z_0, \phi) = \sum_{t=1}^{T} D(Z_t \mid Z_{t-1}, \phi)$$

Now Y does not Granger-cause X if

$$D(X_t \mid Z_{t-1}, \phi) = D(X_t \mid X_{t-1}, Y_0, \phi)$$

This allows us to write the joint density as

$$D(Y_t, X_t \mid Z_{t-1}, \phi) = D(Y_t \mid X_t, Z_{t-1}, \phi)\, D(X_t \mid X_{t-1}, Y_0, \phi)$$

34. The new requirement then is loosely stated as

$$D(Z_t \mid Z_{t-1}, \phi) = D(Y_t \mid X_t, Z_{t-1}, \phi)\, D(X_t \mid X_{t-1}, Y_0, \lambda)$$

4. THE EVIDENCE ON MONETARIST CLAIMS

In the previous chapters we have surveyed the theoretical debate about monetarism and have reviewed in some depth the rapidly changing techniques for testing theories. Any illusion that testing economic theories is a simple task of looking at two series, plotting them on graph paper, or even of fitting an equation and arriving at unambiguous conclusions, should have been dispelled by now. In the course of the previous chapter, we looked at various examples where evidence had been offered in support of monetarist propositions. Even acceptance or rejection of the hypotheses becomes a changing, almost dialectical, process whereby theory, technique and interpretation change in interaction with each other (e.g. the debate about money—income causality). In such circumstances, there are bound to remain honest differences even among competent, fairminded economists. The topic of monetarism also brings out deep-seated political emotions, which is hardly surprising since, unlike physical sciences, economic theory has a way of immediately affecting individual lives, not to say, party political philosophies and the electoral strategies of parties in and out of power. For the time being we shall avoid such political matters and look at the evidence that has accumulated in the technical economics literature about the various propositions of monetarism.

In reviewing the evidence on monetarism we face several difficulties. Thus there is no agreement even among monetarists as to what monetarism is. When Thomas Mayer sought to define monetarism in 1975, he listed twelve propositions which in his view characterise monetarists and distinguish them from Keynesians. The reaction of a number of economists to Mayer's listing was interesting. It emerged that there were several variants of monetarism: one could label them Chicago (Friedman) monetarism, Brunner—Meltzer monetarism, international monetarism and so on. Even for Chicago monetarism, one could get somewhat different testable propositions from Friedman in 1956 as against Friedman in 1963 or 1967. And even when we have done that, the Mayer survey of monetarism has to be supplemented with an account of the *New Monetarism* or the *New Classical Macro-economics* of Lucas, Sargent and Sims.

Purvis and Mayer's Propositions

A later survey of monetarism by Douglas Purvis (1980) lists eight propositions (plus a base proposition) some of which overlap with Mayer's twelve propositions. We can therefore take the common ground between the two surveys as our starting point. In terms of the evolution of monetarist theory that we survey in Chapters 1 and 2, it will be seen that some of these propositions are of different vintage from others. Thus we have:

(A)
The Quantity Theory of Money: This can be taken to lead to different propositions:

(i) the velocity of circulation is constant or at least stable (Fisher (1911))

(ii) the demand for money is interest inelastic (Friedman (1959), Friedman and Meiselman (1963));

(iia) the demand for money has low interest elasticity (Friedman (1959), Laidler (1906));

(iii) the demand for money is more stable than the consumption function: that is, the money multiplier is larger than the fiscal multiplier (Friedman (1959), Friedman and Meiselman (1963), Andersen and Jordan (1968)); and

(iv) the money stock and changes in the money stock are the most important determinants of aggregate economic activity as represented by nominal GNP (Friedman (1956), (1958)), or, money causes income (Friedman and Schwartz (1963), Sims (1972)).

(B)
A Self Regulating Economy: This proposition concerns the existence of a competitive general equilibrium along the lines indicated by Walrasian theory and entails the acceptance of the classical dichotomy (demand and supply are functions only of relative prices) and the ability of the economy to return to equilibrium if disturbed by a random shock (stability of equilibrium). This implies that observed unemployment must be voluntary except for a random component. The testable propositions here are:

(i) public expenditure competes with private expenditure for a given level of savings; public expenditure 'crowds out' private expenditure (Friedman–Meiselman (1963)) (where the proposition is implicit if the LM curve is vertical and the IS curve is not), Stein (1974), (1976); and

(ii) the long-run Phillips Curve is vertical, i.e. the coefficient of expected inflation in the wage inflation or price inflation equation is unity (Friedman (1967)).

(C)

The Natural Rate Hypothesis: A corollary of the Self Regulating Economy proposition, it is stronger and has several testable implications. It states that equilibrium output and equilibrium unemployment are independent of the nominal price level and changes in the nominal price level. This leads to:

(i) the Phillips Curve is an aggregate supply equation where the deviation of actual from (rationally) expected inflation explains short-run deviation of output (employment) from its equilibrium path (Lucas and Rapping (1969), Lucas (1972), (1975));

(ii) the path of real variables (output, employment) is independent of the path of the nominal money stock or of any other indicator of systematic policy action denoted in nominal terms (Lucas (1972), Sargent and Wallace (1975), Sargent (1976)); and

(iia) only unanticipated change in money stock has any influence on economic activity (Barro (1977)).

(D)

The Exogeneity of Money Supply: This sustains the above propositions, is implied in the Quantity Theory of Money and is rarely explicitly stated. It is taken as uncontroversial that money supply changes are exogenous. This may mean that they are determined autonomously by the policy makers or that they merely predate the change in real economic activity. This has been a long debate since the days of Hume and Steuart. It can be stated as:

(i) changes in money stock are *not* demand determined but supply determined.

(E)

The Law of One Price: This is the international aspect of monetarism. The transmission mechanism via stable demand functions of real balances in each country to the relative price levels of traded goods will mean that the exchange rate movements will reflect the relative rates of domestic inflation. The testable propositions are:

   (i) exchange rate movements are fully determined by changes in relative price levels — the 'naive' Purchasing Power Parity theory (Frankel (1979)); and

   (ii) exchange rates reflect the international price of a country's money and hence changes in the determinants of the demand for real money balances — income and prices — determine exchange rate movements — the monetary approach to balance of payments (Frenkel and Johnson (1976), Dornbusch (1976)).

There are various interconnections between these propositions and I am sure, many another can be added or some deleted.[1] The policy implications of these propositions lead in the Friedman view to the desirability of a fixed money growth rule, in Hayek's view to a constant money stock, and in the new classical macro-economics to the irrelevance of any systematic rule (subject to some minor qualifications) in stabilising the economy. There are further differences under regimes of flexible exchange rates as against fixed exchange rates, especially concerning the exogeneity of money supply.

   Those who do not agree with monetarist propositions have offered systematic evidence against some of these propositions or just expressed scepticism. A major ground of scepticism concerns the measurability and controllability of money supply. The proliferation of measures of money stock M_1, M_2, M_3, and now in the USA, M1A, M1B, or in the UK PSL$_1$ (Private Sector Liquidity), PSL$_2$, lends some support to the view that in saying 'money causes income (or inflation)' more questions are begged than answered if the policymaker is to use that as a guide. The determinants of changes in the money stock have not received quite the same attention as factors affecting the demand for money. A principal plank of the anti-monetarist attack thus concerns the volatility and endogeneity of money supply and even the elusiveness of the very concept of money. In the UK, this has the name of the *Radcliffe view* after the Radcliffe Report and recently Nicholas Kaldor has used it for a sustained critique of monetarism.[2] We shall look at this later when reviewing the success of UK monetarist policies. Let us now examine the propositions in A–D.

A(i) Is the velocity of circulation constant or stable? This is a very old proposition, now superseded by more sophisticated versions. For Irving Fisher, velocity, defined as the ratio $P_T T/M$, was stable and much more important it was independent of P_T, T and M. As we saw in chapter 1 above, he tested QT plotting MV/T against P_T.

The more recent definition of velocity is the Marshallian one as we saw in Chapter 1 above. Here one looks at M/Py or M/Y — the ratio of money stock to nominal income. In Chart 1, we have plotted the logarithm of $k = M/Y$ for UK data 1881—1980. This chart at once exhibits the variability in ln k but also shows us the reason for the great appeal of the quantity theory in the nineteenth century. For 1881—1913, the income velocity is quite stable, the fluctuations being largely random around a constant level. Then Britain was an open economy, the apex of a vast formal and informal political empire, with London the main financial centre of the world. The prevalence of Gold Standard meant that changes in the metal's supply could be due to random factors such as gold discoveries and hence money supply would be exogenous and beyond policy control. But London's position meant that the Bank of England could manage the Gold Standard in Britain's favour since very small movements in interest rates caused large inflows and outflows of gold. The position of India was also crucial in affording monetary stability for the metropolitan power. The precise mix of reasons for the stability of the observed velocity are thus hard to guess; suffice it to say it was not natural or automatic, nor merely the result of pricate decisions about money demand (de Cecco (1974), Brown (1940)).

This is not meant to 'explain away' the observed constancy of k in nineteenth century data but merely to point out that we have not so far seen any well developed model where the constancy of k would be an *outcome* rather than an *assumption*.

It is surely obvious that the interwar period shows a complete collapse in the constancy of k and the postwar period does not support any hypothesis of constancy if we merely look at the data.

The US data on casual inspection tell the same story. Thus Friedman in his 1959 article on "The Demand For Money" charts the observed and the computed measures of $P_p y_p / M$ (Friedman (1969), p. 127). While the fit is close, the fluctuations in actual velocity are quite remarkable when we note that these are smoothed or cyclical averages, i.e. these are movements in normal or long-run velocity rather than year to year changes as in our Chart 4.1. Thus velocity of money circulation is not stable.

In reaching the conclusion that velocity is not stable we have only taken a crude look at the data. Obviously this is not enough. The next step is therefore to look at the shape and stability of the demand for money. This involves looking at propositions A(ii), A(iia), and part of A(iii).

A(ii) Is the demand for money interest inelastic? The answer to this is no. We have already seen that in the 1959 study of the secular demand for

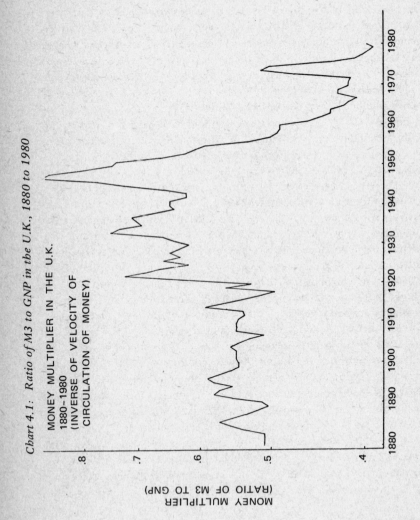

Chart 4.1: Ratio of M3 to GNP in the U.K., 1880 to 1980

MONEY MULTIPLIER IN THE U.K.
1880–1980
(INVERSE OF VELOCITY OF
CIRCULATION OF MONEY)

MONEY MULTIPLIER
(RATIO OF M3 TO GNP)

money, Friedman assumed zero interest elasticity. Also in FM, a zero interest elasticity was implicitly assumed for the short-run (annual) demand for money. AM's tests showed that this restriction was rejected as we saw in Chapter 3. Laidler's work on the demand for money also showed that interest elasticity was non-zero, though low.

Recently there has been a debate in the UK about the demand-for-money function. Much of the discussion centres around the need to avoid naive specification and take proper account of serial correlation properties of the errors. Thus the estimated parameters of the demand-for-money—income-and-interest-elasticity — as well as response of the demand for real balances to the rate of inflation — are highly sensitive to the specification of the error structure and a likely dynamic misspecification.

The debate bagan with a study by Hacche (1974) of the demand for money where he set up the following model

$$\ln M_t^* = a_0 + a_1 \ln y_t + a_2 \ln P_t + a_3 \ln (1 + r) + e_{1t} \qquad (100a)$$

$$\Delta \ln M_t = (1 - \gamma)(\ln M_t^* - \ln M_{t-1}) + e_{2t} \qquad (100b)$$

Hacche did not specify the error terms, e_1, e_2 but we have done so to facilitate subsequent discussion. In (100a), M^* denotes the desired demand for money, y is real output, P price level and r the (long-term) rate of interest. Equation (100b) then describes the partial adjustment process of actual demand to desired demand. For (100a) to be a proper neoclassical demand for money a_2 should be equal to unity. For Friedman's view to hold a_3 should be zero or small.

Writing $m = \ln M$, $y' = \ln y$, $p = \ln P$ and $(1 + r)' = \ln (1 + r)$, taking first differences and imposing $a_2 = 1$ as Hacche did; we get

$$\Delta(m - p)_t = b_1 \Delta y_t' + b_2 \Delta(1 + r_t)' + b_3 \Delta(m - p)_{t-1} + v_t \qquad (101)$$

Hacche did not specify error terms e_{1t}, e_{2t} in his equations but once we have done that, notice that

$$v_t = (1 - \gamma)\Delta e_{1t} + \Delta e_{2t} \qquad (101a)$$

Hacche further thought that v_t may be autocorrelated so he transformed it as

$$(1 - \rho L)\Delta(m - p)_t = b_1(1 - \rho L)\Delta y_t' + b_2(1 - \rho L)\Delta(1 + r_t)'$$
$$+ b_3(1 - \rho L)\Delta(m - p)_{t-1} + \epsilon_t \qquad (102)$$

where

$$(1 - \rho L)\, v_t = \epsilon_t \tag{102a}$$

In (102), we have imposed the restriction $a_2 = 1$ as well as the view that first differencing and evidence of autocorrelation in v_t are not due to mis-specification. Thus estimation of (102) by OLS with a search procedure for ρ will lead to the optimal estimates for the parameters.

In the light of our discussion in Chapter 3 it can be seen that adding e_1 and e_2 at the outset clarifies the similarity of (102) and (102a) to equations (73a)–(73b) above. We have to separate the systematic dynamics due to the partial adjustment process in (100b) from the error dynamics as in (101a) and (102a).

Hendry and Mizon (HM) subjected Hacche's specification to a proper test of the autoregressive restrictions as well as the prior restrictions arising from economic theory ($a_2 = 1$).

Recall from (74a), (74b) above, which were

$$\rho(L)\beta(L)\,Y_t = \rho(L)\delta(L)X_t + \gamma(L)u_t \tag{74a}$$

$$\psi(L)\,Y_t = \phi(L)X_t + \gamma(L)u_t \tag{74b}$$

Now HM point out that if $\psi(L)$ and $\phi(L)$ polynomials had arisen from error dynamics rather than systematic dynamics, i.e. if $I = 0$, $P = J$ then the estimated $\psi(L)$, $\phi(L)$ polynomials should have common characteristic roots due to the common $\rho(L)$ element on both sides. They tested (102) and (102a) written in (74b) form for common roots. They tried up to $J = 4$ and found they could not reject $P = 3$. Thus these common factors can be extracted from the data and that will leave only the systematic dynamics.

But also notice that an equation such as (101) has no steady state solution. If we set all the growth rates equal to zero (or a constant) then we are unable to discover a long-run demand function for money. This can however be accomplished by respecifying a much simpler model that allows the short-run data to reflect disequilibrium dynamics around a long-run steady state. (Compare Phillips' finding of the long-run curve with short-run loops). This simplifies the dynamics considerably. Hendry and Mizon specify the demand for money equation as:

$$\Delta(m - p)_t = \beta_0 + \beta_1 \Delta y_t' + \beta_2 \Delta(1 + r_t)' + \beta_3 \Delta(m - p)_{t-1} + \beta_4 \Delta p_t$$
$$+ \beta_5 (m - p - y')_{t-1} + \beta_6 (1 + r)_{t-4}' + \xi_{1t} \tag{103}$$

In (103) the crucial terms are β_5 and β_6. If we set the rates of growth equal to constants, then, in steady state, (103) converges to a long-run demand for money function. If $\beta_6 = 0$ then the interest elasticity of the long-run demand for money is zero. If $\beta_5 = 0$ as well, then a long-run demand for money function *does not exist*. Equation (103) then describes the short-run path of demand for money around such a long-run relationship. For the short-run disequilibrium to converge to a stable long-run function we need $\beta_5 < 0$.

In carrying out the estimation of (103), Hendry and Mizon also test ξ_1 for first order autoregression (rejected), and for whether the lag should be longer (rejected) and whether the residuals exhibit any residual serial corelation of up to twelfth order (rejected). Their steady state demand for money equation is then derived as

$$M/Py = k(1+r)^{-2.6}\, y^{0.6}\, p^{-1.7} \tag{104a}$$

$$k = \exp\left[7 + \dot{y}' + 3.2\,(\dot{p} - \dot{m})\right] \tag{104b}$$

Now (104a) and (104b) are comparable to (28) above which was Friedman's long-run demand for money equation: $\dot{y}'$, $\dot{p}$ and $\dot{m}$ are the growth rates of y, P and M, i.e. $\dot{y}' = \Delta y'$ etc.

The income elasticity is large but much less than the 1.8 found by Friedman for the US. The interest elasticity measured as $(\partial \ln M / \partial \ln r)$ has to be extracted from (104a) at the mean values of r and turns out to be -0.2 but it is not constant and increases with increases in r. Also, k the Cambridge coefficient is not constant but is a function of income growth and negatively related to the (steady state) growth of real balances. So we conclude that the velocity is unlikely to be constant in the long run or in the short run, but that a stable demand for money equation can be extracted from the data if proper econometric practice is followed. (See also Hendry (1980a), Courakis (1978) and the references therein.)

Similar work for US money demand has not so far been carried out to our knowledge. Laidler (1980) confines himself to estimation of models of the (101) type. Laidler in a recent article on monetarism is, however, very pessimistic about the stability of the demand for money.

Ten years ago it was possible to argue that this characteristic monetarist belief in a stable demand for money function was well supported by empirical evidence, as I did in Laidler (1971). However, the last decade has produced a good deal of evidence to suggest that the *relationship has shifted in an unpredictable way* in a number of countries.

(Laidler (1981) emphasis added)

Among the reasons for the unpredictable shift are the regime of flexible exchange rates after 1973, the innovations in financial markets whereby many more highly liquid interest-bearing assets were introduced to compete with the liabilities of the banking sector (i.e. traditional 'money') and, perhaps most interesting of all, the very attempt by governments to follow monetarist policies. To quote Laidler's 1980 paper, 'The Demand for Money in the United States — Yet Again',

> The United States is far from being the only country in which, in the 1970s, far more attention has been paid to the behaviour of the money supply than in the past not merely by commentators on policy, but also by policy makers themselves. Unfortunately, this increased attention to the behaviour of the money supply has coincided with the onset of apparent instability in the demand-for-money relationship not just for the United States but for other countries as well, Britain and Australia, for example. Anyone who remembers the late 1960's, when a well-determined unemployment-inflation trade off vanished as soon as policy makers attempted to exploit it, must find this extremely disturbing, not least because such commentators as Kaldor (1970) warned that instability in the demand-for-money function would materialize the moment attempts were made to control the behaviour of the money supply.
>
> (Laidler (1980) pp.223–4)[3]

It would not be unfair to conclude from this survey that

> the demand for money is either *unstable* or, if by suitable econometric practice a stable equation can be extracted from the data, it exhibits a variable but significant interest elasticity while the velocity measured as *k* is *not constant* but a function, even in steady state, of income, price and money stock growth.

This then means that Fisher's condition for the velocity to be independent of the other variables in the equation of exchange is violated. Friedman's assertion of a stable money demand is also found to be either rejected by new data or heavily qualified.

A(iii) The Greater Stability of the Demand for Money as compared to the Consumption Function. We have already seen the AM evaluation of FM evidence which led to a severe qualification of A(iii). Also above, we have surveyed the evidence on the stability of the demand for money. It need only be added that much previous work on the estimation of these relationships being defective on grounds surveyed in Chapter 3, all previous conclusions need to be re-examined. Thus, while Hacche (1974) and Laidler (1980) find instability in the demand for money, Hendry and Mizon (1978) and Hendry (1980a) found a long-run relationship by using an appropriate econometric specification. Davidson, Hendry, Srba and Yeo (1978) also found a stable long-run consumption function, using techniques similar to those in Hendry and Mizon.

It does not however make much sense to run a race about relative stability between single equations even when they are as well estimated as those cited above. This is because, as we have said before, such relationships yield causal information only if specified and estimated as part of a complete simultaneous equation system. So while a stable demand for money equation as well as a stable consumption function have been found, we must remain sceptical as to the value of even proposing A(iii) or similar predictions as they cannot be tested.

A(iv) Money Income Causality. This is controversial as we saw in chapter 3. Friedman asserted causality analysing the data by National Bureau methods and Tobin produced a theoretical model whereby the evidence was consistent with an ultra Keynesian model. Then Sims, adapting Granger's definition of causality, found in favour of Friedman. The Sims causality criterion when extended, as in Sims (1977), still leaves a possibility open for the influence of a third variable or of spurious correlation due to policy intervention; while Sims doubted the importance of these factors in explaining away his finding, doubts persist as we saw in Chapter 3. Laidler's conjecture that the money demand equation broke down because of policy attempts to control money supply lends some support to the view that policy intervention may cause distortions in a well established relationship. Indeed following Sim's conditions described in Chapter 3, if authorities define their objective solely in terms of the money supply and minimise its variance, and a stable income-money causality existed, we should now observe that in the seventies the observed causality by Sims' method should be *reversed*. Indeed the more accurate and autonomous the control of the money supply, the stronger should be the result that income 'Sims-causes' money.

For the time being however, no further work seems to have been carried out to bring Sims' results up to date. For the UK, Goodhart et al. (1976) found that the income–money causality result was not reproduced. There was a feedback relationship in UK data. (See below for Sims' recent work on exogeneity under C.)

All the propositions A(i) to A(iv) involve single equation predictions. Even the causality test in A(iv) can be carried out without setting up a complete model. The propositions under B and C, however, require that we set up some complete system. Since our samples are obviously small in size — never more than 200 observations, such models have to be compact or condensed structural form models as we have called them above. The IS—LM framework was surveyed in Chapter 2 and again, in AM's scheme, in equations (51)—(59). This is highly aggregated, as it is, but even that is condensed to four equations, (51a)—(54a).

Following AM's development of a framework for testing rival theories in terms of restrictions on the coefficients of an IS—LM model, no further work was done on the systems estimation of a small model. Large models such as the FMP model or Wharton model were fitted but these could not be estimated by systems methods. Meanwhile discussion continued on the specification of small theoretical models. A debate took place on various issues around Friedman's attempts to formulate his theory and distinguish it from Keynesian and old fashioned quantity theoretic approaches. This debate between Friedman, Tobin, Patinkin and others neither settled the issue at a theoretical level nor was it followed up by systematic tests of the various restrictions proposed by Friedman as characterising his approach. (See Gordon (1974) for the debate.)

We have to turn therefore to an attempt by Jerome Stein, in a series of papers, to construct a small but comprehensive model containing the basic IS—LM framework of the goods, money and labour markets. The model purports to nest the Keynesian and the monetarist schemes in a simple way by allowing us to test the 'crowding out' effect. Although Stein did not himself estimate it by systems methods, we have done so and shall use our results in what follows. (For Stein's model see Stein (1974), (1976), (1978). See Purvis (1980) for a review article of Stein (1976). A discussion of Stein's model is in Desai (1981a) and Desai and Blake (1980), (1981a).)

B(i) Is there Crowding Out? Crowding out is a proposition that says that if the government finances its budget deficit by issuing bonds rather than printing money, this will raise the rate of interest and thereby crowd out private expenditure, especially private investment. This was known as the *Treasury view* in the interwar period in Britain. The idea here is that in the absence of the (stimulating) effect of a government deficit, the economy is perfectly capable of achieving a full employment equilibrium. There is no shortage of effective demand that Keynes asserted caused an under-employment equilibrium. So, if there is crowding out, then the economy behaves in accordance with neoclassical theory. If there is no crowding out, then the economy is Keynesian (Blinder and Solow (1973) have forcefully argued the case for fiscal policy).

Before we describe Stein's model in detail, let us immediately remark that this may be setting up a false dilemma. It may be that the existence of crowding out depends on the phase of the business cycle; like all multiplier effects, this too may be variable and not constant (see our reference to the

Morishima and Saito model in Chapter 3, footnote 11). So it is possible that the economy may be neither exclusively neoclassical nor exclusively Keynesian.

Stein specifies a Friedman–Phelps type expectations-augmented Phillips Curve. Recall our equation (23a) above, Stein has

$$\dot{w} = \dot{p}^e + b_0 - b_1 U \tag{105}$$

Here $\dot{w}$ is $D\ln W$ or growth rate of money wages as before and $\dot{p}^e$ is expected inflation as before; U unemployment is a proxy here for excess demand of 'labour in efficiency units per unit of capital'. The coefficient of expected inflation is restricted *a priori* to unity and unemployment enters linearly and the rate of change of unemployment does not appear in the equation. Thus (105) has imposed some prior restrictions and not left them in testable form.

The next equation expresses the excess demand-for-labour measured by unemployment as a function of real wage per effective unit of labour and of real government expenditure as a proxy for government purchase of labour services. Thus let $x = AL/K$ where A is the efficiency factor for labour L and K is the stock of capital. Then W/PA is real wage per unit of effective labour and A grows at a Harrod-neutral constant rate α. We then have

$$(X^a - X^s)\big/X^s = H^{-1}(U) = g(W/PA, G/K; X^s). \tag{106}$$

H transforms the excess demand for efficient labour into measured unemployment. Stein then works with a differentiated and linearised version of (106), which gives

$$DU = \beta_1(\dot{w} - \dot{p} - \alpha) - \beta_2 D(G/K) \tag{107}$$

The method of differentiating and linearising eliminates all level effects such as the level of government expenditure or of unemployment. Putting (105) and (107) together we get

$$DU = \beta_1(b_0 - \alpha) - \beta_1 b_1 U - \beta_1(\dot{p} - \dot{p}^e) - \beta_2 D(G/K) \tag{108}$$

In equilibrium we set $DU = DGK = 0$ and $\dot{p} = \dot{p}^e$ and get the natural rate of unemployment U^* as

$$U^* = (b_0 - \alpha)\big/b_1 \tag{109}$$

This makes U^* appear invariant to fiscal policy or to inflation, actual or expected but this is entirely due to the lack of level terms G/K and U in (107) and to the unit coefficient of $\dot{p}^e$ in (105). To appreciate the restrictive nature of (105) and (107), let us generalise them as

$$\dot{w} = b_0 - b_1 U + b_2 \dot{p}^e + b_3 DU \tag{105a}$$

$$DU = \beta_1(\dot{w} - \dot{p} - \alpha) - \beta_2 D(G/K) - \beta_3(G/K) - \beta_4 U \tag{107a}$$

Putting them together we get

$$DU = [\beta_1(b_0' - \alpha_1) - (\beta_1 b_1 + \beta_4)U - \beta_1(\dot{p} - \dot{p}^e) +$$
$$+ \beta_1(b_2 - 1)\dot{p}^e - \beta_2 D(G/K) - \beta_3(G/K)]/(1 - \beta_1 b_3) \tag{108a}$$

Now putting $DU = D(G/K) = 0$ and $\dot{p} = \dot{p}^e$, we get

$$U^* = [\beta_1(b_0 - \alpha_1) + \beta_1(b_2 - 1)\dot{p}^e - \beta_3(G/K)]/(\beta_1 b_1 + \beta_4) \tag{109a}$$

In (109a) the influence of expected inflation as well as that of the *level* of real government expenditure is clear. The long-run Phillips Curve has no argument in $\dot{w}$ but fiscal policy does shift it about. Equation (109) is then asserting a restrictive relationship biased towards monetarism rather than Keynesianism.

For inflationary expectations, Stein has an adaptive scheme which in the continuous time framework becomes

$$\dot{p}^e = [\lambda_1/(D + \lambda_1)]\dot{p} \tag{110}$$

λ_1 being the speed of adjustment of expected to actual inflation. We shall examine below a rational expectations variation of this.

It is in the specification of the third equation that Stein condenses a number of structural equations for the goods market (consumption and investment) and financial markets (money and bonds) into a single equation for the rate of inflation. Unlike the Phillips Curve literature, prices are not related to unit labour costs alone but also to the excess demand for goods:

$$\dot{p} = (\dot{w} - \alpha) + \lambda_2 E/K \tag{111}$$

E is the excess demand for goods. This is made up of the difference between the sum of private investment and government expenditure, and savings. The existence of excess demand implies some fixed-price elements in the economy which prevent the savings–investment equilibrium condition from holding. The goods market equations are tied to the financial markets via the expected real rate of interest which equals the difference between the nominal rate of interest r and the expected rate of inflation. The nominal interest rate is determined by the demand for bonds by the private sector and the supply of bonds by the government. Bonds and money constitute private wealth. When more bonds are unloaded by the government on the private sector entailing a change in the nominal rate of interest, the share of government bonds in private wealth goes up, ceteris paribus. This sets up a wealth effect on consumption and interest rate effects on investment. The sum of these two effects as a result of the change in the private sector portfolio constitutes a measure of the crowding out effect for Stein. If this sum is negative, then there is crowding out, if positive then bond financed government expenditure is stimulating of economic activity. Various manipulations and substitutions then give

$$\dot{p} = P(U, \dot{p}^e, G/K, M/PK, B/M) \tag{112}$$

In (112), B is the nominal value of government bonds and K is capital stock as before. B/M thus is the ratio of bonds to money in private wealth (which equals $B + M$). U enters into (112) via its direct effect on the unit labour cost term $(\dot{w} - \alpha)$ in (111) and also via its effect on excess demand via its role as a proxy for output. M/PK is real balances per unit of capital. G/K is the fiscal policy effect. Stein then differentiates (112) and linearises it to get

$$D\dot{p} = P_1 DU + P_2 D\dot{p}^e + P_3(\dot{m} - \dot{p} - \dot{k}) + P_4 D(G/K) + P_5 D(B/M) \tag{113}$$

Once again differentiating and linearising remove the effect of levels of variables such as U and M/PK. Thus $\dot{m} - \dot{k}$ (= $D\ln M - D\ln K$) captures the effects of money supply growth per unit of capital stock. Stein thus reduces the IS–LM curves to a single condensed equation (112) by allowing fixed price elements but also introducing the mechanism for government deficit financing via B/M. He then adds a condensed equation for the labour market (108) and an equation for the generation of inflationary expectations (110). Stein's main claim is that he has captured the flavour of the major differences between Keynesians and monetarists. Now one test as to which model better explains reality is the *sign* of $\partial \dot{p}/\partial(B/M)$ in (112) or that of P_5 in (113). Note that these two need not be equivalent if the omission of level terms introduces specification errors.

The equivalence of the two implies that the impact of a change in (B/M) on prices is *immediate* and not spread out over time.

While Stein's theoretical framework is not free from criticism and was so criticised by various participants in the 1974 Conference at Brown University, his model was also described as 'ingenious, original, interesting and thought-provoking'. As Douglas Purvis says in his review article of the conference volume, 'His attempts to estimate the model and test the monetarist hypothesis must be viewed as a positive and constructive step.'[4] Thus, to estimate and evaluate Stein's thesis is an important step in the continuing debate between Keynesians and Monetarists.

There are of course various qualifications to be made at the outset. Thus, Stein's model is highly condensed and in the course of condensing he introduces various prior restrictions — unit coefficients on variables, absence of level effects — which are not strictly germane to the original question. Thus crowding out or the shape of the long-run Phillips Curve are statements about steady states or about comparative static equilibria. Estimable econometric models are couched in terms of short run stochastic difference or differential equations. Such models may include incidental restrictions which may bias the results and hence fail, despite econometric evidence, to settle the issue. The task of a critical researcher then becomes the difficult one of separating the incidental restrictions from the essential ones.

Stein's model well illustrates this. He himself specified the system in equations (108), (110) and (113) but when it came to estimation he omitted equation (110) on the (mistaken) grounds that it may cause multi-colinearity. He then failed to estimate the structural form parameters and instead estimated the solved out unrestricted reduced form of (108) and (113) in terms of U and $\dot{p}$. This URF gave the result that the sign of (B/M) in the U equation was positive and in the $\dot{p}$ equation negative. This he concluded meant that the data supported a monetarist interpretation, albeit subject to various qualifications. (For further details of various minor errors in Stein's procedure, see Desai and Blake (1980)).

As will be clear after a reading of Chapter 3, estimates of *unrestricted reduced form* coefficients of *incomplete* dynamic models by *single equations methods* can never be satisfactory econometric practice. Indeed as in the case of AM's criticisms of FM surveyed in Chapter 3, it can lead to misleading conclusions. This happens also to be the case with Stein's model. A proper econometric practice is to estimate the structural parameters of equations (108), (110) and (113) as a *system* subject to the prior restrictions. These restrictions then need to be tested. If they are validated (not rejected) by the data, then *conditional* upon such nonrejection, we test the discriminating hypothesis concerning the sign of P_5, the parameter of interest.

We carried out this exercise for three bodies of data. Firstly for the same data set that Stein had used to arrive at his pro-monetarist conclusions, i.e. US quarterly data from 1960.I to 1973.IV. Secondly for the data from an extended period from 1960.I to 1978.IV. Lastly, because Stein's model included long-run effects via the deflation by capital stock (which he did not incorporate in his US results), for UK annual data for 1881–1965, since consistent data series on money and capital stock as well as other variables are available for this period.

To estimate the system in (108), (110) and (113) it is necessary to solve out the unobservable variable $\dot{p}^e$ by substituting out equation (110) into (108) and (113). This gives the following system

$$
\begin{bmatrix} -1 & 0 \\ P_1 & -1 \end{bmatrix} \begin{pmatrix} D^2\,U \\ D^2\,\dot{p} \end{pmatrix} - \begin{bmatrix} (\lambda_1 + \beta_1 b_1) & \beta_1 \\ -P_1\lambda_1 & (\lambda_1 - P_2\lambda_1 + P_3) \end{bmatrix} \begin{pmatrix} DU \\ D\dot{p} \end{pmatrix}
$$

$$
- \begin{bmatrix} \beta_1 b_1 \lambda_1 & 0 \\ 0 & P_3\lambda_1 \end{bmatrix} \begin{matrix} U \\ \dot{p} \end{matrix} + \begin{bmatrix} \beta_1 \lambda_1 (b_0 - \alpha) \\ 0 \end{bmatrix} + \begin{bmatrix} -\beta_2 & 0 & 0 \\ P_4 & P_3 & P_5 \end{bmatrix}
$$

$$
\begin{pmatrix} D^2(G/K) \\ D(\dot{m} - \dot{k}) \\ D^2(B/M) \end{pmatrix} + \begin{bmatrix} -\beta_2\lambda_1 & 0 & 0 \\ P_4\lambda_1 & P_3\lambda_1 & P_5\lambda_1 \end{bmatrix} \begin{pmatrix} D(G/K) \\ (\dot{m} - \dot{k}) \\ D(B/M) \end{pmatrix} = \begin{pmatrix} 0 \\ 0 \end{pmatrix} \qquad \text{(I)}
$$

This system incorporates the various zero restrictions as well as nonlinear restrictions embodied in (108), (110) and (113). There are ten parameters λ_1, $(b_0 - \alpha)$, b_1, β_1, β_2, P_1, P_2, P_3, P_4 and P_5. As can be seen from (I) there are sixteen coefficients excluding the zero's and the 1's for $D^2 U$ and $D^2\dot{p}$. There are, in all, twelve zero and nonlinear restrictions on the system. We thus need to estimate (I) in a way that we can extract estimates of the ten parameters (label them θ_i) from the sixteen coefficients (label them a_j) and derive tests for the restrictions.

System (I) is in differential equations (continuous time) terms so we need to approximate it in discrete terms before we can use data with appropriate averaging restrictions. We then need to add error terms which will be due partly to the approximation errors of casting a continuous system in discrete terms and partly to the unspecified stochastic terms in the various constituent equations which have been specified in deterministic terms as (I) makes clear.

So we have in system (I), a structure such as

$$A(\theta)\, z(t) \equiv B(\theta)\, y(t) + C(\theta)\, x(t) = 0 \qquad (114)$$

$A(\theta)$ makes it explicit that the elements a_j of A are functions of θ_i. Also, $z(t)$ expresses the endogenous and exogenous variables as continuous functions of time. After approximating it by discrete time and adding error terms u_t we get

$$A(\theta)\, \tilde{z}_t = u_t$$

where z_t indicates the discrete time approximation to $z(t)$. For the approximation, we used a method due to Sargan (1974). The results for the three samples are then given in Table 4.1. (Details are described in Desai (1981a), Desai and Blake (1980a), (1981a).)

The first thing to note about Table 4.1 is that the χ^2 value for each of the three calculations indicates that the Stein model is *misspecified*. It imposes invalid restrictions, though we cannot separate out the incidental restrictions from the essential ones. Thus, the above system, as a whole, is inappropriate for answering the question posed. A theoretical model such as Stein's proves its usefulness for pedagogic purposes precisely because it is simple, i.e. replete with untested restrictions. It is when we come to the estimation of the system empirically that we realise that the restrictions, plausible though they may sound in theory, are invalid.

The mispecified nature of the system implies, of course, that Stein's pro-monetarist conclusion about the crowding out effect have to be rejected. On that score, our results are mixed. P_5 is positive for the US in 1960–73 with a 't value' above one and also for the UK in 1881–1965 though with a very low t value. It is negative for the US in 1960–78 but all three conclusions are based on inappropriate standard errors since the model is misspecified. Thus in this highly simplified model, we can reach no conclusion about the sign of P_5.

The significance of P_5 in the US in 1960–78 is curious since so many other parameters have wrong signs in that period. Thus if we were to accept $P_5 < 0$ as crowding out in 1960–78, we have to live with $P_3 < 0$ implying that higher money growth leads to lower inflation!

The only robustly estimated parameter seems to be λ_1 the speed of adaptive expectations. This value is very high for the UK indicating adjustment within about six months. For the US there seems to be some speeding up of the adaptation of inflationary expectations in the mid-seventies since the value of λ_1 doubles between the two samples.

Table 4.1: *Maximum Likelihood Estimates of Stein's Model*

	US 1960. I– 1973. IV	US 1960. I– 1973. IV	UK 1881–1965
λ_1	0.6386 (0.20)	1.2733 (0.51)	1.7759 (0.37)
β_1	0.1405 (2.37)	–0.1515 (0.09)	–0.6733 (4.27)
b_1	0.4281 (7.00)		–0.1840 (1.16)
$\dfrac{(b_0 - \alpha)}{b_1} =$		0.0455 (0.013)	
$(b_0 - \alpha)$	2.2555 (37.43)		–0.8229 (5.21)
β_2	0.5442 (0.39)	0.0140 (0.006)	0.7293 (0.35)
P_1	0.7907 (0.77)	–4.8697 (2.440)	–0.2651(10^{-4}) (0.01)
P_2	–7.0331 (4.54)	0.1950 (0.892)	0.2154 (0.21)
P_3	0.4844 (0.25)	–0.5386 (0.123)	0.3563 (0.11)
P_4	0.3036 (0.48)	–0.0438 (0.050)	0.0087 (0.012)
P_5	0.1414 (0.12)	–0.2977 (0.052)	0.0285 (0.051)
$\chi^2(12)$	28.80	49.46	33.80

Figures in parentheses below parameter estimates are the asymptotic standard errors and besides the χ^2 are the number of restrictions on the system. The critical value of $\chi^2(12)$ for 95% confidence level is 21.03. Some loss of observations occurred in each case due to creation of lagged values of variables.

The number of restrictions equals the number of instruments (number of predetermined variables) times the number of equations less the number of parameters.

For the rest, the parameter estimates have wrong signs, high standard errors and are generally not very enlightening. In the UK in 1881–1965 as well as in the US in 1960–73, λ_1, β_2 and P_3 are the three significant coefficients. These indicate that fiscal policy can lower unemployment and that money growth can lead to inflation. The effect of a one per cent growth in money supply is a one per cent point addition to the rate of inflation. A unit change in government expenditure can, however, lower unemployment by one half of one per cent. There is no simultaneous interaction between $\dot{p}$ and U (except in the rather dubious results of the US in 1960–78 where β_1 has the wrong sign). If taken at their face value, these results would indicate that an increase in government expenditure financed by money creation will lead to lower unemployment and higher inflation reflecting the negative inflation–unemployment trade-off.

The main conclusion however has to be that if estimated with appropriate systems techniques, i.e. by maximum likelihood methods, the Stein model is shown to be misspecified. This leads us to remain sceptical about the crowding out question, contrary to Stein's conclusion. Indeed the results on Stein's exercise parallel AM's conclusion about FM — a misspecified single equation estimation whose results are reversed on careful re-estimation by more appropriate methods. It also points to the immense difficulties involved in testing predictions of theoretical models in which there is much *a priori* restriction. Thus the existence of crowding out is asserted as a basic proposition of new classical macro-economics but its empirical validity seems difficult to test.

Stein's model though simple has proved data inadmissible. Much of the literature in recent years about the propositions of new classical macro-economics has arrived at dramatic conclusions based on equally simple, i.e. highly restrictive, models. Thus Lucas' derivation of the aggregate supply function is based on a highly restrictive model; the Sargent–Wallace 'theorem' about the independence of the path of the private economy of changes in the nominal money stock is based on a highly restrictive IS–LM model as we saw in chapter 2. While theoretical debates can be won on logical grounds by constructing such simple models, it is only when they are empirically tested that we can have confidence in their validity. Thus, for example (108) above is very similar to Lucas' aggregate supply function except that Lucas would set $\beta_2 = 0$. Putting $\beta_2 = 0$ in (108) and using (109) we get

$$D(U - U^*) = -\beta_1(U - U^*) - \beta_1(\dot{p} - \dot{p}^e) \qquad (115)$$

Now (115) is very much the Lucas aggregate supply function where we expect $\beta_1 > 0$. The only change is that Stein writes $\dot{p}^e$ in terms of an adaptive framework while Lucas prefers rational expectations. Our Stein results in Table 4.1 show that β_1 is either positive and nonsignificant (US 1960–73), negative and nonsignificant (UK), or negative and with a t value of about 1.66 (US 1960–78). None of these correspond to Lucas' view although the *a priori* arguments of Stein as well as Lucas sound plausible.

We tried to check whether the major misspecification in Stein's model was the specification of the inflationary expectations scheme. Could we, for example, respecify the model in terms of rational expectations and obtain better estimates? Alas, no. We respecified the Stein equation (108) along Lucas lines and dropped (110) in favour of a rational expectations scheme. For the $\dot{p}$ equation, we retained (113) but added a plausible restriction that on the parameter $P_2 = 1$. Thus our new scheme became

$$DU = -\beta_1(U - U^*) - \beta_1(\dot{p}_t - E_{t-1}\dot{p}_t) \tag{116}$$

$$D(\dot{p} - E_{t-1}\dot{p}) = P_1 DU + P_3(\dot{m} - \dot{p} - \dot{k}) + P_4 D(G/K)$$

$$+ P_5 D(B/M) \tag{117}$$

The restriction $P_2 = 1$ is not strictly necessary but allows for weakly rational expectations. In (117) we use the linearity property of the expectations operator and put $ED\dot{p} = DE\dot{p}$. Then instead of (110) we have

$$E\dot{p}(t) = E(\dot{p}(t) \mid G(t), K(t), \ln M(t), B(t), U(t), p(t)) \tag{118}$$

In (118), the information set is the continuous time analog of the discrete system which assumes that all information up to the beginning of the period t is available.

The RE version of the Stein model can then be written analogous to (I) as

$$\begin{bmatrix} -1 & 0 \\ P_1 & -1 \end{bmatrix}\begin{pmatrix} DU \\ D\dot{p} \end{pmatrix} - \begin{bmatrix} -\beta_1 b_1 & \beta_1 \\ 0 & P_3 \end{bmatrix}\begin{pmatrix} U \\ \dot{p} \end{pmatrix} - \begin{bmatrix} 0 & 0 \\ 0 & -P_2 \end{bmatrix}\begin{pmatrix} DEU \\ DE\dot{p} \end{pmatrix}$$

$$- \begin{bmatrix} 0 & -\beta_1 \\ 0 & 0 \end{bmatrix}\begin{pmatrix} EU \\ E\dot{p} \end{pmatrix} + \begin{pmatrix} \beta_1 b_1 U^* \\ 0 \end{pmatrix}$$

$$+ \begin{bmatrix} -\beta_2 & 0 & 0 \\ & & \\ P_4 & P_3 & P_5 \end{bmatrix} \begin{pmatrix} D(G/K) \\ (\dot{m} - \dot{k}) \\ D(B/M) \end{pmatrix} = \begin{pmatrix} 0 \\ 0 \\ 0 \end{pmatrix} \qquad (II)$$

In (II) we have created an expectational variable for unemployment EU but set all its coefficients equal to zero. Note also that since we no longer have (110), System (II) is distinguishable from (I) by being a lower order differential equation system. There is no chance of (I) and (II) being observationally equivalent, although, as Sargent has noted, in other specifications, Keynesian and monetarist models often are observationally equivalent (Sargent 1976).

After discrete approximation of the differential equations, (II) can be written in Wallis' notation described in Chapter 3 as

$$B_0 y_t + B_1 y_{t-1} + A_0 y_t^* + A_1 y_{t-1}^* + c + C_0 x_t + C_1 x_{t-1} = \epsilon_t \quad (119)$$

where $y_t = (U_t, \dot{p}_t)'$ and $x_t = [(G/K), (M/K), (B/M)]'$, where primes indicate transposes. The estimation of (119) was then carried out by maximum likelihood methods following Wallis' procedure. Nonlinear across-equation restrictions were imposed and tested. (For details, readers are referred to Desai and Blake (1981b).) The estimation was carried out for the period from January 1960 to April 1978 to make it comparable to the adaptive expectation case in Table 4.1.

We set U^* the natural rate of unemployment equal to 0.05 (5%) *a priori* and of course put $P_2 = 1$. In (II) there are many fewer restrictions than in (I) but as Table 4.2 shows the χ^2 value was 110.92 which far exceeded the critical $\chi^2(5)$ value at the 95% level. Thus respecification of the expectation scheme is not sufficient to rescue the Stein model. The model is still grossly misspecified, even when we have eliminated terms in second differentials (D^2) of the variables.

Subject to that very important caveat, Table 4.2 shows that β_1 is negative rather than positive and significant. P_5, Stein's crucial parameter, is positive and significant. The value of P_3 is now positive, as it should be, unlike in the adaptive expectation case. On the whole the rational-expectations parameter-estimates look sharper but we cannot draw any inference from them due to the misspecification of the model. In as much as the system in (II) is not too unlike the basic rational expectations model put forward by McCallum (1980) that we discussed in chapter 2, it is worth noting that the data reject the restrictions implied therein. We may add here that, to our knowledge, all other models incorporating an RE scheme have, to date, been estimated by much less efficient methods than used by us.

Table 4.2: *Maximum Likelihood Estimates of the rational expectation version of Stein's Model*

	US 1960. I to 1978. IV	
U^*	0.05	(fixed)
b_1	1.5851	
	(0.078)	
β_1	−0.9940	
	(0.063)	
β_2	0.1540	
	(0.034)	
P_1	0.6020	
	(0.102)	
P_2	1.00	(fixed)
P_3	0.4578	
	(0.146)	
P_4	−0.0232	
	(0.018)	
P_5	0.1013	
	(0.03)	
$\chi^2(5)$	110.92	

Figures in parentheses below the parameter estimates are standard error and beside the χ^2 value are degrees of freedom.

Considerable identification problems were encountered if we left U^* unrestricted so we put it equal to 0.05. This is consistent with adaptive expectations estimate in Table 4.1.

Thus the evidence on crowding out is that we lack a suitable model to test the presence or otherwise of this effect. In the context of two different specifications of the Stein model, an adaptive expectations and a rational expectations one, in each of four cases, the model is rejected by the data. Conditional on that, P_5 is found negative and significant in one case (adaptive expectation; US 1960–78), positive and significant in another case (rational expectations; US 1960–78), positive, with a 't value' above one, in a third case (US 1960–73) and positive and nonsignificant in the UK case. Note also that β_1 the crucial parameter in the neoclassical demand for labour/supply of aggregate output equation, is negative in three out of four cases (but significantly only once) and nonsignificant in three out of four cases. The evidence for the surprise-only supply hypothesis thus seems weak. Since however the model is misspecified we must look at other evidence.

At various points above we have already surveyed the evidence on B(ii) which concerns the shape of the long run Phillips curve. Work by Solow, Parkin and others, now extensively surveyed, showed that both the speed of adaptive expectations and the coefficient of $\dot{p}^e$ in the Phillips Curve as less than unity. This literature has already been superseded by Lucas' work on the expectations scheme. So now $\alpha_2 = 1$ is not regarded as a proposition worth testing. In a rational-expectations world $\alpha_2 = 1$ by the requirements of rationality. So despite lack of evidence on $\alpha_2 = 1$, the economics profession has shifted its attention away from this hypothesis to the natural rate hypothesis.

C(ii) Is the path of 'real' variables independent of the path of policy variables? In turning to the natural rate hypothesis, we will look directly at the evidence for C(ii) because this involves testing the NRH in the context of a complete model rather than by a single equation approach as C(i). (See however Lucas (1973) for some tests favourable to his hypothesis in a single equation context.) Thomas Sargent (1976) has specified and estimated 'A Classical Macro-econometric Model of the United States' whose avowed aim was to be monetarist ('more monetarist than . . . the St. Louis model') and to incorporate the Sargent–Wallace (1975) proposition that an x percent model growth rule as suggested by Friedman is superior to any feedback rule.

Sargent describes his paper thus:

> This paper formulates, tests and estimates a version of the classical model that has its origin in hypotheses that place severe restrictions on the random behaviour of unemployment output and the interest rate. The model implies *that these three "real" variables are econometrically exogenous with respect to variables measuring monetary and fiscal policies.* As a consequence, government manipulations of monetary and fiscal policy variables have no predictable effects on unemployment, output or the interest rates and hence are useless for pursuing counter-cyclical policy.
>
> (Sargent (1976), p. 208, emphasis added).

Sargent therefore specified a model embodying a natural rate hypothesis along with rational expectations. He was thus implementing the research begun by Lucas in his 1972 paper on the 'Econometric Testing of the Natural Rate Hypothesis'.

Sargent's model had five equations:

a Lucas–Phillips Curve

$$\lambda(L)U_t = \gamma_1(p_t - E_{t-1}p_t) + \gamma_2 t + e_{1t}; \gamma_1 < 0, \tag{120}$$

a Labour Force Participation Equation:

$$\omega(L)f_t = \beta_1(p_t - E_{t-1}p_t) + \beta_2 U_t + \beta_3 t + e_{2t};$$

$$\beta_1 > 0, \beta_2 < 0, \tag{121}$$

a Production Function

$$y_t' = \alpha_0 t + \alpha_1(L)(f_t + pop_t - U_t) + e_{3t}; \tag{122}$$

an Interest Rate Equation

$$\delta_1(L)r_t = \delta_2(Z_t - E_{t-1}Z_t) + e_{4t}; \tag{123}$$

a Demand for Money Equation

$$(m_t - p_t) = \mu_1(L)r_t + \mu_2(L)y_t' + \mu_3(m_{t-1} - p_{t-1}) +$$
$$+ \mu_4 t + e_{5t}; \tag{124}$$

(We have generalised the presentation to take account of changes at the estimation stage.)

Here, m, p and y' are as before logarithms of the money stock (M), price level (P) and real output (y); U is unemployment, r the interest rate, f the logarithm of the labour force participation rate, which is defined as (L/POP) where L is total labour supply for POP, the total population; pop is the logarithm of POP, and Z a vector of exogenous variables. The errors e_i are assumed to be *mutually* and serially independent. Z, m and pop are exogeneous so the five equations solve for U, f, y', r and p, given the rational expectation of p and Z. In addition the exogenous variables are generated as autoregressive processes:

$$\phi_1(L)m_t = \epsilon_{1t} \tag{125}$$

$$\phi_2(L)Z_t = \epsilon_{2t} \tag{126}$$

$$\phi_3(L)pop_t = \epsilon_{3t} \tag{127}$$

Notice that (124) will be the LM schedule when combined with (125). So the IS curve is represented entirely by (123) which solves the interest rate in terms of exogenous variables. Then (120), (121) and (122) yield an aggregate supply curve to match the aggregate demand curve from (123) and (124). In (120) to (127), $\lambda(L)$, $\omega(L)$, $\alpha_1(L)$, $\delta_1(L)$, $\mu_1(L)$, $\mu_2(L)$, $\phi_j(L)$ are lag polynomials of various length determined at the estimation stage.

The model is recursive in its equilibrium formulation or, as Sargent puts it, for one-period-ahead forecast purposes. This is because

$E_{t-1} (P_t - E_{t-1} P_t) = 0$. So we can solve in turn for

$E_{t-1} U_t, E_{t-1} f_t, E_{t-1} y'_t, E_{t-1} R_t = \hat{\delta}_1 (L) R_t$ and so, given

$E_{t-1} y'_t$ and $E_{t-1} R_t$ and $E_{t-1} M_t$ (from (125)), we can

generate $E_{t-1} P_t$.

Thus all the real variable predictions are independent of the money supply which only affects prices. The recursive nature of the model dissolves when solving for actual values of variables since γ_1, β_1 are non-zero, these being the only two coefficients 'above' the diagonal in the B_0 matrix.

Sargent first carried out Granger-causality tests and Sims-causality tests on the endogenous variables with respect to a set of possible causal variables consisting of W the money wage, m, government surplus in real terms ($Rsur$), government expenditure in money terms ($\$G$) and in real terms ($G$). Of the various tests the most damaging to Sargent's prior restrictions seems to be the one that indicates W as causing U on both the Sims and the Granger causality tests. According to the Granger test, m causes U but not according to the Sims test. Also according to both the Sims and the Granger tests, r seems to cause m and W seems to cause r as well as U.

Thus by his own findings Sargent's model is misspecified in assuming m exogenous when it is not and omitting W which causes U and r. He does not however worry about the rejection of these restrictions, even by his own chosen method of estimation, i.e. by causality tests rather than likelihood ratio tests on restrictions. He proceeds to estimate the model in (120) to (124), but by IV methods rather than maximum likelihood methods. In particular the intra- and inter-equation, non-linear restrictions imposed by the rational expectations hypothesis are not incorporated as we did above in Table 4.2. (Of course, when Sargent estimated his model, Wallis' procedure had not been proposed.) Sargent estimated the equations for US quarterly data from 1951.I to 1973.III. All the lag lengths of $\lambda(L)$, $\omega(L)$, $\alpha_1(L)$ and $\delta_1(L)$ were four quarters. For the demand for money equation, Sargent set $\mu_3 = 0$ and experimented with four forms, (i) $\mu_2(L) = \mu_{20} = 1$, (SE = 0.0086) (ii) $\mu_2(L) = \mu_{20} = 1$, $\mu_4 = 0$, (SE = 0.01085), (iii) $\mu_2(L)$ of seven periods in length, (SE = 0.0056), (iv) as in (iii) but with $\mu_4 = 0$, (SE = 0.0058). Here SE is the standard error of the regression and in each case $\mu_1(L)$ is seven periods in length. While Sargent does not provide any likelihood ratio tests for the restrictions on the (i) to (iv) versions of equation (124), it would seem that $\mu_2(L) = \mu_{20} = 1$, i.e. specifying velocity as a dependent variable and $\mu_4 = 0$ can both be rejected and (iii) must be the preferred form.

For the other parameters, Sargent obtained

$$\tilde{\gamma}_1 = -0.287, \ \tilde{\gamma}_2 = 0.7(10^{-6}), \quad \tilde{\beta}_1 = 0.15, \tilde{\beta}_2 = -0.075,$$
$$\quad (2.0) \qquad (0.5) \qquad\qquad (0.9) \qquad\quad (1.9)$$

$$\tilde{\beta}_3 = 0.4(10^{-4}).$$
$$\quad (2.1)$$

Thus the labour force participation variable was independent of the deviation of price from expected price, the only simultaneous element being the significant value of $\tilde{\gamma}_1$. ($\tilde{\ }$ as before indicates IV estimates.)

At the conclusion of his paper, Sargent felt that despite the causality evidence from W on U and r,

> the tests have turned up little evidence requiring us to reject the key hypothesis of the model that government monetary and fiscal variables do not cause unemployment or the interest rate. The fact that such evidence has been hard to turn up ought to be disconcerting to users of the existing macro-econometric models, since as usually manipulated those models all imply that monetary and fiscal policy *do* help cause unemployment and the interest rate

> (Sargent (1976) p.236)

As we have already noted, his own analysis showed that the model on which Sargent bases these strong conclusions is misspecified. The crucial question then is, does the independence of U and r of monetary and fiscal policy arise from misspecifications in the model or do the data support such a conclusion? It turns out that, as in the cases before of FM and Stein, Sargent's conclusions are not borne out by the data when a proper systems test of the restrictions is carried out.

Such a test was carried out by Cuddington (1980). Cuddington formulates Sargent's exogeneity hypothesis in terms of Geweke's multi-equation tests described in chapter 3. Let the model be

$$B(L)y_t + C(L)x_t = \epsilon_t \qquad (128)$$

In a system such as (128), for x_t to be exogenous we require

Sims-causality: no future values of x enter (128), i.e. if we write $C(L)x_t$ as $C_1(L)x_t + C_2(L^-)x_t$ with L^- indicating future values then $C_2(L^-) = 0$.
Granger-causality: x_t can be determined without any influence of y_t.

In the context of (128) the real variables say $y = (U, r, y', f)$ are to be exogenous to the policy variables $x = (M, Rsur, G, SG)$ then writing down the system as a final form system as in (129) below the coefficients of x should be zero.

$$y_t = F(L)y_{t-1} + G(L)x_{t-1} + \eta_t \qquad (129)$$

So exogeneity requires $G(L) = 0$.

Cuddington estimates the four equations for each of the y variables by specifying eight lagged values of each of the four y, i.e. $F_1 y_{t-1}, \ldots$ $\ldots F_8 y_{t-8}$ where each F_i is a 4×4 matrix, and then adding for each x variable *separately* a sixth order lag, i.e. $g_j(L)x_{jt}$. So he had in each y_{it} equation 38 independent regressors and the joint test was that for each x_{jt} the twenty four coefficients in the four equations $g_{ij}(L) = 0$ for each j in all i.

When Cuddington carried out the exogeneity test equation by equation, he confirmed Sargent's results. But a systems test on all the equations together led to a *rejection* of Sargent's exogeneity hypothesis. The conclusion then is that the real variables U, r, f and y' are 'jointly caused' by each of the policy instruments. Thus Sargent's results seem to arise from his single equation assumptions imposing recursiveness as a restriction. This restriction is rejected when appropriate econometric techniques are used.

Thus a major plank of the new classical macro-economics, the natural rate hypothesis is rejected even when taking Sargent's model which, as we saw, already imposes an inappropriate restriction through the exclusion of money wages. Policy variables do seem to have predictive or causal information in them. The strong claims made for the natural rate hypothesis and rational expectations models have yet to be substantiated empirically.

This conclusion is strengthened if we examine some results provided in a study of the US and Germany by Sims (1980). Eschewing the use of economic theory for providing restrictions, Sims estimated a purely vector-autoregressive model on six variables — money wage (W), money stock (M), real GNP (y), unemployment (U), price level (P) and import price (Pm). For these six variables he estimated an unconstrained vector auto-regressive model of the form

$$y_t = \Sigma \, \phi_i \, y_{t-i} + \xi_t \tag{130}$$

This exercise will then involve 144 (6 × 6 × 4) parameters when there are four lags. Sims uses quarterly data for the US for the period 1949–75 and for West Germany for the period 1958–76. While there are some thorny technical problems (which are discussed by Sims) in using the standard F tests etc. when there are so many parameters to be estimated (24 in each equation), his results on exogeneity are similar to those of Cuddington. The block-exogeneity of the real sector with respect to money, i.e. the same assumption that Cuddington tested, was rejected for both the US and West Germany. An arbitrary shock (an 'innovation') in unemployment has feedback effects on the money supply and unemployment is also connected with output in the same way. The difference in the behaviour of the variables in the two countries to a monetary shock (innovation), Sims concludes, contradicts the classical rational expectation hypothesis (Sims (1980) p.32). He finds however that y, U and M are jointly exogenous with respect to W and P in the US though not in Germany. This implies that in Phillips Curve studies, unemployment can at least be taken as exogenous in the US, if not in West Germany.

The precise interpretation that one can put on these exogeneity tests is not clear. As Sims points out (Sims (1980), p.30), protagonists of the new classical macro-economics want real variables to be exogenous with respect to the money supply because they wish to argue for a monetary policy with no feedback, e.g. an x percent rule. If y is not exogenous, then that means in an equation such as (129), $G(L) \neq 0$. The strange thing here is that an old fashioned monetarist such as Friedman would base much of his argument on $G(L) \neq 0$ but then he would go on to say that lags as shown by coefficients of $G(L)$ were too long and variable to use monetary policy. New classical macro-economists wish to assign no part of the systematic variation in y to systematic components of monetary policy and thus they need exogeneity. For a Keynesian exogeneity is no problem at all either way. If y were found to be uninfluenced by x, then he would take it that money adjusted passively. But lack of exogeneity fits in with the inter-ventionist neo-Keynesian position where one uses monetary and fiscal policy actively for stabilisation purposes. Thus the rejection of exogeneity undermines the new classical position. These results, derived from systems tests of models, give a different message from single equation exercises.

Robert Barro has recently claimed empirical support for the proposition that only unanticipated changes in the money supply influence unemployment (Barro (1977)). We can look at this evidence briefly. Barro sets up a two equation recursive system

$$\beta_{11}(L)\Delta m + \beta_{12}(L)U = \gamma_{10} + \gamma_{11}(g - \lambda(L)g) + e_{1t} \qquad (131a)$$

$$\beta_{21}(L)(\Delta m - E_{t-1}\Delta m) + \beta_{22}U_t = \gamma_{20}$$

$$+ \gamma_{22}MIL + \gamma_{23}\overline{W} + e_{2t} \qquad (131b)$$

We have deliberately written a general version of Barro's models where he puts down *a priori* the lag length in each case. In (131a), $(g - \lambda(L)g)$ indicates the difference between the log of actual and 'normal' real government expenditure, 'normal' expenditure being derived by an adaptive scheme; $\beta_{11}(L)$ is the lag distribution attached to Δm, the growth of money supply with $\beta_{11}(0) = 1$. To impose recursiveness, Barro supposes that U_t does not appear in (131a), i.e. $\beta_{12}(0) = 0$. In (131b), MIL is a dummy variable for military conscription and $\overline{W}$ is the minimum wage (although this is a money wage and not a real wage as would be required by a fully neoclassical model).

Barro's method was to generate predictions of Δm from the *OLS* estimation of (131a) and treat the OLS residuals as $(\Delta m - E\Delta m)$. Then he regarded the significance of the $\beta_{21}(L)$ coefficients as a test of the RE hypothesis. From our discussion of the appropriate estimate of RE models, it is clear that the *OLS* residuals from (131a) ignore vital information in the structure unless we cannot reject the restriction that $\beta_{12}(0) = 0$, and that the errors are mutually uncorrelated at time t and serially uncorrelated with their own past values and the past values of the other error term. Barro certainly did not test these prior restrictions and hence his test of the rational expectations hypothesis is misspecified. Indeed the fact that the leading term in $\beta_{21}(L)$, i.e. $\Delta m_t - E_{t-1}\Delta m_t$

is significant in his *OLS* estimate of (131b) *prima facie* leads to the conclusion that $\hat{e}_{1t}$ and $\hat{e}_{2t}$ are likely to be correlated thus rejecting the recursiveness restriction.

Before we look at Leiderman's improved estimation of Barro's model (Liederman (1980)), let us examine the logic of Barro's model. Thus, surprisingly, prices appear nowhere in the model. The minimum wage is defined in money terms and not real terms and, *apropos* the Lucas–Rapping results and Lucas' aggregate supply hypothesis, (131b) must be misspecified since in equilibrium with $\Delta m = E\Delta m$, U depends on the minimum money wage as the only economic variable. Also if $g = \lambda(L)g$, then the steady state growth of the money supply is a function of equilibrium unemployment, i.e.

$$\Delta m^* = - \left(\sum_{i=1} \beta_{12i} \Big/ \sum_{j=0} \beta_{11j} \right) U^* \tag{132a}$$

$$U^* = \gamma_{20} + \gamma_{22} \, MIL + \gamma_{23}\overline{W} \tag{132b}$$

Where * indicates equilibrium value. Since no one, neither Keynesian, neo-Keynesian nor monetarist of any kind, has seriously argued that money growth depends on the minimum money wage, one must treat (131a)–(131b) as a system having no theoretic foundations. Barro's model also implies that, even in the steady state, money growth is uncorrelated with inflation, hardly a monetarist result!

Even treating it as a statistical artifact requires that we pay proper attention to the definition of rational expectations which imposes cross equation restrictions. Leiderman writes down (131a) and (131b) as

$$\beta_{11}(L)\Delta m + \beta_{12}(L)U = \gamma_{10} + \gamma_{11}(g - \lambda(L)g) + e_{1t} \tag{133a}$$

$$\beta_{21}(L)\Delta m + \beta_{22}U = \gamma_{20} + \gamma_{22} MIL$$

$$+ \gamma_{23}\overline{W} + \gamma_{24}(L)E_{t-1}(\Delta m) + e_{2t} \tag{133b}$$

The first requirement is to test $\beta_{21}(L) = \gamma_{24}(L)$. Leiderman calls this *structural neutrality*, i.e. systematic changes in money growth do not influence unemployment.

This however does not constitute a test of the rational expectations hypothesis. Leiderman substitutes the *single equation prediction* of Δm from (133a)

$$\Delta m = E_{t-1}\,\Delta m + e_{1t} = \beta_{11}\,(L)\Delta m_{-1} - \beta_{12}\,(L)U + \gamma_{10}$$

$$+ \gamma_{11}\,(g - \lambda(L)g + e_{it}$$

into (133b) to get

$$-\beta_{21}\,(L)\Delta m = \gamma_{24}\,(L)\,\beta_{11}\,(L)\Delta m_{-1} + (\beta_{22} + \beta_{21}\,(L)\beta_{12}\,(L))\,U$$

$$+ (\gamma_{20} - \gamma_{10}\,\sum_{j} \beta_{21j}) - \beta_{21}(L)\gamma_{11}(g - \lambda(L)g)$$

$$+ \gamma_{22}MIL + \gamma_{23}\bar{W} + e_{2t} - \beta_{21}(L)e_{1t} \tag{134}$$

An appropriate test of the rational expectations hypothesis then requires that (134) satisfies the restrictions across the different coefficients. Using the methods of Mizon (1977), Leiderman carried out a test of the restriction using a likelihood ratio test. He found that he *could not reject* either the structural neutrality assumption or the rational expectations hypothesis.

Thus Leiderman *confirmed* Barro's results. We need however to point out that his test is not comprehensive. Thus unlike Cuddington and Sims, he did not test the recursiveness assumption imposed on the system in (131a)–(131b). Nor as far as we can gather from reading his paper, did he check for dynamic misspecification caused by the omission of important variables like prices. Indeed Leiderman treated e_{1t} and e_{2t} as jointly normally distributed but not serially correlated. These would be good *a priori* reasons to doubt the validity of that assumption. Thus to strengthen Leiderman's confirmation of Barro's results it would be necessary to check that the system is not misspecified. It would be surprising if it came out that the system was not misspecified since the U equation violates the neoclassical homogeneity postulate!

We have found thus far that various pieces of empirical evidence advanced in favour of the monetarist argument, starting with Friedman's work in the 1950's through to recent work by Sargent and Barro, have been found to rest on invalid prior restrictions. Proper econometric estimation has shown that the claims made are either not sustained or, as in Barro's case if true, contradict elementary propositions of economic theory. Of course, this is hardly the end of the story. Much work is being done to provide additional support for the variants of monetarism, and future work may show some irrefutable evidence in favour of some monetarist proposition or other. For the present we may conclude that the velocity of circulation is not stable, the demand for money function has either not shown stability (Laidler), or, if stable, has nonmonetarist features such as the nonconstancy of *k* or the income velocity (Hendry—Mizon). We must also conclude that monetary and fiscal policy variables do have some effect on output, unemployment, prices and wages and interest rates and that the economy shows features of simultaneity rather than block recursiveness (Cuddington/Sims). There is just no evidence that commodity and labour markets work with the rapidity and flexibility required by neoclassical competitive general equilibrium theory. Only perhaps in sowing some *a priori* doubts on the naive Phillips Curve specification has the monetarist literature succeeded. Even here empirical evidence is lacking either for the absence of money illusion if expectations are adaptive, or for the natural rate hypothesis if expectations are rational.

The fashionable success of a theory has never been impaired by the lack of empirical support, or at least not very rapidly, in any science. It was pointed out early on, for instance, that Newton's theory did not account for the motion of the moon but this did not prevent the triumph and spread of his system. Similarly, monetarism in its old and new forms has spread. One particular variant of interest to us here is what is known as international monetarism.

International monetarism gained in fashion with the breakdown of the Bretton Woods system of fixed exchange rates. Persistent dollar deficits of the US, a result of the Vietnam War, the key currency position of the dollar which made dollar liabilities internationally acceptable but beyond the control of domestic monetary authorities of the countries on the receiving end of Eurodollar deposits, the deteriorating competitive position of the US and UK *vis-à-vis* Japan and the Newly Industrialized Countries, the 'global reach' of multi-national corporations — all this led to the establishment of flexible exchanges and the accompanying belief that domestic economic problems were both caused by, and the cause of, international influences. There was a great deal of interdependence among the advanced capitalist countries tied together by trade and capital flows.

Flexible exchange rate regimes revived interest in the *purchasing power parity* (PPP) theory. This theory has its roots in the Hume—Ricardo theory of the price—species flow mechanism which analysed the effects on domestic prices and economic activity caused by the flow of 'treasure' or of balance of payments surpluses and deficits. An automatic equilibrating mechanism was postulated whereby no permanent discrepancy in relative prices of commodities could persist between freely trading economies. In the aftermath of World War I, this idea was revived by Gustav Cassel to propose a theory of how flexible exchange rates would move. This is known as the law of one price or the PPP theory.[5]

The PPP theory states that the exchange rate (E) of any currency in terms of units of a foreign currency would be proportional to the ratio of the price level of the domestic country (P) to that of the price level of the foreign country (P'). Thus, the absolute version of PPP asserts

$$E = C(P/P') \tag{135}$$

where C is some constant. The transmission mechanism whereby variations in the ratio of price levels got reflected in the exchange rate was variously stated. Cassel's argument worked mainly through the effects of relative price changes on the export and import of goods. Rapid adjustment in prices (including wages) through demand and supply fluctuations were then postulated in order to derive (135). In a sense, the whole apparatus of the neoclassical market mechanism assumed by both old and new classical macro-economists is also assumed in the PPP. Of course, since not all goods get traded, some assumptions have to be made about the adjustment of prices of nontraded goods, (e.g. services, public goods) to those of traded goods.

Perhaps the best example of a policy based on PPP theory was Britain's attempt to get back on the pre-1914 dollar–pound parity. As Keynes forcefully argued in his *The Economic Consequences of Mr. Churchill* (1925), the Bank of England followed price movements in the US and the UK closely in deciding the timing of the restoration of the Gold Standard. It was perhaps this episode that finally turned Keynes against the PPP. Whatever the ratio of US to UK price levels in the months leading up to the restoration of the parity, subsequent events amply proved the folly of the decision.

In recent years, an alternative monetarist transmission mechanism known as the *monetary approach to the balance of payments* (MABP) has been proposed. This is to regard exchange rates as price of a country's money (and indirectly other financial assets denominated in the currency) for the world at large. Given a stable demand function for money in each country, exchange rate movements can be deduced from PPP working through the money and other asset demand functions (Frenkel and Johnson (1976)).

In the seventies, PPP and the MABP were all the rage. PPP was regarded in most international trade models or even in models for open economies (such as the UK) as a maintained rather than a testable hypothesis. It was the international equivalent of the absence of money illusion, the long-run vertical Phillips Curve, etc. As experience of flexible exchange rates has accumulated, early confidence in the truth of PPP has evaporated. Thus

Jacob Frenkel, one of the originators of the MABP, writes in his paper 'The Collapse of the Purchasing Power Parities During the 1970's',

> One of the striking facts concerning the relationship between prices and exchange rates during the 1970s has been the dismal performance of the predictions of the simple versions of the purchasing power parity doctrine (PPP) . . .. During the 1970s short-run changes in exchange rates bore little relationship to short-run differentials in national inflation rates and frequently, divergences from purchasing power parities have been cumulative.
>
> (Frenkel (1981))

In testing PPP, we come across the same set of econometric problems as we saw in reviewing Hacche's work on the demand for money. Thus normal econometric practice (Frenkel (1978), Frenkel (1979)) is to test (135) directly by taking logarithms and writing

$$e_t = \alpha_0 + \alpha_1 (p - p')_t + u_t \tag{136a}$$

where $e = \ln E$ etc. Many researchers wish to test the relative version of PPP which predicts that *changes* in E will be proportional to *changes* in the price ratio, i.e.

$$\Delta e_t = \alpha_0' + \alpha_1' \, \Delta(p - p')_t + \eta_t \tag{136b}$$

As we have seen above in our discussion of Granger–Newbold and Hendry–Mizon, both these equations may involve misspecifications. To take care of serial correlation in residuals, (136a) is often re-estimated after computing the first-order autocorrelation coefficient ρ from *OLS* on (136a) as

$$(1 - \hat{\rho}L)e_t = \alpha_0(1 - \hat{\rho}) + \alpha_1(1 - \hat{\rho}L)(p - p')_t + v_t \tag{137}$$

Equations such as (136a), (136b) and (137) are rather ad hoc and do not do justice either to the PPP theory or the problem of dynamic specification. Equation (136a) treats PPP as a theory which predicts that, at every moment, E should be proportional to (P/P'). This certainly is not the case, since theorists since Cassel have thought of (135) as a *long-run or equilibrium* level towards which actual exchange rates tend. The distinction between short-run disequilibrium movements and long-run equilibrium loci, which we encountered above in the works of Phillips, Friedman, Tobin, Hendry–Mizon, applies here. We must distinguish between the short-run and the long-run and at the same time make sure that the serial correlation properties of the errors are incorporated into our estimation.

Equation (136b), of course, does not yield a long-run equilibrium value at all.

Hali Edison has, in a series of studies of dollar–pound exchange rates, applied the methods of Hendry and Mizon (1976) to test the PPP theory. As a first step (135) is cast in testable form and then prior restrictions are specified. So we can write

$$\Delta e = \delta_0 + \delta_1 \Delta p + \delta_2 \Delta p' + \delta_3 e_{-1} + \delta_4 p_{-1} + \delta_5 p'_{-1} + \epsilon_t \qquad (138)$$

If PPP is to hold we require

   (i) Symmetry: $\delta_1 = -\delta_2$
  (ii) Homogeneity: $\delta_1 = -\delta_2 = 1$
 (iii) Long-run equilibrium $\delta_3 = -\delta_4 = \delta_5, \delta_3 < 0$

If restrictions (i), (ii) and (iii) are not rejected then the long-run equilibrium value of the exchange rate is given by

$$e^* = (p^* - p'^*) + (\delta_0/\delta_3) \qquad (139)$$

On taking exponents, (139) yields (135) with $C = \exp(\delta_0/\delta_3)$.

Equation (138) is a general specification which nests (136a), (136b) and (137) within it. Thus (136a) imposes

$$\delta_1 = -\delta_4 = \alpha_1$$

$$\delta_2 = -\delta_5 = -\alpha_1$$

$$\delta_3 = 1.$$

Equation (136b) imposes

$$\delta_3 = \delta_4 = \delta_5 = 0$$

$$\delta_1 = -\delta_2$$

These restrictions can of course be tested. The desirability of (138) is that it treats the equilibrium exchange rate as unobservable and allows the actual exchange rate to move in response to immediate changes in relative prices and to correct the discrepancy, if any, between previous values of the exchange rate and the predicted equilibrium value as given by the ratio of prices in the previous period. If the restrictions (i) to (iii) on (138) are satisfied, then we can be confident that *eventually* the actual exchange rate will tend to its PPP value.

The approach in (138), along with restrictions (i) to (iii) embodies the 'naive' PPP. It is naive because it does not fully specify the transmission mechanism whereby changes in relative prices get translated into changes in exchange rate. The *monetary approach to exchange rate determination* (MAEx), allows for this by treating the exchange rate as the price of a currency.[6] It postulates the following model:

There is a demand function for money in both countries which embodies the short-run–long-run distinction along the lines suggested by Hendry and Mizon:

$$\Delta(m - p) + \beta_0 + \sum_{i=1}^{5} (\beta_i \Delta(L) + \gamma_i L) x_i + \delta(L) m_{-1} + \xi_t \qquad (140a)$$

$$\Delta(m' - p') = \beta_0' + \Sigma(\beta_i' \Delta(L) + \gamma_i' L) x_i' + \delta'(L) m_{-1}' + \xi_t' \qquad (140b)$$

In (140a), the vector of independent variables x comprises real income, wealth, the short-term interest rate, the long-term interest rate and the price level, all in logarithmic form as is money supply. Then (140b) defines similar variables for the foreign country. The steady state demand functions can then be extracted from (140a)–(140b) by setting the dependent variable and all Δx_i equal to zero. The static demand for money equation only then becomes a special case of these dynamic demand functions.

We add to this a general dynamic version of equation (138).

$$\Delta e_t = \alpha_0 + \Sigma(\alpha_{1i} \Delta(L) + \alpha_{2i} L) q_i + \alpha_3(L) e + \epsilon_t \qquad (138a)$$

Here q comprises both p and p'. From (140a) and (140b), we can derive p and p' as functions of the x, x' variables and the money supplies m and m'. We substitute them into (138a) to derive our econometric equation for the MAEx version of the PPP. Such a reduced form equation would again need to be estimated bearing the restrictions in mind. Let us write generally

$$\Delta e_t = a_0 + \Sigma(a_{1i} \Delta(L) + a_{2i} L) z_i + a_3 e_{-1} \qquad (141)$$

where $z = (y, y', 1, 1', r_s, r_s', r_L, r_L', m, m', p, p')$

In z, y is income, 1 wealth, r_s the short-term interest rate and r_L the long-term interest rate. Just as we derived restrictions (i) to (iii) for (138), we can derive restrictions for (141).

(i) Homogeneity between prices and exchange rates $a_{2,11} = {}^-a_{2,12} = a_3$. The coefficient of levels of p, p' and e must match to appear in the form $(e - p + p')_{-1}$ as in (138).

(ii) Symmetry. Given (i) holds, coefficients of the independent variables of the two countries must appear with equal and opposite coefficients i.e. $a_{21} = {}^-a_{22}$, $a_{23} = {}^-a_{24}$, $a_{25} = {}^-a_{26}$, $a_{27} = {}^-a_{28}$, $a_{29} = {}^-a_{2,10}$, $a_{2,11} = {}^-a_{2,12}$.

(iii) Strong Proportionality. Subject to (i) and (ii), all the variables other than p, p' and e_{-1} must not appear in level form i.e. $a_{21} = {}^-a_{22} = a_{23} = {}^-a_{24} = a_{25} = {}^-a_{26} = a_{27} = {}^-a_{28} = a_{29} = {}^-a_{2,10} = 0$. This means that in the long-run E depends on (P/P') and C is a constant.

Edison calls condition (i) a weak test since it only assures that e, p and p' appear together in one expression. Condition (ii) is called a semi-strong test and (iii) the strong test.

Previous work on PPP and MAEx is shown by Edison to suffer from theoretical specification errors (lack of a well defined long-run equilibrium solution) and from econometric errors (serial correlation indicating dynamic misspecification, parameter instability). She carried out her analysis on three samples: the \$/£ exchange rate for the flexible exchange rate period January 1973 − September 1979 on a *monthly* basis; the twenties experience of \$/£, \$/FF, FF/£ where FF is the French franc (previously analysed by Frenkel (1978) who found his results supported PPP); and the long-run period from 1892 to 1972.

Since the results are similar across the three samples and as there would be a lot of numbers to list, we summarise the main points here.

For the twenties the naive PPP *did not* hold for the \$/£ exchange rate, though the \$/FF and FF/£ rate were well tracked by the price ratio. This implies, curiously, that triangular arbitrage conditions did not hold as far as the parameters were concerned. One suggestion to explain this is that the Bank of England was deliberately manipulating the Bank Rate to deflate the economy so as to affect the relative price level between the UK and the USA. This would indicate a sort of dirty floating on the part of the Bank. Since naive PPP implicitly assumes a purely competitive adjustment process, it fails to take account of policy variables of this sort. One would obviously need to analyse the PPP theory in an enlarged model allowing for the effects of dirty floating.

For the seventies data, Edison found that the weak test of homogeneity and the semi-strong test of symmetry were passed, i.e. the restrictions on the coefficients under (i) and (ii) attached to (141) *were not rejected*. But the strong test on the coefficients of the other independent variables failed, i.e. the restriction under (iii) *were rejected*. This result parallels Hendry and Mizon's result about the UK demand for money equation. In a stylised way, we can write the UK exchange rate behaviour as

$$E = C(^r s/^r_s, \, ^r L/^r_L, \, y/y', \, ^1/1', \, m/m') \, (P/P') \qquad \qquad (135a)$$

These results would indicate that there is a lot of scope for government policy in affecting the exchange rate even in long-run equilibrium. This then denies the neutrality results claimed by neoclassical, and especially by the new classical, macro-economists.

For the long period, there was a need to split the data since 1892–1913 was the period of the Gold Standard and 1914–25 and 1931–45 were periods of floating exchange rates with 1925–31 the brief adventure back on the Gold Standard. The post war period 1945–72 was again a period of fixed exchange rates. When exchange rates are fixed then in an equation such as (138), we need to reverse the order of variables as between dependent and independent. We can merely check if p moved in such a way in response to a change in p' so as to preserve the price ratio to the equilibrium level implied by the fixed exchange rate, i.e.

$$\Delta p = \delta'_0 + \delta'_1 \Delta p' + \delta_2 (e + p' - p)_{-1} + \epsilon'_t \qquad \qquad (138a)$$

Now when Edison ignores these structural breaks, takes the period 1892–1972 as a single homogeneous period and estimates (138), she finds that PPP cannot be rejected, i.e. she gets $e^* = 1.565 + (p - p')^*$ as the long-run solution and the restrictions (i) to (iii) attached to (138) are *not* rejected. This however leaves the causality question open since we know that for parts of the period Δe was zero or nearly zero (1892–1914, 1925–31, 1949–67, 1968–72).

When she tried a version of the MAEx model for the same period, 1892–1972, it turns out that she gets

$$e^* = 2.54 + (p^* - p^{*\prime}) - 0.421 \, (m^* - m^{*\prime}) \qquad \qquad (139a)$$

So again as in the seventies homogeneity and symmetry are *not* rejected but strong proportionality *is* rejected. The same pattern is repeated for each subperiod. While homogeneity and symmetry cannot be rejected, strong proportionality is always rejected. This is so even for the period of the Gold Standard where she gets

$$p^* = 1.57 + (p^{*\prime} - e^*) - 0.41 \, (y^* - y^{*\prime}) \tag{139b}$$

By contrast the Bretton Woods period showed

$$p^* = 1.33 + (p^{*\prime} - e^*) - 12.3 \, (r^* - r^{*\prime}) \tag{139c}$$

In all these cases the short-run variation in the dependent variable Δe or Δp was very well explained, and the fitted equation passed various diagnostic tests on a random residual correlogram, post sample parameter stability, possible high order autoregression in the residuals etc. Thus the long-run results do not arise from the underlying parameters being badly determined or nonsignificant. There is a persistent failure of the PPP hypothesis in its strong version.

The results on PPP and MAEx are in line with those on the demand for money and the natural rate hypothesis. The requirements for the strong monetarist doctrine to be upheld such as neutrality of real variables with respect to policy variables, independence of the velocity of circulation (or the Cambridge k) of any economic variables, the long-run strict proportionality of exchange rates to price ratio — are not fulfilled by the data. In each case the gains to be made by proper econometric care and the very partial basis of the support claimed for monetarist propositions are obvious. In the case of AM's reply to FM, Hendry and Mizon's to Hacche, Desai and Blake's to Stein, Cuddington's to Sargent and in Edison's work on PPP, the monetarist propositions are shown to be very restrictive with the data rejecting the restrictions.

In all these exercises, the model proposed by the monetarist school was accepted as a starting point. Rather than run a race between two rival models (among which it may often be difficult to decide anyway due to problems of testing non-nested hypotheses), we have summarised the accumulated experience over the last twenty years of testing the claims of monetarism on the monetarist's own specified basis. While such conclusions are always tentative and much more work will emerge in the future, we find that results of tests do not favour monetarism.

Is the Money Supply Exogenous?

We now turn to an objection of a different sort. In all the discussions so far, we have accepted the monetarists' argument that the money supply is exogenous and that it is controllable by the authorities. Many antimonetarists have questioned this assumption. It is argued for example by Galbraith in his book *Money* and elsewhere that the quantity theory may work well for an economy with only gold (or any single commodity) acting as a means of payment but with a credit-economy where money is created by the act of banks giving advances, the simple truths of the quantity theory no longer hold. Kaldor in his memorandum to the Select Committee already cited has most forcefully reiterated this proposition and backed up his argument by a quantitative study of many OECD countries' data.

Kaldor begins by ascribing three propositions to monetarists. These are: (a) that the economy, left to itself, is self regulating — the Invisible Hand, Walrasian Equilibrium or the natural rate hypothesis; (b) that there is no difference between a commodity-money economy and a credit-money economy; and (c) 'that successful control of the growth of the money supply will *in itself* exert a "downward pressure" in prices and thereby moderate the rate of inflation . . .'.

We have already dealt with (a). Kaldor's main contribution to the debate is to argue that in a credit-money economy since money is created by banks in response to loan-demands by private agents, the money supply is demand determined. Thus, while a commodity-money economy may suffer from excess supply involuntarily thrust upon it (e.g. by gold discoveries), in a credit-money economy individuals borrow money voluntarily and thereby allow banks to create money. Thus if there were an excess, since borrowing is costly, individuals will retire the excess by paying back the money. Thus the supply of money is demand determined and hence endogenous not exogenous.

This then ties in with the difficulty of defining what money is. Thus the proliferation of definitions of money, M_1, M_2, M_3, M1B, PSL_1, PSL_2 (matching the interwar discussion by Hawtrey and Keynes as we saw in Chapter 1), illustrates that narrowly or broadly defined money is only a part of liquidity in general. Kaldor thus reiterates the Radcliffe Report view as the correct one. This then means that a Central Bank cannot control the money supply directly.

> The Central Bank has no direct control over the amount of money held by the nonbanking public in the form of deposits with the clearing banks; its power is in determining the short rates of interest either directly through announcing a minimum lending rate, (or a re-discount rate) or indirectly through influencing the money market rates by open market operations. In the absence of quantitative controls over the clearing banks' lending or borrowing activities, it can only influence the rate of change in the volume of bank deposits held by the public through the effect of changes in the interest rates; these effects . . . . are highly uncertain. In the case of credit-money therefore in contrast to commodity-

money it is *never* true to say that the level of expenditure on goods and services rises in *consequence of* an increase in the amount of bank-money held by the public. On the contrary, it is a rise in the level of expenditure which calls forth an increase in the amount of bank-money . . . . In a credit-money economy, therefore the causal chain between money and incomes or money and prices is the reverse to that postulated by the quantity theory of money.

(Kaldor, pp.103–104).

Kaldor does not test his proposition by setting up an econometric model. He points to evidence listed in Table 4.3 about the inter-country variability in the velocity measure as well as the intra-country variability in different measures of velocity. Kaldor concludes that these differences cannot be systematically explained, as he had done previously in his evidence to the Radcliffe Committee. (Kaldor, p.108).

Table 4.3: *Percentage Changes in Ratio of Money to GNP for Various Definitions of Money: 1958–78*

	K_1 % change	K_3 % change	K_4 % change
Belgium	−35.6	2.2	1.0
France	−15.1	53.3	68.9
West Germany	2.9	86.1	NA
Italy	85.3	85.9	64.5[b]
Japan	47.8	74.6	9.9[c]
Netherlands	−24.8	31.5	24.5
Sweden	−16.4	7.0	−6.1[d]
Switzerland	−8.9	27.8	NA
UK	−16.6[a]	−14.0	12.9
US	−45.9	0.4	16.0

K_1 is M_1/Y, K_3 is M_3/Y and K_4 uses an even broader definition of money than M_3.

(a)   For 1966–78
(b)   For 1958–77
(c)   For 1970–77
(d)   For 1958–70

For his next piece of evidence on the endogeneity of the money supply, Kaldor shows that changes in Sterling M3 are better explained by bank lending to the private sector ($R^2 = 0.83$) than the unfunded element in the Public Sector Borrowing Requirement ($R^2 = 0.05$). This is for the years 1966–79. In turn, bank lending to the private sector is not well explained by PSBR ($R^2 = 0.01$. While the R^2 alone is not conclusive evidence in support of a hypothesis and Kaldor's equations need to be recalculated, the difference in the explanatory power of the two variables is quite striking. Both $R^2 = 0.05$ (ΔM_3 on PSBR) and $R^2 = 0.01$ (bank advances on PSBR) are not significantly different from zero.[7]

We can only conclude this chapter by saying that there are obviously many more articles we could have surveyed but we have chosen for their monetarist evidence the better writers — Friedman, Sargent, Stein, Sims and Barro. We have also dealt with writing where a certain degree of econometric sophistication was used. We hope to have shown that the evidence in favour of monetarism is less than overwhelming.

Notes

1. I have especially left out the proposition that 'there are long and variable lags between changes in money and its influence on income and prices'. This is because it seems that this proposition is irrefutable since any lag of a non-zero finite length can be described as long rather than short and since all our estimates are statistical point estimates with non-zero variance, they imply variability. Lags (as indeed all multipliers) therefore cannot fail to be of some length and some variability. This is then a portmanteau proposition. If a claim had been made that lags are short and constant (or stable) that would be a refutable proposition. Of course, refutability of any proposition has to be hedged by the complicated dialectical process about testing that I described in Chapter 3.
2. Professor Lord Kaldor: *Memorandum of Evidence on Monetary Policy* to the Select Committee on the Treasury and the Civil Service in the House of Commons Treasury and Civil Service Committee, Session 1979–80, Memoranda on Monetary policy, (HMSO, 1980) pp.86–130.
3. This phenomenon whereby, as soon as some statistical regularity is used for devising policy, it breaks down, has now come to be known as Goodhart's Law after Charles Goodhart of the Bank of England. See the correspondence in *The Times*, Brian Griffiths (4 February 1980), Charles Goodhart (8 February 1980).
4. The quotations are from Purvis (1980, p.115) which also surveys other contributions at the conference which concentrated almost exclusively on the theoretical aspects of the crowding out hypothesis. Criticisms of the crowding out hypothesis were made at the conference by Tobin and Buiter and by Ando and Modigliani from a theoretical viewpoint. Stein's was the only testable model. Stein's model was criticised on various grounds by Niehans and his empirical findings by Christ and Solow. See Stein (1976). Also for other criticisms Desai and Blake (1980).
5. This section on the PPP has benefitted very much from the research done by Hali Edison towards her Ph.D. dissertation on 'Testing PPP' under my supervision. I am grateful to her for allowing me to cite her results.
6. My treatment of MAEx is heavily derived from Hali Edison's unpublished Ph.D. dissertation.

7.   See Memorandum by Hendry in the House of Commons Treasury and Civil
      Service Committee: Monetary Policy Volume III Appendix 1 pp. 1–21 and
      S.G.B. Henry, D. G. Mayes and D. Savage: Memorandum by the National
      Institute of Economic and Social Research: House of Commons Treasury and
      Civil Service Committee, Session 1979–80. Memoranda on Monetary Policy
      (HMSO, 1980) pp.147–159.

5. HAS MONETARISM FAILED?

The question we now pose is a direct one and, if less amenable to a precise, technical answer, it is nonetheless urgent. Monetarism is an issue which engages the talents as well as the passions of economists because it is seen to have had a profound effect on the economic life of the advanced capitalist countries (we leave out, quite deliberately, other countries such as Chile and Israel that have also been subjected to a monetarist policy). As of the moment of writing (August 1981), unemployment in the UK is 2.85 million and rising. There are nearly half a million people who have been unemployed for over a year and the incidence of unemployment among the school leavers and the young is more than 30 per cent. There has been a decline in total output of 7 per cent since May 1979, when the present government came to power and a loss of 20 per cent in manufacturing output.

Yet despite the rise in unemployment and loss of output, the rate of inflation seems to be declining far too slowly. By June 1981, the annual rate of inflation was still 11.3 per cent, barely below its level the year previously. After a long spell of a high exchange rate for the pound sterling, there has been a fall in the exchange rate over the second quarter of 1981 renewing fears of a revival of inflationary pressures. The UK economic policy was seen as a deliberate monetarist experiment by various international observers such as the IMF, the Bank for International Settlements (BIS). As the BIS said in its 1980 report, 'economists and policy makers have for once been offered the possibility of observing an experiment akin to those available in the natural sciences. The outcome will no doubt have wider implications than its effect on the United Kingdom alone'. In its report a year later, the BIS warned 'that severe monetary restraint can hurt an economy's ability to produce'. Can we then conclude, as the Economics Editor of *The Times* did recently, that monetarism has failed? As he rather dramatically put it, 'The 1970s was the decade of monetarism. The 1980s are clearly shaping up to be the time when the theory is pushed back into the economic history section of the world's textbooks'.[1] As John Kenneth Galbraith put it recently,

> In a highly organised society, monetary policy works against inflation. But it works, experience now tells us, both unequally and by producing a high and enduring volume of unemployment and a severe recession in business activity. It is one of Britain's great, useful and painful contributions to economic understanding that it has shown that this is not an economist's construct; it is a matter of practical experience
>
> (Galbraith, (1981))

Enough has been said in the previous chapters to make it obvious that even in natural sciences, one should not expect a quick and unambiguous answer to emerge from an experiment. In the social sciences and even more in the realm of economic policy, any answer we glean from an experiment is bound to be controversial. We need therefore to put the question in a perspective so that before we arrive at an answer, we already can appreciate the limits of agreement.

To begin with, we concentrate on UK monetary policy partly as a result of much more intimate knowledge of this environment but also because the UK experiment is agreed by many to be crucial. In the US by contrast, though monetarism gained in influence through the seventies, we cannot say that a fully fledged monetarist policy has been adopted. This is partly because of the much greater diffusion of economic policy-making power in the US as between the Executive, the Legislature and the Federal Reserve System. While the Federal Reserve System took a much more 'monetarist' stance in the seventies compared to the sixties, it was only in October 1979 that it went over to publicly announced quantitative money supply targets. The Executive was not wholly committed to a monetarist stance until the advent of the Reagan Administration in January 1981. So while we shall refer to the US experience, our main emphasis is on the UK.[2]

Secondly we must define what we mean by a 'monetarist policy'. A monetarist policy, if it is to mean anything, must involve a declared emphasis on the regulation of growth of the money stock (however defined). Also the targets must be quantitative. The target growth rate need not be but may be constant — an x per cent money growth rule. The policy may be to announce targets for each year in advance or to announce a medium-term financial strategy. Lastly, the reliance may be purely on a policy of restraint on money growth or the monetary policy may be used in combination with other *macro-economic* policies such as incomes policy. (Of course there is a wide choice in structural or micro-economic (i.e. supplyside) policies to accompany monetarist or Keynesian policies.)

To be a pure monetarist policy, there should be no attempt to peg interest rates.

Policies can then be ranked on a scale of commitment to monetarism by the degree of variability in the monetary growth target (the less variable the more monetarist), the height of the growth rate (the less the height the more monetarist), the length of the pre-announcement (the longer-run the more monetarist) and by the predominance of monetary policy in the overall macro-economic policy mix (sole reliance on monetary policy being the most monetarist).

By this token, the Callaghan–Healey government from the fall of 1976 onwards was, partly as a result of IMF insistence, set on a mild monetarist course. After the first target announcement for 1976–7 (a growth rate of 9–13 per cent) in December 1976, already eight months into the year, targets were announced for the next twelve months in March 1977 (9–13 per cent), April 1978 (8–12 per cent), November 1978 (8–12 per cent). But there was also the use of incomes policies alongside monetary targets (plus various job subsidy schemes). All this makes the Callaghan–Healey experience a mild monetarist policy. (Mr. Healey has labelled his successor's policy 'punk monetarism', so perhaps we should label his policy 'jazz monetarism' since there was a great deal of improvisation in his days.)

By contrast, targets were announced for the 10 months to April 1980 by the new government upon taking office, and, in March 1980, a medium term financial strategy laid down the target growth rate for monetary growth until March 1984. There were also accompanying targets for PSBR and for PSBR as a proportion of GDP. There was also an announced refusal to resort to incomes policy as an additional weapon. Thus the policy from June 1979 onwards was much more of a purist monetarist policy than before (see Table 5.1 and Table 5.2).

This needs to be said because it has been argued already, and it will no doubt be argued in the future, that the Thatcher–Howe policy was not quite monetarist enough. Thus Peter Jay argued in *The Times* in February 1981 that the Callaghan–Healey policies were truly monetarist while those in force when Thatcher and Howe took over were not.[3] As we shall see later, the *outcome* on money supply growth did not match the *intention* of the Thatcher government, but to define policies by outcomes rather than intention can be circular. One may end up by defining a policy as truly monetarist only if it is successful. The failures of the present policy will no doubt be explained by some as due to insufficient severity, but that it was a monetarist policy cannot be denied.

In judging the success of the recent monetarist policy, we must also recognise that throughout the postwar period and especially since the

Table 5.1: Targets for Monetary Growth

Date when Target was set	Period of Target	$\pounds M_3$ Target	$\pounds M_3$ Actual
		(Annual Growth Rates)	
December 1976	12 months to April 1977	9–13%	7.7%
March 1977	12 months to April 1978	9–13%	16.0%
April 1978	12 months to April 1979	8–12%	10.9%
November 1978	12 months to October 1979	8–12%	13.3%
June 1979	10 months to April 1980	7–11%	10.3%
November 1979	16 months to October 1980	7–11%	17.8%
March 1980	14 months to April 1981	7–11%	22.2% (Dec. 1980)

Source: Select Committee on Treasury, Report p. xiv.

Table 5.2: Medium Term Financial Strategy

	March 80–March 81	March 81–March 82	March 82–March 83	March 83–March 84
$\pounds M_3$ Growth	7–11%	6–10%	5–9%	4–8%
PSBR (£billions at 78/79 prices)	6	5	3.5	2.5
PSBR/GDP	3.75%	3.0%	2.25%	1.5%

Source: Select Committee on Treasury: Monetary Policy, Vol III, Minutes of Evidence, pp. 10–11.

beginning of the sixties, the UK economy has had deep structural problems — de-industrialisation, steady loss of competitive power, regional disparities in growth, international adjustment to loss of empire, inner city decay etc. One can describe the UK economy as being perpetually deflated since 1966 except for the Heath–Barber boom. This was done in the early years to restore the balance of payments and to sustain an overvalued pound, and after the devaluation, to cope with inflation. This long record of deflation whereby successive governments were engaged in public expenditure pruning exercises contributed something to the structural problems of de-industrialisation, regional deprivation etc. One cannot expect short-term or even medium-term macro-economic policy to tackle these problems. So one must evaluate the short-run policy in terms of its objectives. What then are the objectives of the current monetarist policy?

Reducing the rate of inflation is the 'overriding priority' of the government. It set out to achieve this objective by setting a proximate target in terms of the control of the — sole instrument — money supply. But since the money supply is not directly controllable, the government set out to regulate public expenditure and PSBR to control the money supply.[4] All this, of course, requires that there be strong *causal* links from PSBR through money supply to inflation. We must also not have any feedback for the policy to work through. It is precisely because many economists are not sure that such one way links exist (Granger causality in the sense of Chapter 3), that there are doubts about a purely monetarist strategy. These doubts arise on many grounds.

In simple IS–LM models which are used in theoretical debates (Sargent–Wallace (1975), Stein (1974), McCallum (1980), one can construct situations with only one instrument and assume it to be controllable and causal. In such models, a budget deficit represents a net addition to excess demand and if translated into money growth leads to inflation. So by that logic a cut in the deficit and a cut in money growth leads to beneficial effects.

But as we have often said above, the high level of abstraction of these models while desirable for settling logical puzzles makes them a poor *descriptive* guide to the way the economy behaves. Thus in the UK, the government is also a seller of goods and resources whose prices enter the Retail Price Index. An element of subsidy in the prices of these goods can be financed from taxation or by borrowing. If such subsidy is cut in an attempt to cut PSBR, the immediate effect is an increase in the prices of those goods. This is not however only a once-for-all increase, since with a medium term financial strategy, targets for money growth being lower for each succeeding year, further cuts in the subsidy and a further increase in prices can only be expected. Similar arguments apply to the attempt to reduce the deficit by an increase in indirect taxes such as VAT. So we have a *rise* in the inflation rate as a consequence of a planned *cut* in PSBR.

Similarly in these models there may be no output or employment effects except temporary ones due to deviations of actual from (rationally) expected inflation. In actual economies, these conclusions have to be qualified unless one can believe, as do some rational expectations theorists, that it is the world's fault if it does not conform to the model. But while the monetarist view has had its best success in explaining how inflation can accelerate, it has had less success in modelling how the economy will react to a cut in money supply designed to bring about a deceleration of inflation. It is often readily assumed that just as the rise in inflation is steep with only a mild increase in unemployment, the decline in inflation will be similarly mild.

The House of Commons Select Committee posed this question explicitly to its witnesses.

> What evidence is there of the magnitude of output and employment reduction required to achieve a reduction of inflation from its current level [April 1980, when it was rising from 16 per cent during 1980.I to about 20 per cent during 1980.II] to single figures by 1982? What will be the effects on investment and the potential for future growth?
>
> (Question B18).

To this, Milton Friedman replied

> The best evidence is from the prior experience of the UK and other countries. As I read that experience . . . and the experience of Japan since 1973 seems to me most relevant, I conclude that (a) only a *modest reduction in output and employment will be a side effect of reducing inflation to single figures by 1982* and (b) *the effect on investment and the potential for future growth will be highly favourable*
>
> (Select Committee (1980), Memorandum on Monetary Policy, p. 61)

Patrick Minford, in answer to the same question, said

> The simulations of our model suggest that on the assumptions that policies are properly understood when they are announced and implemented, *the disturbance to output and employment from reduction in the money supply and in the PSBR would be minimal*

The qualifying clause is a possible let-out for the witness but in his written evidence after arguing that the Liverpool model had a better 'track record' than the National Institute model on inflation and was about the same on output, Minford reproduced a table of comparative forecasts (Table 5.3). Thus Minford was in general agreement with Friedman. David Laidler as the other leading monetarist witness was somewhat more cautious,

> I do not believe that we have any idea to within two or three percentage points just what the level of unemployment would currently be sustainable in the British economy if indue upward pressure on inflation was to be avoided.

Table 5.3: Comparitive Forecasts

	Output Growth				Inflation			
	Treasury	NIESR	LBS	Liverpool	Treasury	NIESR	LBS	Liverpool
1980	−2.5	−0.5	−1.7	0	16.5	15.8	17.7	16.5
1981	−0.7	2.0	0.4	1.6	13.0	13.0	14.1	9.0
1982			2.4	2.9			9.0	8.1
1983			2.5	2.7			7.7	4.3

Source: Select Committee, op. cit., pp. 131–143.

Let us now take a look, by contrast, at the actual outturn of events. In Chart 5.1, we illustrate the UK experience of inflation ($\dot{P}$) and unemployment (U) from 1956.I to 1981.II. In the left hand corner are squeezed the first thirteen years of the period where the P/U pattern is much as was predicted by the Phillips Curve (magnified in Chart 5.2). Many of the loops are counterclockwise and there appears to be a negative relationship between $\dot{P}$ and U. From 1969.I we see a contrast. The Roy Jenkins policy of post devaluation deflation (bringing the budget into a *surplus* the only year in the postwar period) raised the level of unemployment, after a lag, to a postwar high of 4 per cent by 1971.I. Inflation had risen from around 5 per cent in 1969 to about 8 per cent in 1971. The Heath-Barber boom then worked to lower the level of unemployment to a low figure of 2 per cent by 1973.IV. Inflation was still in single figures at this time. But while the government was using an incomes policy to restrain wage growth it was fuelling the economy to run at very high levels of employment. The OPEC oil price rise of October 1973 thus came on top of a booming economy. In the next two years, the rate of inflation more than doubled to reach a peak of 24 per cent by 1975.IV. Unemployment rose to 5 per cent by then.

Looking at the diagram for 1969.I to 1975.IV, we see the similarity with Friedman's analysis of hyperinflation in a Phillips Curve context. This is now reproduced as Fig. 5.1. We have drawn a vertical long-run Phillips Curve with several short-run Phillips Curves rising up with

Chart 5.1: Inflation and unemployment in the UK, 1956.I to 1981.I

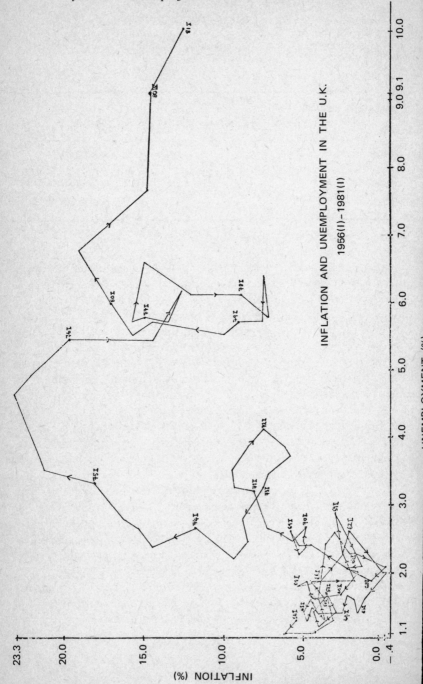

INFLATION AND UNEMPLOYMENT IN THE U.K.

1956(I)–1981(I)

Chart 5.2: Inflation and unemployment in the UK, 1956.I to 1968.IV

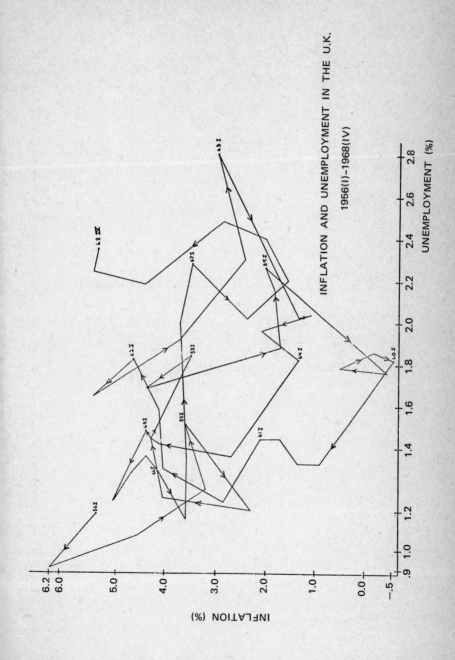

INFLATION AND UNEMPLOYMENT IN THE U.K.

1956(I)–1968(IV)

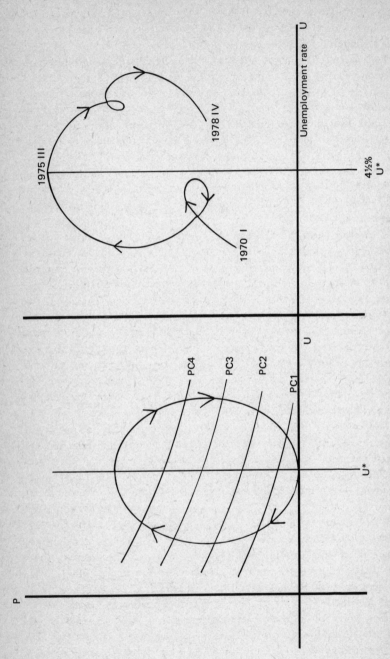

Figure 5.1: A Stylised Interpretation of UK Inflationary Experience 1970–1978

different levels of expected inflation PC_1 to PC_4. The stylised clock-wise loop around the long-run Phillips Curve then shows the process of hyperinflation.

The effects of monetary deceleration are symmetric to those of monetary acceleration. This is the message behind Friedman's citing of the UK experience of 1972–5 as relevant for predicting limited effects of deceleration. When we look at the data a slightly different picture emerges. From the peak inflationary rate in 1975.IV, inflation came down, not steadily (see the upward loop in 1977), to a low level of under 10 per cent by 1978.I and stayed below 10 per cent throughout 1978. The annual rate was 24.2 for 1975, 16.5 for 1976, 15.8 for 1977 and 8.3 per cent for 1978. In Fig. 5.2 we have drawn a stylised picture of the British data alongside the Friedman diagram. These two seem to match quite closely.

Remember however that the Callaghan–Healey macro-economic policy was not purely monetarist. While money supply growth was thought to be curbed and for two out of the three years the government even succeeded by some miracle in keeping the actual M_3 growth within the target, the role of incomes policy must not be forgotten. The breakdown of Phase 4 of the Callaghan–Healey policy in 1979.I has been taken to be a general failure of all incomes policy, but the lessons to be learnt there are perhaps different as we shall see later. In any case there was a combination of monetary and incomes policies. Unemployment had now gone up to 6 compared to about 4 per cent in 1975. This rise in unemployment was no doubt partly due to the deflationary policies pursued but also partly due to the longer run structural reasons mentioned above.[5]

The events of the economy from 1979.III onwards fall mostly in the realm of the new government. Inflation was at 10 per cent in 1979.II and unemployment was at about 5½ per cent. In the next year, from 1979.III to 1980.III, inflation rose from 10 per cent to a peak of 20 per cent and unemployment to 7 per cent. In terms of numbers of unemployed (excluding school leavers) the figures (annual averages) were 1.27 million for 1976, 1.377 for 1977, 1.376 for 1978, 1.303 for 1979 and 1.646 for 1980. These figures being annual averages even hide the dynamics of the unemployment variable which is best seen in Chart 5.1. While inflation fell from a peak of 20 per cent in 1980.II to 15 per cent in 1980.III and about the same level in 1980.IV, unemployment increased from 7 to 9 per cent inside six months. Taking one percentage point of unemployment to represent around 250,000 people, half a million were added to the unemployed register in those six months. By 1981.I inflation had fallen to just under 14 per cent and unemployment had reached 10 per cent. In 1981.II, inflation was about 12.5 per cent and unemployment higher still. The shape of the $\dot{P}/U$ scatter in Chart 5.1. from 1979.I to 1981.II looks totally unlike the Friedman picture in Fig. 5.1. There is another upward loop and if anything the curve lunges out towards high unemployment with very little gain in reducing inflation.

How would a monetarist explain away this large increase in unemployment for a very small (if any) gain in inflation reduction over two years? We offer two likely explanations. In Fig. 5.3, we postulate that the monetarist may argue that the natural rate of unemployment increased (and is still increasing?). Thus the vertical Phillips Curve shifted from, say 4½ per cent in 1975 to 6 per cent in 1978. The Callaghan–Healey episode of decline in inflation between January 1976 and April 1978 will be explained away as a temporary loop not indicating any fundamental improvement. By this token, the natural rate of unemployment may have again increased. As to why it should increase, various answers may be given in terms of the levels of unemployment benefits, the low-income tax-trap which puts a more than 100 per cent marginal tax rate for those coming off the dole and into low wage employment etc. But since the real value of benefits has not been increasing over the last two years, this explanation

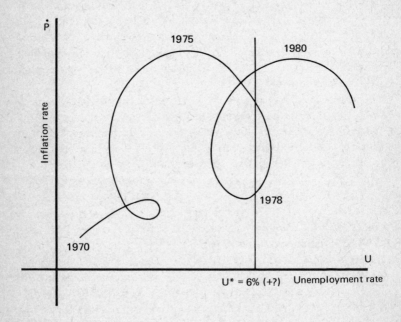

Figure 5.3: Broad Loop Around a Constant NRU

is hardly adequate. It may also be a little circular since it may only say the natural rate of unemployment is whatever the actual level is.

An additional explanation with a shifting natural rate of unemployment is to blame the rise in unemployment on misinformation on the part of the workers. This story is that the government having announced a target for M_3 growth, workers should immediately translate this into an appropriate (lower) rate of expected inflation and adjust their wage bargaining accordingly. If they don't, then unemployment will result with employers going bankrupt due to monetary stringency. We examine this explanation in some detail below.

An alternative monetarist explanation could be that the natural rate of unemployment is constant say at 6 per cent but that the adjustment loop is larger. This is the picture in Fig. 5.4, where again a stylised diagram is drawn. By this token, it will be a long time before the adjustment is completed. The Callaghan–Healey success in reducing inflation will again have to be explained away here. This would imply that the two year experience was a temporary 'blip' but that the full adjustment will take many years. This is the convenient long-run of the economist.

It is not entirely obvious whether the adjustment will either ever take place, or, if it does, will do so at a reasonable cost. The confidence that it

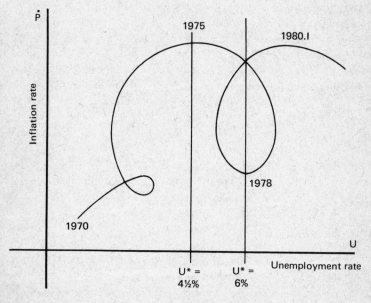

Figure 5.4: Narrow Loop Around Shifting NRU

will take place 'eventually' requires confidence in the natural rate hypothesis either in the Friedman adaptive expectations version or in the Lucas–Sargent rational expectations version. As we have seen in Chapter 4 however, the evidence does not favour either of these hypotheses. While *a priori*, one may want to believe that a Walrasian world of rational competing individuals ought to behave like this, it seems unlikely that the actual economic world does behave like this.

What then is the explanation of the UK experience? There is no doubt that the monetary restraint has worked on output and unemployment directly and severely. It has affected inflation indirectly if at all. The effect of reduced money growth on inflation comes via depressing wage rises by increasing unemployment. Since the government is working with only one instrument — money supply — and its effect on its objective — inflation — is indirect, there would appear to be a long period of painful adjustment at the end of which there is no guarantee that either inflation or unemployment will come down. The Callaghan–Healey policy was to affect inflation and inflationary expectations via incomes policy directly and to use monetary policy to keep unemployment at a level consistent with that desired level of inflation.

A simple argument can be sketched here. (For details see Desai (1981c). This is not as yet fully worked out on the empirical side but the evidence so far seems to indicate that the model has good data support. Preliminary results are in Desai and Blake (1981c).

We have a short run Phillips Curve with $\dot{p}^e$ and U as arguments in the $\dot{w}$ equation but the previously achieved level of real wage sets a floor which the workers fight to preserve. The real wage resistance hypothesis has much support in UK data (Henry, Sawyer and Smith (1976)). So we have

$$\dot{w} = a_0 + a_1 U + a_2 \dot{p}^e + a_3 (w-p)_{-1}. \tag{140}$$

Prices are determined by unit labour costs but employers try to maintain an equilibrium share of profits (or an equilibrium mark-up) by adjusting prices upward in the face of real wage resistance:

$$\dot{p} = b_0 + b_1 (\dot{w}-\dot{q}) + b_2 (w-p-q)_{-1}. \tag{141}$$

Here q is log of output per worker. The term $(w-p-q)$ is the logarithm of the share of wages in total income or the reciprocal of the mark-up factor. Notice that we have added the term $(w-p)$ in the wage equation and $(w-p-q)$ in the price equation in order to obtain satisfactory equilibrium solutions, as we illustrated in the Hendry–Mizon study of the demand for money and the Edison study of PPP.

Unemployment, in our argument, is not independent of monetary (or fiscal) policy. This is where we depart from the monetarist view of both the Friedman and Lucas variety. The rejection of the exogeneity assumption required by the natural rate hypothesis in the Cuddington and Sims papers seems a fairly comprehensive settlement of the argument. We posit a connection between money supply and unemployment via a mechanism, outlined in the *General Theory* (Chapter 19) that Tobin has again recently brought to our attention under the label of the *Keynes Effect* (Tobin (1980c)). Keynes, in analysing the impact of a money wage cut on aggregate employment (with a given level of money supply), traced the effect as equivalent to a rise in money stock per wage unit (with wage unchanged). This, he said, left entrepreneurs with more money than they needed for meeting prime labour costs and hence, via the speculative motive, led to a fall in the interest rate and hence an increase in aggregate demand and employment. Thus it was the effect of a change in (M/W) that, for Keynes, had an effect on U via the rate of interest.

Though this is a rather brief sketch of Keynes' argument, it can be used to illustrate our point that the money supply acts on income and employment primarily, and not on inflation. So we add to the above

$$\Delta U = \delta_0 + \delta_1 (\dot{m} - \dot{w}) + \delta_2 \Delta r + \delta_3 (m-w)_{-1} - \delta_4 U_{-1} \quad (142)$$

We expect $\delta_1 < 0, \delta_2 > 0, \delta_3 > 0, \delta_4 > 0$.

With this model, let us now seek to understand the monetarist diagnosis and its failure. Recall that we cited Minford's evidence concerning the effect of a money supply deceleration on output and unemployment: 'on the assumption that policies are properly understood when they are announced and implemented', he said there should be no adverse effects. Again, he said, in reply to the question

How do you expect the change in the objectives of economic policy, indicated in the letter from the Chancellor to affect economic performance? Specifically, is there any risk that ending the postwar commitment to high employment may permit a return to prewar conditions of unemployment?

The objectives of the present government do not in any view imply any likelihood of a return to prewar conditions of unemployment. The view that this could be so is based, wrongly in my view, on the assumption that expectations of inflation and of equilibrium real wages will not adjust to the new policies. Clearly if unions demand and firms concede real wages that are not appropriate to changed market conditions then unemployment will result. Similarly if wage increases, for

example of 20-30 per cent are awarded systematically, when money supply growth is running systematically at say 7 per cent, that too implies an increase in unemployment. But there is *no reason either in economic theory or from empirical evidence* to expect this
(Select Committee, vol. II, Minutes of Evidence, p. 17, emphasis added).

To make sense of this answer in the light of experience we would have to say that either the economic theory or the evidence which led to this conclusion must have been grossly in error. We have already cited our reservations concerning both in previous chapters. But we can see the flaw in the model implicit in Minford's statement by putting it in the context of our simple framework above. The steps are as follows.

Unemployment is determined by 'real forces' and is exogenous to the money supply (despite evidence from Cuddington and Sims, cited above, against exogeneity). So we drop our ΔU equation.

Inflation is explained by the quantity theory as

$$\dot{p} + \dot{y}' = \dot{m}$$

where $\dot{y}'$ is the rate of growth of real output, also exogenous to the policy sphere. So we replace our $\dot{p}$ equation by the equation above.

In the wage bargain, there is no money illusion ($a_2 = 1$), there is no real wage resistance ($a_3 = 0$).

On these bases, the monetarist sees the government as setting a desired level of money supply growth $\hat{m}$ which signals a desired rate of inflation $\dot{p}^d$ plus an allowance for productivity growth. The latter is there because with $U = U^*$, $\dot{y}'$ equals $\dot{q}$. So we have

$$\hat{m} = \dot{p}^d + \dot{q} \tag{143}$$

Now if the above assumptions are granted, then unemployment will stay at its natural level if workers adopt as their $\dot{p}^e$, the government's signal $\dot{p}^d$. So the workers, to maintain U at U^*, must completely disregard the experience of past inflation or even the previous inability of governments to achieve their targets. If they do not do these things, unemployment is the workers' own fault.

Since wage settlements have been falling over the last two years while unemployment has been going up, since the government has shown a singular inability to achieve M_3 targets in 1980-81 and since inflation has proved resistant to monetary control, we believe the blame, for unemployment being at the 1930's level, rests with faulty theory and not with those who bargain.

Consider our alternative explanation: that workers expect inflation to be similar to past inflation (adaptive expectation), that there is some money illusion but there is also real wage resistance, that prices are governed by labour costs and a desire on the part of employers to maintain the mark-up at some equilibrium level and that unemployment is influenced by money growth. In such a world in equilibrium with $\dot{p} = \dot{p}^e$, $\Delta r = 0$ we get from (142) – (144)

$$\dot{w} = [(a_0 + a_2 b_0 - a_2 b_1 \dot{q}) + a_1 U + (a_2 b_2 + a_3)(w-p) - a_2 b_2 q]/$$

$$(1 - a_2 b_1) \tag{144}$$

$$U = \delta_0 / \delta_4 + \delta_1 / \delta_4 (\dot{m} - \dot{w}) + \delta_3 / \delta_4 (m - w) \tag{145}$$

Fig. 5.5: The Phillips Curve and the Keynes Effect Curve

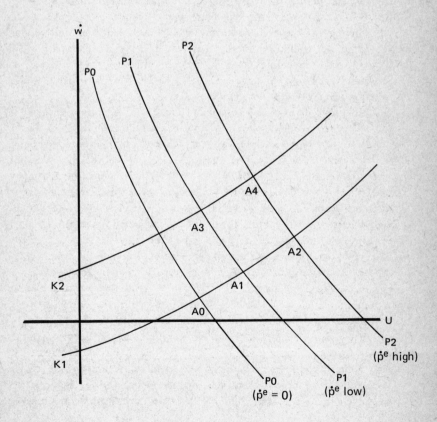

We have here a long run Phillips Curve (146) which is not vertical $(1 - a_2 b_1) > 0$ and another curve (147), the Keynes Effect Curve, which traces the simultaneity between U and $\dot{w}$. Fig. 5.5. illustrates these two curves. The Keynes Effect curve shifts about as money supply growth changes for a given level of money stock in wage units. Similarly the position of the Phillips Curve is determined by the equilibrium real wage level.

The long-run Phillips Curve slopes down, of course, since $a_1 < 0$ and the Keynes Effect curve slopes upwards, since $\delta_1 < 0$ and $\delta_4 > 0$. In Fig. 5.5, $P_1 P_1$ is a Phillips Curve with low inflationary expectations, the effects of which come through the constant term $a_2 b_0$. $P_2 P_2$ is a higher Phillips Curve which has shifted due to higher inflationary expectations. $K_1 K_1$ is the Keynes Effect curve with $\dot{m}$ low and $K_2 K_2$ has $\dot{m}$ high.

Now we can conjecture that incomes policy works directly by lowering price expectations (i.e. lowering $a_2 b_0$) so $P_1 P_1$ is the curve with an effective incomes policy. If the government then also maintains a low $\dot{m}$, then we shall have a low inflation, medium unemployment equilibrium at A_1. Abandoning incomes policy and relying solely on $\dot{m}$ gives us a high unemployment and medium inflation. If we run an incomes policy plus a high $\dot{m}$, we have low unemployment and medium inflation at A_3, but such an incomes policy may break up, shifting the Phillips Curve, to give high inflation and medium unemployment at A_4.

This simple diagram in our opinion illustrates the various episodes in the UK economy in the seventies and makes sense of chart 5.1. In the late sixties the Phillips Curve was over to the left of $P_1 P_1$ and $\dot{m}$ was low under Jenkins. We draw this $P_0 P_0$ ($\dot{p}^e = 0$) for illustrative purposes. The equilibrium is at A_0. Rising inflationary expectations lead to a rightward shift of the Phillips Curve to give A_1 as the new position. The Heath-Barber policy then is to have high $\dot{m}$ with incomes policy taking the economy to A_3. The breakdown of incomes policy, rising inflationary expectations and high $\dot{m}$ in 1974-5 led the economy to A_4. From there, a combination of low $\dot{m}$ and incomes policy brought the economy to A_1 under Healey-Callaghan. The breakdown of that incomes policy and the abandonment of any incomes policy in 1979-80, together with high $\dot{m}$, moved the economy to A_4. As money supply growth comes down the economy shifts towards A_2 with high unemployment.

We can only claim that this is a plausible alternative explanation. It allows for price expectations without invoking a vertical Phillips curve and monetary policy acts here through its effect on unemployment. No doubt when econometric evidence emerges to back up this story, it will be subjected to the same rigorous tests we have insisted on for other models, but it seems to make sense of UK experience of the seventies that the simple monetarist models do not.

Our explanation also indicates that the reliance on $\dot{m}$ alone will continue to mean high unemployment unless means are somehow found to soften the impact of monetary restraint on output. If the government relies on inflationary expectations coming down then the only hope is that over the long run the Phillips Curve would shift to the left along the $A_1 A_2$ portion of the $K_1 K_1$ curve.

The problems in the US economy, which we can only briefly discuss, are different. For one thing, the structural problems of the British economy have not yet visited the US economy. The main structural change it faced ..ı the seventies was the realisation of external limits to its growth potential. While the dollar was the key currency in the sixties, its overvaluation imposed little external constraint on the ability of the economy to grow by means of domestic stimuli. But the Vietnam war deficits, the reluctance of European countries to hold dollar liabilities, and the OPEC oil price rise in the context of its energy intensive production structure made the US much more of an open economy in the seventies than before. This meant that the price of domestic inflation was a loss of international competitiveness, the threat of inroads by foreign capital into the US and an erosion of profitability.

In his summary of the US economy, Tobin emphasises the rise in the prices of raw materials and energy as the main cause of the US recession. He also traces some of the macro-economic problems to the greater variability of monetary policy. But he shows how policies to control the nominal money stock in the US, as in the UK, made real output much more volatile rather than let prices make the adjustments, as monetarists would have it. In a simulation study of the possible effects of a steady monetarist disinflation, Tobin shows that to bring down the growth of nominal income from 12 to 2 per cent, at a quarterly rate, over ten years would have a great impact on unemployment. Such a policy in Tobin's model leads to unemployment increasing for seven years before it starts falling. Tobin starts the economy at 1980 values of 10 per cent inflation and 6 per cent unemployment. The latter is also the natural rate of unemployment. It takes twenty years before the economy is even close to the desired inflation rate of zero, at $U = 6$ per cent. These twenty years form a loop in which unemployment increases from 6 to 10 per cent in seven years, then falls in the eighth year to 4 per cent and then rises again to 7 per cent.

This is of course a stylised story but it agrees closely with the UK experience. But as Tobin says,

> It is far from certain that society has consensus on how the burdens of real economic reverses should be shared, or even how such questions could be decided. An economic path anything like [the one described above] will probably be politically divisive.[6]

When the monetarist experiment was initiated in the UK by the present government, it was said the American politicians were watching with interest. The social stability for which Britain was renowned promised a better testing ground for the experiment than the US could have provided. The riots in the summer of 1981 have shaken much of the complacency about social stability in Britain.

None of what we have said above will solve the longer run problems of growth, employment and investment. The steady erosion in British productive capacity, the wastage of human potential, the long run effects of continuous cuts in capital expenditure on health, education and social services by successive governments, have not been touched by our analysis. These problems are not easy of solution, but a short-run macro-economic policy should not aim to tackle them. What it should do is to establish the environment for confidence for private and public agencies to invest in the future. The present policy is to rely on a reduction of inflation by monetary means as the sole key to future growth. Apart from invocation of the free market, there is no other policy but the medium term financial strategy. Its effect has been to impose enormous short-run costs in terms of unemployment and lost output without holding out any hope that the future will be better.

Monetarist theory and monetarist policy put overwhelming if not exclusive emphasis on the reduction of inflation through reduction of money supply. They invite us to ignore the appalling effects on unemployment by alternately invoking the long-run or rational expectations or some incantation of laissez faire theory which treats all unemployment as voluntary. The doctrine has won support despite persistent attempts at pointing out theoretical and empirical flaws in its argument. The appeal of monetarism is ultimately the appeal of all conservative economic theory. It uses the reduction of inflation via monetary control to create a condition in the labour market similar to that which prevailed in the years before the Second World War. Such conditions alone it believes can permanently weaken the strength of labour so as to moderate their inflationary wage demands. To restore profitability one needs to cut real wages. The reduction of inflation via the control of money supply increases unemployment in the hope of cutting real wages. But such a policy has to contend with political realities.

Laissez faire theory prevailed in government policy practice in the nineteenth century since workers were weakly organised, did not have the franchise and had only limited access to the state. This allowed the state to ignore with impunity the cyclical and secular course of unemployment. The growth of the franchise, of political rights of free speech and association weakened the hold of laissez faire. Statesmen and politicians were required to be responsive to popular demands. It was Keynes' genius to propose an economic arrangement which could reconcile political democracy with the economic market place. Some, like Beveridge and Kalecki, saw that there were tensions inherent in maintaining full employment in a political democracy with the economic market place.

But full employment and economic prosperity were maintained at an unprecedented level for nearly twenty-five years. Indeed full employment itself made the neoclassical doctrines come back into full play. The economic marketplace (especially in the labour market), full employment and political democracy have proved an explosive combination. Profit shares declined in most advanced countries. When finally the upsurge in raw material prices provided the catalyst which converted the mild inflation of the fifties and sixties into hyperinflation of the early seventies, the laissez faire theorists saw their chance and took it.

But a monetarist policy can only work if a government can stay immune from popular pressure, as nineteenth century governments could. It requires a long period of high and increasing unemployment to achieve its true goal of altering the balance of power between labour and capital in post-Keynesian societies. This is the long period for which unemployment must remain unnaturally high before converging to its natural rate. Cycles could be long or short in the nineteenth century. In this day and age, it would be surprising if such a long period was allowed to any government, any government that seeks to maintain democratic institutions. This is the real test of monetarism.

Notes

1. David Blake: Why has Monetarism Failed, *The Times*, July 13, 1981. The quotation from the BTIS report is taken from this article.
2. See for a survey of US policies in the 1970s Tobin (1980a) and (1981).
3. Peter Jay, *The Times*.
4. See on this, the House of Commons Select Committee on Treasury and the Civil Service Report, Chapter 5.
5. We no doubt wish to enter into the debate as to whether this was a socialist policy or into other e.g. income distributional consequences of this policy.

Nor should our analysis be implied to suggest that this was the only policy available to the Labour government at that time. We merely wish to concentrate on macroeconomic policy as it was actually implemented.

6.   Tobin (1980a). The interpolation in the square brackets is a reference to Figure 6 on p. 67 in Tobin's article which embodies the results of the simulation in $\dot{P}/U$ space.

BIBLIOGRAPHY

Andersen, L.C. and J.L. Jordan (1968) "Monetary and Fiscal Actions: A Test of their Relative Importance in Economic Stabilisation", *Federal Reserve Bank of St. Louis Review*, 50, 11–24.

Ando, A. (1977) "A Comment" in Sims (1977b), 209–212.

Ando, A. and F. Modigliani (1965) "Velocity and the Investment Multiplier", *American Economic Review*, September, 693–728.

Ando, A., F. Modigliani and R. Rasche (1972) "Equations and Definitions of Variables for the FRB–MIT–PENN Econometric Model, November 1969" in Hickman (1972).

Barro, R.J. (1977) "Unanticipated Money Growth and Unemployment in the United States", *American Economic Review*, March, 101–115.

Barro, R.J. and H. Grossman (1971) "A General Disequilibrium Model of Income and Employment", *American Economic Review*, March, 82–93

—— (1976) *Money, Employment and Inflation,* (Cambridge University Press, Cambridge).

Bassmann, R.L. (1963) "The Causal Interpretation of Non-Triangular Systems of Economic Relations", *Econometrica*, July, 439–48.

Benassy, J.P. (1975) "NeoKeynesian Disequilibrium Theory in a Monetary Economy", *Review of Economic Studies*, 4, 503–24.

Bird, R., Desai, M., Enzler, J. and P. Taubman (1965) "Kuznets Cycles: The Meaning", *International Economic Review*, May, 229–39.

Blake, D. (1981) "Why Has Monetarism Failed?", *The Times*, July 13.

Blaug, M. (1968) *Economic Theory in Retrospect*, (Heinemann, London).

—— (1981) *On the Methodology of Economics*, (Cambridge University Press, Cambridge).

Blinder, A.S. and R.M. Solow (1973) "Does Fiscal Policy Matter?" *Journal of Public Economics*, Vol. 2, 319-37.

Brown, W.A. (Jnr) (1940) *International Gold Standard Reinterpreted*, Columbia University Press, New York.

Brown, W.A.(1976) *Applied Econometrics* (Phillip Allen, Deddington, Oxon)

Brunner, K. (1968) "The Role of Money and Monetary Policy", *Federal Reserve Bank of St. Louis Review*, 50, July.

Brunner, K. and A. Melter (Editors): The Carnegie-Rochester Conference Series on Public Policy, published as a supplement to *Journal of Monetary Economics*, in which series
(1976) The Phillips Curve and Labor Markets: Vol 1
(1980) On the State of Macro-Economics: Vol 12.

Buiter, W. (1980) "The Macroeconomics of Dr. Pangloss: A Critical Survey of the New Classical Economics, *Economic Journal*, March, 34–50.

Cannan, E. (ed.) (1919) *The Paper Pound of 1797-1821* (London).

Casarosa, C. (1981) "The Microfoundations of Keynes' Aggregate Supply and Expected Demand Analysis, *Economic Journal*, March, 188–94.

Clower, R.W. (1965) "The Keynesian Counter-Revolution: A Theoretical Appraisal", in Hahn, F. and F.P.R. Brechling (1965).

Cobbett, W. (1830) (Reprinted 1967) *Rural Rides*, (Penguin, London).

Cohn, N. (1976) *Europe's Inner Demons*, (Paladin, Frogmore, St. Albans).

Cooper, J.P. and C.R. Nelson (1975) "The *Ex-Ante* Prediction Performance of the St. Louis and FRB-MIT-PENN Econometric Models and Some Results on Composite Predictions", *Journal of Money, Credit and Banking*, February, 1–32.

Corry, B.A. (1962) *Money, Saving and Investment in English Economics: 1800-1850*, (Macmillan, London).

Courakis, A. (1978) "Serial Correlation and a Bank of England Study of the Demand for Money: An Exercise in Measurement without Theory", *Economic Journal*, September, 537–48.

Cuddington, J. (1980) "Simultaneous-Equations Tests of the Natural Rate Hypothesis", *Journal of Political Economy*, June, 539–49.

Davidson, J.E.H., D.F. Hendry, F. Srba, and S. Yeo (1978), "Econometric Modelling of Aggregate Time Series Relationship Between Consumers' Expenditure and Income in the United Kingdom", *Economic Journal*, Dec.

Davidson, P. (1972) (Revised Edition 1978) *Money and the Real World*, (Macmillan, London).

Davidson, P. and E. Smolensky (1964) *Aggregate Demand and Supply Analysis*, (Harper and Row, New York).

de Cecco, M. (1974) *Money and the Empire: The International Gold Standard 1890-1914*, (Oxford University Press, Oxford).

de Prano, M. and T. Mayer (1965) "Autonomous Expenditures and Money", *American Economic Review*, September, 729–52.

Deaton, A. and J. Muellbauer (1980) *Economics of Consumer Behaviour*, (Cambridge University Press, Cambridge).

Desai, M.J. (1975) "The Phillips Curve: A Revisionist Interpretation", *Economica*, February, 1–19.

— (1978) "Inflation, Unemployment and Monetarism in the UK 1880–1965: A Test of Professor Stein's Model", paper read at NBER Conference on Economics and Control, Austin, Texas.

— (1981a) "Testing Monetarism: An Econometric Analysis of Professor Stein's Model of Monetarism", *Journal of Economic Dynamics and Control*, May, 141–56.

— (1981b) "The Tasks of Monetary Theory: Hayek-Sraffa Debate in Modern Perspective", in M. Baranzini (ed.), *Essays in Economic Analysis* (Blackwell); see also note by McCloughry in same edition.

— (1981c) "Inflation, Unemployment and Monetary Policy — the UK Experience", *British Review of Economic Issues*, November.

Desai, M.J. and D.P.C. Blake (1980) "Monetarism and the US Experience", LSE/SSRC Econometric Programme Discussion Paper.

— (1981a) "Monetarism and the US Economy: A Re-evaluation of Stein's Model 1960–1973", forthcoming in *Journal of Monetary Economics*.

— (1981b) "Adaptive Expectations vs. Rational Expectations in the Monetarist Black Box", LSE/SSRC Econometrics Programme Discussion Paper.

— (1981c) "Inflation, Unemployment and the Keynes Effect: An Alternative Econometric Assessment of the UK Experience", LSE/SSRC *Methodology, Inference and Modelling in Econometrics*,

Dornbusch, R. (1976), "Expectations and Exchange Rate Dynamics", *Journal of Political Economy*, 84, No. 6, Dec., pp. 1161-76.

Dow, J.C.R. (1964) *The Management of the British Economy 1945–1960*, (Cambridge University Press, Cambridge).

Dreze, J. (1975) "Existence of an Exchange Equilibrium Under Price Rigidities", *International Economic Review*, 301–20.

Eckstein, O. (1972) *The Econometrics of Price Determination*, (Board of Governors of the Federal Reserve System, Washington DC).

Edison, H. (1981) "Short-Run Dynamics and Long-Run Equilibrium Behaviour in Purchasing Power–Party Theory: A Quantitative Reassessment", unpublished doctoral thesis, University of London.

Ellis, H.S. (1951) "The Rediscovery of Money", reprinted in F.A. Lutz and L.W. Mints (eds.) (1952) *American Economic Association: Readings in Monetary Theory*, (Allen and Unwin, London).

Engle, R., Hendry, D.F. and J-F. Richard (1981) "Exogeneity", unpublished paper, University of California, San Diego, July.

Eshag, E. (1963) *From Marshall to Keynes: An Essay on the Monetary Theory of the Cambridge School*, (Basil Blackwell, Oxford).

Fand, D. (1970) "Monetarism and Fiscalism", *Banca Nazionale del Lavoro Quarterly Review*, September.

Fisher, F.M. (1972) "Comment on Lucas", in Eckstein (1972).

Fisher, I. (1911) (Revised Edition 1922) *The Purchasing Power of Money*, (Macmillan, New York).

Frankel, J. (1979), "On the Mark: A Theory of Floating Exchange Rates Based on Real Interest Rate Differentials", *American Economic Review*, Sept., pp. 610-22.

Frenkel, J. (1976), "A Monetary Approach to the Exchange Rate: Doctrinal Aspects and Empirical Evidence", *Scandinavian Journal of Economics*, 78, No. 2, May, pp. 200-24.

— (1978) "Purchasing Power Parity: Doctrinal Perspective and Evidence from the 1920s", *Journal of International Economics*, 8, 169-79.

Frenkel, J. (1981), "The Collapse of Purchasing Power Parities During the 1970s", *European Economic Review*, Vol. 1, No. 1, May.

Frenkel, J. and H.G. Johnson (1976), *The Monetary Approach to the Balance of Payments*, George Allen and Unwin, London.

Friedman, M. (1956) "The Quantity Theory of Money: A Restatement" reprinted in Friedman (1969), 51–68.

— (1958) "The Supply of Money and Changes in Prices and Output", reprinted in Friedman (1969), 171–88.

— (1959) "The Demand for Money: Some Theoretical and Empirical Results", *Journal of Political Economy*, August, reprinted in Friedmam (1969), 111–40.

— (1961) "The Lag in Effect of Monetary Policy", *Journal of Political Economy*, October, reprinted in Friedman (1969), 237–60.

— (1966) "Interest Rates and the Demand for Money", *Journal of Law and Economics*, October, reprinted in Friedman (1969), 141–56.

— (1967) "The Role of Monetary Policy", Presidential Address to the American Economic Association, published in the *American Economic Review*, March, 1968, reprinted in Friedman (1969).

— (1969) *The Optimum Quantity of Money and Other Essays*, Macmillan, London).

— (1970) "Comment on Tobin", *Quarterly Journal of Economics*, May, 318-27.

— (1970a) "The Counter-Revolution in Monetary Theory", First Wincott Memorial Lecture, London, September 16, *Institute of Economic Affairs Occasional Paper 33*.

— (1975) "Unemployment vs. Inflation: An Evaluation of the Phillips Curve with a British Commentary by David Laidler", *Institute of Economic Affairs Occasional Paper 44*.

Friedman, M. (1976) "Inflation and Unemployment: The New Dimension of Politics", The 1976 Nobel Memorial Lecture, *Institute of Economic Affairs Occasional Paper 51*.

—— (1980a) Memorandum to *House of Commons Select Committee on the Treasury and Civil Service: Monetary Policy*, H.C. 720, London).

—— (1980b) "Monetarism; a reply to the critics", *The Times*, March 3.

Friedman, M. and R. Friedman (1980) *Free to Choose*, (Penguin, London).

Friedman, M. and D. Meiselman (1963) "The Relative Stability of Monetary Velocity and the Investment Multiplier in the United States, 1897-1958" in *Commission on Money and Credit, Stabilisation Policies*, (Englenord Cliffs, N.J.).

Friedman, M. and A. Schwartz (1963) *A Monetary History of the United States 1867-1960*, (Princeton University Press, Princeton, N.J.).

Frisch, R. (1933) "Propagation Problems and Impulse Problems in Dynamic Economics" in *Economic Essays in Honour of Gustav Cassel*, (George Allen and Unwin, London).

Galbraith, J.K. (1980) Letter to *The Times*, March 3.

—— (1981) "Up from Monetarism and Other Wishful Thinking", *New York Review of Books*, August 13.

Gersovitz, M. (1980), "Misspecification and Cyclical Models: The Real Wage and the Phillips Curve", *Economica*, November 1980.

Geweke, J. (1978) "Testing the Exogeneity Specification in the Complete Dynamic Simultaneous Equation Model", *Journal of Econometrics*, 163–85.

Gilbert, C. (1976) "The Original Phillips Curve Estimates", *Economica*, February, 51–57.

Goodhart, C.A.E., P. Williams and D. Gowland (1976) "Money, Income and Causality: The UK Experience", *American Economic Review*, Vol. 66, pp. 417-23.

Gordon, R.J. (ed.) (1974) *Milton Friedman's Monetary Framework: A Debate with His Critics*, (The University of Chicago Press, Chicago, Illinois).

Gould, B., Mills, J. and S. Stuart (1979) "The Politics of Monetarism" Fabian Tract, 462, May, Fabian Society, London.

—— (1981) *Monetarism or Prosperity*, (Macmillan, London).

Gourieroux, C., J.J. Laffont and A. Monfort (1979) "Rational Expectations: Analysis of the Solutions" (*INSEE Discussion Paper 7907*, Paris).

Granger, C.W.J. (1969) "Investigating Causal Relations by Econometric Models and Cross Spectral Methods", *Econometrica*, July, 424–35.

Granger, C.W.J. and P. Newbold (1974) "Spurious Regressions in Econometrics, *Journal of Econometrics*, 2, 11-20.

Haavelmo, T. (1943) "The Statistical Implications of a System of Simultaneous Equations", *Econometrica*, January, 1–13.

— (1944) "The Probability Approach in Econometrics", *Econometrica*, July, Supplement (118 pp.).

Haache, G. (1974) "The Demand for Money in the United Kingdom: Experience Since 1971", *Bank of England Quarterly Bulletin*, No. 3, 284–305.

Hahn, F. (1965) "On Some Problems of Proving the Existence of an Equilibrium in a Monetary Economy", in Hahn and Brechling (1965).

— (1977a) "Unsatisfactory Equilibria", unpublished paper, Stanford.

— (1977b) "Exercises in Conjectural Equilibria", *Scandinavian Journal of Economics*, 210–26,

— (1978) "On Non-Walrasian Equilibria", *Review of Economic Studies*, January, 1–17.

— (1980a) "Monetarism and Economic Theory", *Economica*, February, 1–18.

— (1980b) "Unemployment from a Theoretical Viewpoint", *Economica*, August, 285–98.

— (1981) "The Preposterous Claims of the Monetarists", *The Times*, April 28.

Hahn, F. and F.P.R. Brechling (1965) *The Theory of Interest Rates*, (Macmillan, London).

Hahn, F. and R. Nield (1980) "Monetarism: Why Mrs. Thatcher Should Beware", *The Times*, February 25.

Hansen, A. (1953) *A Guide to Keynes*, (McGraw Hill, New York).

— (1949) *Monetary Theory and Public Policy*, (McGraw Hill, New York).

Hansen, L. and T. Sargent (1980) "Formulating and Estimating Dynamic Linear Rational Expectations Models, *Journal of Economic Dynamics and Control*, February, 7–46.

Harcourt, G.V. (ed.) (1977) *The Microeconomic Foundations of Macroeconomics*, (Macmillan, London).

Harvey, A.C. (1981) *The Econometric Analysis of Time Series*, (Phillip Allan, Deddington, Oxfordshire).

Hayek, F.A. (1931) *Prices and Production*, (Routledge and Kegan Paul, London).

— (1933) *Monetary Theory and Trade Cycle*, (Jonathan Cape, London).

— (1980) Letter to *The Times*, March 5.

Hazlitt, H. (1959) *The Failure of the "New Economics"*, (Arlington House, New Rochelle, N.Y.).

Hendry, D.F. (1977) "Comments on Granger-Newbold's 'Time Series Approach to Econometric Model Building' and Sargent-Sims 'Business

Cycle Modelling without Pretending to Have Too Much *A Priori* Economic Theory' ", in Sims (1960b).

Hendry, D.F. (1980) "Econometrics: Alchemy or Science?" *Economica*, November, 387-406.

Hendry, D.F. (1980a), "Predictive Failure and Econometric Modelling in Macroeconomics: The Transactions Demand for Money", in Omerod, P.A. (ed.) *Economic Modelling*, Heinemann, London.

— (1980b) Technical Note in Appendix 3 to Report of *House of Commons Select Committee on the Treasury and Civil Service: Monetary Policy*, H.C. 163 III, (HMSO, London).

Hendry, D.F. and G. Mizon (1978) "Serial Correlation as a Convenient Simplification, Not a Nuisance: A Comment on a Study of the Demand for Money by the Bank of England", *Economic Journal*, September, 549-63.

Henry, S.G.B. *et al* (1980) in Memorandum to *House of Commons Select Committee on the Treasury and Civil Service: Monetary Policy*, H.C. 720, (HMSO, London).

Henry, S.G.B., Sawyer, M. and P. Smith (1976) "Models of Inflation in the U.K.", *National Institute Economic Review*, 77, August, 60-72.

Hester, D. (1964) "Keynes and the Quantity Theory: Comment on Friedman and Meiselman CMC Paper", *Review of Economics and Statistics*, November, 364-8.

Hickman, B.G. (1972) *Econometric Models of Cyclical Behaviour*, 2 vols, (Columbia University Press, New York).

Hicks, J.R. (1937) "Mr Keynes and the Classics: A Suggested Interpretation", *Econometrica*, April, 147-59.

Hood, W. and T.C. Koopmans (eds.) (1953) "Studies in Econometric Method", *Cowles Commission Monograph No. 14*, (John Wiley, New York).

House of Commons (1974) *Expenditure Committee, Ninth Report (Public Expenditure, Inflation and the Balance of Payments)*, H.C. 328, (HMSO, London).

— (1980) *Select Committee on the Treasury and Civil Service, Third Report (Monetary Policy)*, (HMSO, London).

   (i) Memoranda on Monetary Policy 2 vols. (Session 1979-80, H.C. 720, 720—II).

   (ii) Monetary Policy Vol. 1 Report (Session 1980–81, H.C. 163—I).

   (iii) Monetary Policy Vol. 2 Minutes of Evidence (Session 1980–81, H.C. 163—II).

   (iv) Monetary Policy Vol. 3 Appendices (Session 1980-81, H.C. 163—III).

Hume, D. (1826) (i) "Of Money" and (ii) "Of the Balance of Trade", in *The Philosophical Works Vol. III*, reprinted in E. Rotwein (1955) *Writings On Economics*, (Nelson, Edinburgh).

Institute of Economic Affairs (1975) *Crisis 1975*.

— (1976) *Crisis 1976*.

Jay, P. (1976) "Employment, Inflation and Politics", *Institute of Economic Affairs Occasional Paper 46*.

Johnson, H.G. (1971) "The Keynesian Revolution and the Monetarist Counter-Revolution", *American Economic Review*, May, 1–14.

Johnson, H.G. *et al* (1972) *Memorial to the Prime Minister*, (Economic Radicals, London).

Kareken, J. and R.M. Solow (1963) "Lags in Monetary Policy" in *Commission on Money and Credit Stabilization Policies*, (Englewood Cliffs, N.J.).

Keynes, J.M. (1923) A Tract on Monetary Reform, JMK, 4.

— (1925) Economic Consequences of Mr. Churchill, JMK, 9.

— (1930) Treatise on Money, 2 volumes, JMK, 5 and 6.

— (1936) The General Theory of Employment, Interest and Money, JMK, 7.

JMK indicates *The Collected Writings of John Maynard Keynes*. All books published by Macmillan, London.

Klein, L.R. (1947) *The Keynesian Revolution*, (Macmillan, London).

— (1950) "Economic Fluctuations in the United States", *Cowles Commission Monograph 11*, (John Wiley, New York).

— (1963) "Post-War Quarterly Model: Description and Application", in *Models of Income Determination*, (NBER, Princeton, N.J.).

— (1977) " Comments on Sargent and Simms 'Business Cycle Modelling etc' ", in Sims (1977b), 203–08.

Koopmans, T.C. (1947) "Measurement Without Theory", *Review of Economics and Statistics*, August, 161–72.

— (1950) Statistical Inference in Dynamic Economic Models, Cowles Commission Monograph, 10 (John Wiley, New York).

Kors, A.C. and E. Peters (eds.) (1972) *Witchcraft in Europe 1100–1700: A Documentary History*, (University of Pennsylvania Press, Philadelphia).

Laidler, D.E.W. (1966) "Some Evidence on the Demand for Money", *Journal of Political Economy*, February, 55–68.

— (1971) (1977 rev. ed.) *The Demand for Money: Theories and Evidence*, (Crowell, New York).

— (1974) Evidence to *House of Commons Expenditure Committee, Ninth Report*, H.C. 328, (HMSO, London).

— (1975) "The End of 'Demand Management', How to Reduce Unemployment in the 1970s", in Friedman (1975).

Laidler, D.E.W. (1980a) Memorandum to *House of Commons Select Committee on the Treasury and Civil Service Monetary Policy*, H.C. 720, (HMSO, London).

— (1980b) "The Demand for Money in the United States – Yet Again", in Brunner and Meltzer (1980), 219-72.

— (1981) "Monetarism: An Interpretation and an Assessment", *Economic Journal*, March, 1-28.

Lakatos, I. (1970) "The Methodology of Scientific Research Programmes", in Lakatos and Musgrave (1970), also reprinted in Lakatos (1978).

— (1978) *Philosophical Papers*, edited by J. Worrall and G. Currie, Vol. 1 (Cambridge University Press, Cambridge).

Lakatos, I. and A. Musgrave (1970) *Criticism and the Growth of Knowledge*, (Cambridge University Press, Cambridge).

Laslett, P. (1960) *Introduction to John Locke's Two Treatises of Government*, (Cambridge University Press, Cambridge).

Latsis, S.J. (ed.) (1976) *Methodology and Appraisal in Economics*, (Cambridge University Press, Cambridge).

Leiderman, L. (1980) "Macroeconometric Testing of the Rational Expectations and Structural Neutrality Hypothesis for the United States", *Journal of Monetary Economics*, January, 69-82.

Leijonhufvud, A. (1968) *On Keynesian Economics and the Economics of Keynes*, (Oxford University Press, New York).

Lipsey, R.G. (1960) "The Relation Between Unemployment and the Rate of Change of Money Wage Rates in the United Kingdom, 1862-1957, a further analysis", *Economica*, February, 1-32.

Lipsey, R.G. and M. Parkin (1970) "Incomes Policy: A Re-appraisal", *Economica*, May, 115-38.

Liu, T.C. (1960) "Underidentification, Structural Estimation and Forecasting", *Econometrica*, October, 855-65.

Lucas, R.E. (1972) "Econometric Testing of the Natural Rate Hypothesis", in O. Eckstein (1972), 50-9.

— (1975) "An Equilibrium Model of the Business Cycle", *Journal of Political Economy*, December 1113-44.

— (1976) "Econometric Policy Evaluation: A Critique", in Brunner and Meltzer (1976), 19-46.

— (1980) "Methods and Problems in Business Cycle Theory", *Journal of Money, Credit and Banking*, November, 696-715.

Lucas, R.E. and L. Rapping (1969) "Real Wages, Employment and the Price Level", *Journal of Political Economy*, October, 721-54.

— (1970) "Price Expectations and the Phillips Curve", *American Economic Review*, June.

Lucas, R.E. and T. Sargent (1979) "After Keynesian Macroeconomics", *Federal Reserve Bank of Minneapolis Quarterly Review*, Spring. (Many of R.E. Lucas' articles are being brought together in a book to be published by Basil Blackwell, August 1981).

Luxemburg, R. (1951) *The Accumulation of Capital*, (Routledge and Kagan Paul, London).

Malinvaud, E. (1977) *The Theory of Unemployment Reconsidered*, Yrjo Johanson Lectures, (Basil Blackwell, Oxford).

Malinvaud, E. and Y. Younes (1977) "Some New Concepts for the Micro-economic Foundations of Macroeconomics", in Harcourt (1977).

Mayer, T. (1975) "The Structure of Monetarism, I and II", *Kredit und Kapital*, I in part 2, 191–217, and II in part 3, 293–315.

—— (1980) "David Hume and Monetarism", *Quarterly Journal of Economics*, August, 89–103.

McCallum, B. (1980) "Rational Expectations and Macroeconomic Stabilization Policy: An Overview", *Journal of Money, Credit and Banking*, November, 716–46.

Middlemass, K. (1979) *Politics in Industrial Society. The Experience of the British System Since 1911*, (Deutsch, London).

Minford, P. (1980a) Memorandum to *House of Commons Select Committee on the Treasury and Civil Service Monetary Policy*, H.C. 720, (HMSO, London).

—— (1980b) "Shots in the Economic Counter-Revolution", *The Times*, February 4.

—— (1980c) "Equilibrium Model Defended", a letter to *The Times*, March 3.

—— (1981) "A Dangerous and Dishonest Game", *The Times*, April 7.

Minford, P. and D. Peel (1980) "The Natural Rate Hypothesis and Rational Expectations – A Critique of Some Recent Developments", *Oxford Economic Papers*, March, 71–81.

Minsky, H. (1976) *John Maynard Keynes*, (Macmillan, London).

Mizon, G. (1977) "Model Selection Procedures", in M. Artis and A.R. Nobay (eds.) *Studies in Modern Economic Analysis*, (Basil Blackwell, Oxford).

Morishima, M. and M. Saito (1964) "A Dynamic Analysis of the American Economy", *International Economic Review*, May, 125–64, also reprinted in Morishima, M. (1976).

Morishima, M. (1976) *The Working of Econometric Models*, (Cambridge University Press, Cambridge).

Muth, J.F. (1961) "Rational Expectations and the Theory of Price Movements", *Econometrica*, July, 315–35.

Okun, A. (1980) "Rational Expectations with Misspecifications as a theory of the Business Cycle", *Journal of Money, Credit and Banking*, November, 817-25.

Parkin, M. (1970) "Incomes Policy: Some Further Results on the Determination of the Rate of Change of Money Wages", *Economica*, November, 386-401.

Perry, L.J. (1980) "A Note on Phillips and Phillips Curve Economics", *Economic Record*, March, 87-91.

Phillips, A.W.H. (1958) "The Relationship Between Unemployment and the Rate of Change of Money Wage Rates in the United Kingdom, 1861-1957", *Economica*, August, 283-300.

— (1959) "Wage Change and Unemployment in Australia 1947-1958", *Economic Society of Australia and New Zealand (Victoria Branch)*, Monograph No. 14, August.

Pierce, D.A. (1977) "Comments on Modelling and Interpreting Economic Relationships", in Sims (1977b).

Purvis, D.D. (1980) "Monetarism, A Review: Review article of Stein (1976)", *Canadian Journal of Economics*, February, 96-122.

Rees-Mogg, W. (1976) "Democracy and the Value of Money: The Theory of Money from Locke to Keynes", *Institute of Economic Affairs Occasional Paper 53*.

Ricardo, D. (1810) "On the High Price of Bullion", in P. Sraffa (1951) (ed.) *The Works and Correspondence of David Ricardo Vol. III*, (Cambridge University Press, Cambridge).

Samuelson, P.A. and R.M. Solow (1960) "Analytical Aspects of Anti-Inflation Policy", *American Economic Review*, May, 177-94.

Sargan, J.D. (1959) "The Estimation of Economic Relationships with Autoregressive Residuals by the Use of Instrumental Variables", *Journal of the Royal Statistical Society*, Series B, 91-105.

— (1964) "Wages and Prices in the United Kingdom: A Study in Econometric Methodology", in P.E. Hart *et al* (eds.) *Econometric Analysis for National Economic Planning*, (Butterworth, London).

— (1974) "Some Discrete Approximations to Continuous Time Stochastic Models", *Journal of the Royal Statistical Society*, Series B, 74-90.

Sargent, T.J. (1976) "A Classical Macroeconometric Model for the United States", *Journal of Political Economy*, June, 631-40.

— (1981) "Interpreting Economic Time Series", *Journal of Political Economy*, April, 213-48.

Sargent, T.J. and N. Wallace (1975) " 'Rational' Expectations, the Optimal Monetary Instrument, and the Optimal Money Supply Rule", *Journal of Political Economy*, April, 241-54.

Sargent, T.J. and C.A. Sims (1977) "Business Cycle Modelling Without Pretending to Have Too Much *A Priori* Economic Theory", in Sims (1977b).

Shackle, G.L.S. ((1974) *Keynesian Kaleidics*, (Edinburgh University Press, Edinburgh).

— (1972) *Epistemics and Economics*, (Cambridge University Press, Cambridge).

Shiller, R.J. (1977) "Comments on Granger-Newbold and Sims", in Sims (1977b), 163–6.

Silvey, S. (1970) *Statistical Inference*, (Penguin, London).

Sims, C.A. (1972) "Money and Income and Causality", *American Economic Review*, September, 540–52.

— (1977a) "Exogeneity and Causal Ordering in Macroeconomic Models", in Sims (1977b) 23–44.

— (1977b) *New Methods in Business Cycle Research*; Proceedings from a Conference in November 1975 sponsored by the Federal Reserve Bank of Minneapolis.

— (1980) "Macroeconomics and Reality", *Econometrica*, January, 1–48.

Slutsky, E. (1937) "The Summation of Random Causes as the Source of Cyclic Processes", *Econometrica*, April, 105–46.

Solow, R.M. (1969) *Price Expectations of the Behaviour of the Price Level* (Manchester University Press, Manchester).

— (1976) "Down the Phillips Curve with Gun and Camera", in D. Belsley *et al* (eds.) *Inflation, Trade and Taxes*, (Ohio State University Press, Columbus, Ohio).

Stein, J.L. (1974) "Unemployment, Inflation and Monetarism", *American Economic Review*, December, 867–87.

— (1976a) "Inside the Monetarist Black Box" and "Comments", in Stein (1976b), 183–271.

Stein, J.L. (ed.) (1976b) *Monetarism*, (North Holland, Amsterdam).

Steuart, Sir James (1767) *An Inquiry Into The Principles of Political Economy*; edited in two volumes by Skinner, A.S. (1966) (University of Chicago Press, Chicago).

Stolper, L. (1940) *German Economy 1870-1940, Issues and Trends*, (Allen and Unwin, London).

The Times (1980) *Letters to the Editor*: February 4 (B. Griffiths), 8, (C. Goodhart), 24, 28, 29, March 3 (J.K. Galbraith, N. Kaldor), March 3 (P. Minford), 5 (F. Hayek), June 13 (F. Hayek), *Articles*: February 4 (P. Minford), February 25 (F. Hahn and R. Neild), March 3 (M. Friedman).

— (1981) *Articles*: February 7 (P. Jay), April 7 (P. Minford), April 28

(F. Hahn), June 29 (T. Congdon), July 13 (G. Davies), July 13 (D. Blake).

Tobin, J. (1970) "Money and Income: Post Hoc Ergo Propter Hoc", *Quarterly Journal of Economics*, May, 301–17.

— (1980a) "Stabilization Policy Ten Years After", Brookings Paper on Economic Activity: 1, 19–90.

— (1980b) "Are New Classical Models Plausible Enough to Guide Policy?", *Journal of Money, Credit and Banking*, November, 788–99.

— (1980c) *Asset Accumulation and Economic Activity: Reflections on Contemporary Macroeconomic Theory*, (Blackwell, Oxford).

— (1981) "The Monetarist Counter-Revolution Today — An Appraisal", *Economic Journal*, March, 29–42.

Trevor-Roper, H.R. (1969) *The European Witch-Craze of the 16th and 17th Centuries*, (Penguin, London).

Wallis, K.F. (1971) "Wages, Prices and Incomes Policies: Some Comments", *Economica*, 302–10.

— (1980) "Econometric Implications of the Rational Expectations Hypothesis", *Econometrica*, January, 49–74.

Weintraub, S. (1957) "Micro-Foundations of Aggregate Demand and Supply", *Economic Journal*, March, 455–70.

— (1960) "The Keynesian Theory of Inflation: The Two Faces of Janus?", *International Economic Review*, May, 143–55.

White, A.D. (1876) (1959) (1980) "Fiat Money (Paper Money) Inflation in France", Cato Paper No. 11, (Cato Institute, San Francisco, California).

Wold, H. (1949) "Statistical Estimation of Economic Relationships", *Econometrica*, July, 1–21.

Working, E.J. (1927) "What Do Statistical Demand Curves Show?", *Quarterly Journal of Economics*, February, 212–35.

Zellner, A. (1977) "Comments on Time Series Analysis and Causal Concepts in Business Cycle Research", in Sims (1977b), 167–74.

Index

American Economic Association, 6, 69

Andersen, L.C. (and J. Jordan) (St. Louis Models) 6, 120, 131, 158n, 162

Ando, Albert, 105, 155, 158n, 203n

Ando-Modigliani (AM), 105–113, 116, 119, 121, 123, 157n, 171, 172, 176, 180, 200

Anti-Bullionists, 17

Aquinas, St. Thomas, 36n

Arrow, Kenneth J., 13n, 42, 87

Arrow-Debreu, 74, 87, 155–6

Attwood Brothers, 11

Ball, James, 158n

Bank for International Settlements, 205, 206

The Bank of England, 8, 17, 18, 38, 198

Bank Rate, 6, 38

Barber, Anthony, 7, 76, 209, 211

Barro, R., 77, 156n, 163, 190–2, 203

Bassmann, Robert, 158n

Baumol, William, 55

Benassy, Jean-Pascal, 156n

Bengal, 17

Bentham, Jeremy, 34

Beveridge, William, 225

Bird, Roger, 157n

Blake, D.P.C., 172, 176, 178, 182, 200, 203n, 218

Blake, David, 205–06, 225n

Blaug, Mark, 36n, 156n

Blinder, Alan, 172

Bretton Woods, 7, 76, 199, 200

Brown, A.J., 3, 56

Brown, W.A., 165

Brumberg, E., 55

Brunner, Karl, 36n, 161

Buiter, Willem, 91n, 203n

Bullionist Report, Bullionists, 17

Burt, Sir Cyril, 9

Callaghan, James, 9, 207, 215, 216, 217, 218, 222

Cambridge, 2, 3, 39, 200

Cannan, Edwin, 90n

Cantillon, Richard, 11, 17

Casarosa, Carlos, 90n

Cassel, Gustav, 10, 193–5

Chicago (School), 2, 104, 161

Christ, Carl, 203n

Clower, Robert, 156n

Cobbett, William, 11

Cohn, Norman, 36n

Phelps-Brown, E.H., 56
Phillips, A.W.H., 3, 55, 56, 57, 58,
   80, 134, 168, 195
The Phillips Curve, 3, 4, 5, 7, 13n,
   55, 56, 57, 58, 59, 63, 65, 69,
   70, 72, 73, 74, 76, 77, 78, 79,
   80, 97, 141, 146, 173, 174,
   176, 184, 185, 193, 194, 211,
   215, 216, 221, 222, 223
Pierce, David, 140, 158n
Pigou, A.C., 26, 54, 74
Popper, Karl, 95, 96
Purchasing Power Parity, 39,
   193-200
Purvis, D., 36n, 161, 162, 172, 176

Radcliffe Report (Committee),
   17, 64, 164, 201, 202
Rapping, L., 78, 80, 90n, 163, 191
Rasche, R., 158n
Reagan Administration, 206
Rees-Mogg, William, 8
Ricardo, David, 10, 11, 17-20, 21,
   35, 37, 40, 41, 42
Richard, Jean-Francois, 143,
   153-4, 159n
Robbins, Lionel, 6
Robertson, D.H., 26, 27, 35, 39
Robinson, Joan, 9
Rotwein, E., 16

Samuelson, Paul A., 4, 48, 59,
   63, 69
Sargan, Denis, 120, 126
Sargent, T.J., 76, 83, 86, 87, 155,
   158n, 159n, 163, 182, 184-8,
   192, 200, 203, 209
Savage, David, 204n
Sawyer, Malcolm, 218
Schwartz, Anna, 2, 3, 65, 162
Shackle, G.L.S., 88, 90n

Shiller, Robert, 140, 145, 158n
Silvey, S., 157n
Sims, C., 76, 102, 117, 135-41,
   145, 153, 155, 157n, 158n,
   159n, 162, 171, 186, 189-90,
   192, 193, 203, 220: Sims
   causality, 135-40, 186, 188
Skinner, A.S., 17
Slutsky, Eugene, 157n
Smith, Adam, 5, 10, 42, 87
Smith, P., 218
Smolensky, Eugene, 90n
Solow, Robert M., 4, 59, 69, 90n,
   101, 102, 155, 157n, 172, 184,
   203n
Srba, Frank, 170
Stein, J.L., 163, 172-84, 188, 203,
   203n, 209
Steuart, James, 16, 163
Stolper, N., 18

Thatcher, Margaret, 207
Theil, Henri, 118
Thornton, Henry, 11, 34
The Times, 8, 9, 11, 15, 91n,
   156n, 158n, 205, 206
Tinbergen, Jan, 62
Tobin, J., 55, 87, 132-5, 138,
   155, 172, 195, 203n, 219,
   223-4, 225n, 226n
Tooke, Thomas, 17
A Tract on Monetary Reform, 26, 39
Treasury (UK), 8, 9, 172, 211
Treatise on Money, 11, 27-32, 39,
   40, 44, 47, 49, 50, 60
Trevor-Roper, Hugh, 36n

Unemployment: Natural Rate of, 5,
   173, 216, 217; Involuntary, 5
US Congress, Joint Economic
   Committee, 66